On the Feminine

On the Feminine

Edited by
Mireille Calle

Translated by
Catherine McGann

HUMANITIES PRESS
NEW JERSEY

First English translation published in 1996 by
Humanities Press International, Inc.
165 First Avenue, Atlantic Highlands, New Jersey 07716.

Library of Congress Cataloging-in-Publication Data

Du féminin. English.
    On the feminine / edited by Mireille Calle ; translated by
Catherine McGann.
        p.   cm.
    Includes index.
    ISBN 0-391-03968-7 (cloth).—ISBN 0-391-03969-5 (pbk.)
    1. French literature—Women authors—History and criticism.
2. Cixous, Hélène, 1937-   —Criticism and interpretation.
3. Feminism and literature—France—History.   4. Women and
literature—France—History.   I. Calle-Gruber, Mireille, 1945-
II. Title
PQ149.D813   1996
840.9'9287—dc20   95-49878
                                                   CIP

Printed in the United States of America

10 9 8 7 6 5 4 3 2 1

CONTENTS

INSTITUTIONS AND LITERARY IMAGINARIES

ACKNOWLEDGMENTS

We would like to thank the following for their invaluable assistance in the realization of this work: the Social Sciences and Humanities Research Council of Canada; Queen's University; the Ministry of External Affairs in Ottawa, Canada, in particular Jacques la Rochelle, Directeur Des Echanges; the Ministry of Foreign Affairs in Paris, in particular Yves Mabin, director of the "Bureau du Livre et de l'Ecrit"; the Cultural Services of the French Embassy in Ottawa and of the Consulate General in Toronto. We would also like to thank Maryann Mojsiuk whose careful attention contributed largely to the quality of this publication.

INTRODUCTION

On the Feminine is, first of all, an *attempt.*

An *attempt* to study rather than to affirm its object, object which proceeds by constituting itself in this effort of the approach. Its approximation. An attempt to *deal with* the feminine and, by this oblique designation, to avoid pre-saying. Pre-naming. Definitive designation. *On the Feminine* strives, therefore, not to index thought but to attempt it. To talk *about* it. And to do this, it is necessary to suspend adhesions (to certain doctrines, positions) and to announce that negotiation is necessary: negotiate language, signs, institutions.

In order to evade double nominal reductionism—*feminism, woman* [*"le* féminisme, *la* femme"] a hybrid point of departure has been chosen: and with the adjective's nominalization ("the feminine"), a qualitative evaluation. That is to say, evaluation of what the feminine quality implies.

Such an approach-approximation could consequently only operate plurivocally: forming an essay-book from the compilation of various texts which connect and disconnect, freely composing proximities, perspectives, fluctuating distances.

At the center of the book is Hélène Cixous' poetry-philosophy: like an interval, an interlude which lends a rhythm to the whole, refers to its differences. Neither confidences nor confessions. The writer gives her addresses, errands, position.

Around this is organized, by points of view and nonview, the institutionalized fields of theory and literary imagination: fourteen texts, symmetrically arranged, where different modes of writing are thought and invented according to their signatories. On one side, Philippe Lacoue-Labarthe, Maroussia Hajdukowski-Ahmed, Eberhard Gruber, Verena Andermatt Conley, Gayatri Spivak, Lynn Kettler Penrod, Mireille Calle; on the other, Claire Nancy, Françoise van Rossum-Guyon, Charles Grivel, Anne-Emmanuelle Berger, Claudette Sartiliot, Marie E. Surridge, Nicole Mozet. Tying philosophical thought to literary creation in order to question our cultural representations, these texts attempt to draw the political and ethical paths of another relationship to knowledge and the world.

On the Feminine is also *on friendship.* Affinities, affections, that a date offered the possibility of materialization in encounters, October 15, 16, and 17, 1991 at Queen's University in Ontario. *On the Feminine* is the trace of these encounters. Of gratitude.

THEORETICAL
CROSSINGS

THE ABORTION OF LITERATURE

Philippe Lacoue-Labarthe

As a concept—I am speaking neither of the word and even less of the object—literature came into being during the brief (and intense) years of Romanticism at Jena: the *Frühromantik*. This is the thesis that Jean-Luc Nancy and I attempted to defend in *L'absolu littéraire*, published a little more than ten years ago, and it is not at all out of immodesty or a defensive reflex that I see no reason not to continue defending it today. Literature, as a concept, came into being between 1798 and 1800.

Essentially, but not exclusively, the Romanticism of Jena means the theoretical and critical work of Friedrich Schlegel.

Come into being means: to be born.

Speaking of Friedrich Schlegel—actually of the only novel he wrote—I would like to talk about the birth of literature. That is, about the moment when "women, writing, and society" were thought of together.

The initial hypothesis is the following: the concept of literature is contemporary with the philosophical concept of birth, insofar as it both presupposes and requires it. The philosophical concept of birth is neither Rousseau's concept of origin—with which it will nonetheless often be confused, both terminologically and logically—nor the Kantian concept of the transcendental—even though Schlegel, fully cognizant, spoke of "transcendental poetry." The philosophical concept of birth is situated at the very intersection of the two and embodies, quite literally, the superposition (I am weighing each of these words) of the chronological and the logical, making possible an ontology other than causal ontology, that is, common theology, be it materialist or spiritualist. Raising birth to the level of a concept—and this is an invention of German thought which thereby closes and delineates French thinking, such as it was known in Europe, and forms a philosophical age from Descartes to Rousseau—means that being must henceforth be conceived as history (I am still weighing my words, including "henceforth"). Lending substance to the object—and to the cause—is the obsession which will

3

dominate—and divide—Europe, indeed the world: it is, if you will, that which opposes *The Birth of Tragedy* and *The Origin of Private Property, the Family, and the State*. We are not yet free from this historicization and must certainly not jump to the conclusion that this "history" is finished. For it is there that the fate of reality or effectivity (*Wirklichkeit*) is played out, be it conceived of as a work of art (*Werk*) or as physical labor (*work*, as Marx had to assert in London).

The novel to which I just alluded and which (this is my hypothesis) expressly thematizes the birth of literature, is Friedrich Schlegel's *Lucinde*. Designated as *Erster Teil*, it appears in Berlin in 1799. The second part will never be written: it is an unfinished novel, victimized by the fragmentization of which Schlegel, with such perseverance, had made himself the theoretician. Shortly afterwards, Schlegel will try his hand at tragedy: a disastrous *Alarcos*; and, apart from a few poems here and there, never again will he run the risk of this literature of whose conception he had dreamed, but of which he must have known just that: he had only *conceived* it. Which is why, being the last element of the hypothesis, it is perhaps not aberrant to suppose that the birth of literature, according to his concept, did not go well (literature was stillborn, if you will), and it did not go well precisely insofar that it wanted to give birth to itself—engender itself and conceive itself. I am speaking, therefore, of the abortion of literature.

(I hasten to add that this does not at all prevent literature from existing, neither from being more or less healthy. It is the concept of literature which is at stake, at the philosophical moment when the concept decided upon existence and, consequently, raised the question of its necessity or of its "objectivity."

Moreover, that there have always been more or less obscure procedures of self-engenderment in literature, that is, in what we have called "literature" since its birth, changes nothing. The concept's age—let us say the age of speculative idealism—is that of the absolute Subject and, therefore, that of reflection. It is with complete lucidity—the word-play reappears constantly—that *Lucinde* reflects the possibility of literature.)

*   *   *

Lucinde, a novel was originally subtitled "Confessions of a Blunderer" (*eines Ungeschikten*). Following a brief dialogue (which, incidentally, allies itself with Petrarch, Boccaccio, and Cervantes), this subtitle serves as the title of the first chapter which is in the form of a letter: "Julius to Lucinde" (Rousseau is never very far). Almost always in the position of enunciator, Julius is Schlegel himself; and the novel is, to a large degree, an autobiography. Lucinde, a name probably taken from *Don Quixote* but which also appears to herald the Clara of a future Schelling dialogue, everything indicates—and everything is made to indicate—that it refers to Brendl Mendelssohn, Moses' daughter, known as Dorothy Veit, who, in 1799, divorces to live thereafter with Schlegel. (Moreover, the third issue of the *Athenäum*—we are still in 1799—opens with a letter from Schlegel to Dorothy: this is the famous letter "On Philosophy.") It is obvious that *Lucinde* is also a *declaration*.

Why is it pronounced under the auspices of awkwardness?

(In order to answer this question, it would be necessary to discuss the entire book, an undertaking which is quite obviously not possible here. I will therefore be very schematic and give only the principle of one possible demonstration.)

The awkwardness in question here is, first of all, erotic. Schlegel speaks about his clumsiness in moments of frivolity. Indeed, these "Confessions," which form a prelude to the entire book, begin themselves with a "nostalgic" recollection, a sort of desirous reverie on what a revelation Lucinde's embraces had turned out to be.

The letter, being a letter, bears an address—as does the novel itself. But, as Julius says, it is also a conversation with himself, a deliberation. And we soon see that the deliberation concerns the very project of the novel and Julius' ability to produce it. Which sheds new light on awkwardness: awkwardness is also aesthetic or artistic: "I want to try," says Julius, as a full-fledged lover and writer, "to give chance a shape—to offer a random shape and to fashion it according to my intentions." (We see here the speculative thematic of *Bildung* and *Gestaltung* according to which the subject's formation, whatever it may be, must be accomplished in the same way as a work of art, that is, like fiction, in the strongest sense of the word: at stake is the possibility of a *Gestalt*, a figure, as the finite manifestation of the infinite.)

The lover is therefore the writer, and vice versa. I will not rush to claim here that the erotic is the metaphor of literature, as is so often the case, and even if Schlegel allows himself to be constrained by some very old schemes, I would think, rather, that literature is the erotic.

When he presents his project to Lucinde, Julius tells her of his intention to "unfold before [her] ... the careful and exact history of [their] frivolity and of [his] clumsiness" and "to describe the various fruits of [his] awkwardness, not forgetting the years of apprenticeship in [his] masculinity." The reference to Goethe is clear, for we know that during these years *Wilhelm Meister* was, in Schlegel's eyes, emblematic of the modern along with the French Revolution and the *Critique of Pure Reason*. In *Lucinde*, the mixing of genres is developed to the highest degree; it is therefore a *Bildungsroman*, amongst others, as well, of course, as a *Kunstlerroman*.

These years of "apprenticeship in masculinity" are very carefully placed at the exact center of the book (they form the seventh chapter out of thirteen). There Schlegel tells of his loves and friendships, granting, moreover, an important position to Caroline Michaelis, his brother's wife and the future spouse of Schelling, for whom he had developed a very strong—and very chaste—passion before meeting Dorothy. Then, at the end, comes Dorothy, that is, Lucinde: this is the erotic and amorous revelation I mentioned earlier.

The dominant feature in the figure of Lucinde—for she is definitely a figure—is that she is a mother. Of course, she is also presented as an artist (she is a painter) and a witty and intelligent woman (and consequently of a sociable disposition that Schlegel dreamed of, if only because she had broken all ties of dependence: she is a free woman); she is also sensitive and emotional, one can sense her religious vocation (in the sense of the accomplishment of humanity) and she has a "marked inclination for the romantic." But what is essential is that she is a mother (of a child that had already died, however, at the time of the encounter), and it is quite clearly this, as compared to all other previous experiences, that finally arouses Schlegel's desire along with his love. It is indeed a complicated desire—where exactly is this child which haunts the entire book?—complicated by the fact that Dorothy is ten years his senior. Schlegel's intention is very clear:

> The opulence of her magnificent stature had a more exciting allure for the fury of his love and senses than the cool charm of the breasts and the unified mirror of a virginal body. The strength and the heat roused by her embrace were greater than that of a young girl; they had something fervent and profound that only a mother can have.

This is why Schlegel's erotic revelation, with its mixture of mystical exuberance and frivolity, outpouring or abandon and obscenity, laughter and tears, exaltation and play, is the revelation of an entire being, uniting (and capable of) all opposites, driven by an extraordinary power or force—almost an energy, in the Greek sense of the word. This being is quite simply that which Schlegel calls a "natural being." If Lucinde, the woman, is a figure, it is none other than the figure of *phusis* itself. (And looked at from this angle, although I cannot analyse it here, there is nothing surprising about the metaphors of light and clarity, day and night, veiling and unveiling, being brought together with the equally dialectic metaphors of germination and vegetal growth, sprouting and blossoming, the bud, the flower, and the fruit: the double etymon in the word *phusis*: *phuein/phainein* has been acknowledged for a long time.)

Here we can begin, perhaps, to understand why, if Lucinde is thus the figure of *phusis*, the novel is subtitled "Confessions of a Blunderer." Awkwardness, clumsiness, not-to-know-all-about-it, not-to-know-how-to-go-about-it, is what can be called *atechnie*. Quite obviously, the subject of *Lucinde*, as has been said, is the relationship between *phusis* and *technē*, a relationship where the possibility, the function, and the ontological status of art has been played out ever since Aristotle and Longinus. I don't dare say, yet again, that what is in question is mimesis, but there is nothing to be done—it is a question of nothing but that. *Lucinde* tells of the origin of art.

The two scenes considered most indecent at the time (they displeased Goethe and scandalized Hegel) were the scenes of copulation, including copulation in its logical and ontological sense.

The second scene, entitled "A Reflection," from the key term of Fichtian idealism, describes what one must well call the "sexual relationship"— the little game, says Schlegel—in the speculative vocabulary of Fichte and Schelling (determining, determined, indetermined) and, from this model, creates a general theory of the production of being (of the one and all), of "creation," from nature or the universe to the work of art. Strictly speaking, it is about a *coïtus metaphysicus*. For technical reasons that are self-evident, I cannot analyse this here.

I will therefore be dealing with the first scene only, which stems from the rest in an analogical sense but which undoubtedly illustrates best what I would like to show.

It appears in the second chapter which is entitled "Fantasy in the Dithyrambic Style on the Most Lovely Situation." Schlegel speaks of what he call "joyous situations." And he continues:

> The most *witzig* and the most lovely of them all is when we exchange roles and, with naïve pleasure, we compete to see who can best imitate (*nachschäffen*) the other by creating the greatest illusion, so as to know whether you succeed better at the studied virtuousity of men than I do at the alluring surrender of women. But do you know that for me, this sweet game holds other charms than just those of the game itself? . . . I see in it a marvelous allegory whose signification is laden with meaning: masculinity and femininity complement each other and culminate in consummate humanity. Many things lie enclosed there, and that which lies thus does certainly not rise again as quickly as I do when yielding to you.

One can see that the exchange or inversion of roles is *mimesis* itself. As to what I am concerned with here, it matters little that the established

relationship, conceived of as *Witz*, be thought of in a dialectical manner, as is the exchange of opposites and the "synthetic" effectuation of
"total humanity" that is found in the ancient dream of androgyny. (We
looked at this a little in *L'Absolu littéraire*, using the "Letter to Dorothy"
as an example.) I imagine that the repetition of such pronounced *topoi*
on masculinity and femininity could also be considered wearisome. What
interests me is simply that it is there that one can probably find the
prototypical scene of art: there, too, in erotico-speculative terms, the
possibility of art, that is, the possibility of aesthetic life seeking to re-
solve itself. After having concluded: "Here is the fantasy in dithyrambic style of the most beautiful situation in the most beautiful world!"
he asks Dorothy if she will not forgive him for the indecency of his
words (and it is true, by the way, that they caused her much grief):

> I also know perfectly well how you found and took them. But I be-
> lieve I know just as well how you will find and take them here, in
> this little book, from which you expect more fidelity in the story,
> more simple truth and calm intelligence, indeed morality, the pleas-
> ing morality of love. "How can one want to write what is scarcely
> permissible to even say, that which should only be felt?" This is my
> answer: if one feels, one must want to say it, and that which one
> wants to say also has the right to be written.

And Schlegel invokes—this is his excuse—a "certain clumsy enthusiasm," "originally and in essence [written into] the nature of man" and
which "thoughtlessly recounts all that is delicate and sacred": "which
clumsily stumbles over the artlessness of its own zeal and, in a word, is
easily divine to the point of vulgarity." Discourse of a blunderer, then.
But also of innocence: affirming never to have wanted to be "hand in
glove" with this type or this race (of men), he really only excuses his
liberty and impudence (*Freiheit und Frechheit*) with the example of . . .
a child: little Wilhelmina, probably his niece, whose "characteristics"
are given in the third chapter, two of which, I must say, are particularly noteworthy:

> 1. Wilhelmina is a mimetic being, or rather she *responds* to the game
>   of mimesis. By which she is, like all women, a poetic being—that
>   is, poietic. (The letter to Dorothy places great emphasis on this
>   fact that poetry is natural to women as philosophy is to men):
>
> > If I imitate her movements, she immediately imitates my imita-
> > tion [It would be difficult to better summarize Aristotle]; we
> > have therefore created a language of gesticulations and we com-
> > municate by means of hieroglyphics borrowed from the figurative

arts. She has, I believe, a much greater inclination for poetry than philosophy.

2. Wilhelmina is the very innocence of—feminine—immodesty: she shows and reveals the hidden and the concealed. Her "nature" as it was said in the eighteenth century. As such, she justifies the impudence of the blunderer:

> And to think! this dear Wilhelmina derives great pleasure, and not infrequently, from lifting her little legs into the air while she is lying on her back, kicking about without concern for her dress or people's judgment. If Wilhelmina behaves in this fashion, what am I not authorized to do since I am very much a man, by god, and need not be more refined than the most refined feminine being?

Impudence is therefore the appropriation—an awkward one—of the secret and innocent immodesty of femininity, that is, of *phusis*, of which we know, since Heraclitus (translated by Schleiermacher during these same years), that in the very movement by which she reveals herself or brings herself into the light of day, she "likes to hide herself." Art—literature—would be that: the "atechnical" impudence to say—pure oxymoron—the modest immodesty of "nature." And to divulge it: because what is at stake socially and politically during the years at Jena is immense.

The appropriation of modest immodesty—the oxymoron indicates rather well what Schlegel meant by morality and *Sittlichkeit*, and what he consequently assigned to the ethical and formative destination of art—is nothing other than the appropriation of power or energy itself: of what began to be called, in Kant's wake, formative force, *die bildende Kraft*, without which any art (any *technē*) is impossible. No fiction. Since the rediscovery of Longinus, this was being called "genius" in Europe. Woman is the genius—the natural gift (of nature)—and impudence is therefore quite simply the appropriation of genius. A pure impossibility. How could a gift be appropriated? No erotic can suffice and Schlegel knew very well: genius is innate, there is no technique for the acquisition of the innate. Awkwardness is irremediably the essence of *technē*: it is basically a question of deficiency. The artist can never truly be a woman in her infinite patience for pleasure (I could phrase this differently: there is no restraint in woman, but it is restraint itself, that is, *phusis*), and it is there that literature founders when it should be born.

In Schlegel's obstinacy—in sum, pathetic—impudence remains very much the mother, a paradoxical one, of the novel. Indeed, after the "Characteristics of Little Welhelmina" there follows "The Allegory of

Impudence" where the intention is to show, by means of an equally carefully calculated dream, whence comes—*Lucinde*. Each novel, that is each novel recognized as a real novel, is "allegorized" by a type (the knight in *Meister*, for example). It is not terribly surprising that, following the purest logic of the *mise en abyme*, *Lucinde* be allegorized by a transvestite: exchange of roles obliges.

It is true that the *Witz*, which is the most extreme condensation of the *Geist*, rivals impudence for the paternity (or maternity) of the novel. Impudence says to the Witz:

> If it is you who made what we now call novels, you could have better spent your time. In the best, I can scarcely find anywhere something of this fleeting life's light poetry; but where did it flee, this audacious music of a heart exalted by the passions of love, that music which sweeps everything along after it such that even the most savage man sheds tender tears and the eternal rocks dance?

[Then, after this "Dionysiac" invocation, addressing no one in particular:]

> If, afflicted with spiritual impotence, one wants to procreate children with it [the *Witz*], if, understanding nothing at all, one attempts to live, it is indecent to the utmost degree, because it is, to the utmost degree, against nature and, to the utmost degree, unseemly. But that the wine sparkles and the lightning inflames, this is what is entirely right and entirely in conformity with propriety.

Upon these words, impudence leaves the stage on the arm of the frivolous novel, saying to the knight in passing (Goethe's "beautiful soul"): "We will see each other again." But it is precisely there that, through a sort of dissolution of its exterior countenance, the *Witz* is suddenly interiorized: it becomes, in the purest manner of reflection, the subject itself. It is like an incorporation of genius.

I must be satisfied with citing this text which would call forth an entire, detailed commentary:

> Everything disappeared then, and even the *Witz* grew and expanded until it ceased to exist. It was no longer before and outside of me, but most definitely within me that I believed to find it: it was a fragment of myself, different, however, from me, living in itself and independent. A new sense seemed to be born to me; I was discovering within me a pure profusion of soft light. I returned within myself and within this new sense whose miracles I contemplated. He saw with the same clarity and the same precision as would an eye of the spirit, turned inward; but at the same time, the perceptions were gentle and intimate, like those of hearing, as immediate as those of touch.

And after having conjured up the transfigured world which presents itself before him—the "opulent earth's green carpet" is another matter of *phusis*—, Schlegel adds (the Dionysiac motif is certainly tenacious):

> And thus I soon saw, behind bizarre masks, cherished forms, known and unknown; it was like a great carnival of love and pleasure: inner Saturnalia who, in their diversity and strange dissoluteness, were not at all unworthy of great Antiquity. But this cerebral bacchanalia's disorderly course [Hegel will remember the formula] did not last long: this inner world was torn apart as if by an electrical discharge and, without knowing how or whence they came, I made out these winged words: "Destroy and create: one and all". . . .

(We are obviously in the utopia of the Same and of indiscrimination that no irony or reflection, Hegel will say, can rectify.)

The voice which speaks thus and, by invoking the *ben kai pan*, tells the secret of creation, is the voice of imagination, that is, since Kant, of transcendental schematism which is an "art hidden in the depths of the soul." This is why, during the course of the mysteries which so obsessed the era (Isis, the disciples at Saïs, etc.) it suggests an initiation, the initiation of the Subject itself as subject of literature. The voice says:

> The time has come, a revelation and a presentation of the innermost essence of divinity are possible, we have the right to disclose all mysteries and fear must cease. Initiate yourself and proclaim that nature alone is venerable and health alone is kind.

And the "companion" who helps Schlegel in this self-initiation—the self-initiation of the absolute Subject—adds, after Schlegel has "reflected" upon the fact that his lips "had never learned the art of producing the songs of the spirit":

> You must not want to convey the immortal fire in its purity and in its rough state . . . , give the world and its eternal visages a form. . . . Conceal and confine the spirit in the letter. The true letter which is all-powerful [there are, as we know, similar proposals in Novalis], it is the true magic wand. It is with this that the irresistible free choice of the great magician, imagination, touches the sublime chaos of nature in its plenitude and brings the infinite word forth into the light of day, word which is an image and a mirror of the divine spirit and which mortals call the universe.

*   *   *

One could scarcely go any further in *speculating* on the birth of literature. Not least because the initiation in question is none other, as everything indicates, the initiation into femininity, that is, as we know, into motherhood. Just after the "companion's" statement about the letter (and we must not smile about it: Schlegel is the last to be unaware of or to deny the homosexual nature of his initiatory reverie or of his learning about masculinity), Schlegel adds this remark which apparently has no connection:

> The advantage that feminine dress has over masculine dress is the same that the feminine spirit has over the masculine spirit: a single audacious combination allows one to take a position beyond all cultural prejudices and bourgeois conventions and to all of a sudden find oneself in a state of innocence at the heart of nature.

On that note, more or less, he describes for the benefit of "adolescents"—inasmuch as they are not yet men—that the "rhetoric of love," the three stages of initiation which are the three stages in the art of loving, can hope to be as convincing as women. There is one condition in this initiation: one must have "what Diderot calls a sense of the flesh," as indefinable as pure strains of music or chiaroscuro in painting, if not, but it is vague, as a "superior aesthetic sense of exquisite voluptuousness." And this condition, which is an "innate gift in women," is in fact the "first stage in the art of loving" for adolescents and they can only acquire this sense from women: like a gift, a favor, a blessing. The second stage has "something mystical" about it and consists of satisfying and arousing woman's infinite desire. But, says Schlegel, "let us not speak of these mysteries!" As for the third stage, the "supreme stage," it is quite simply access to androgyny, "to the lasting sense of harmonious warmth": "The adolescent who has this," writes Schlegel, "no longer loves only as a man but at the same time as a woman." This access to "infinite humanity," that which existed, says a fragment of the *Athenäum*, "before donning the veil of sex, the coat of the masculine and feminine," is the sole fortune of the self-conception of literature which, in its essence, is nothing other than the love of femininity:

> Allow me to confess: it is not only you that I love, I love femininity itself. I do not only love it, I adore it, because I adore humanity and because the flower is the culmination of the plant, of its beauty, and of its natural formation.

That is why the self-conception of literature is equally the self-conception of the subject. According to what he calls his "divine vocation," Schlegel can call himself the son of the *Witz*, this word which, we now understand, ultimately signifies *technē*, cleverness itself:

What can he not believe himself capable of, he to whom the *Witz* itself, in a voice come from the heights of the parted sky, says: "This one here is my beloved son in whom I have placed all my love." And why should I not say of myself, by virtue of the powers and the freedom which are peculiar to me: "I am the beloved son of the *Witz*"?

Or again, when he recalls his life with Lucinde (Dorothy) at the end of "The Years of Learning Masculinity,"

His art increased in perfection and that which he was previously incapable of obtaining, in spite of all efforts and striving, now came to him spontaneously: moreover, his existence became for him a work of art without him realizing exactly how this had come about.

Still, no child is born. I mentioned to what degree the obsession with the child runs throughout *Lucinde*, at least as much as the plant and flower and femininity. But all the children in question are already dead or will die. And the child announced in the beautiful dialog about the night, so reminiscent of Novalis' *Hymns* ("Nostalgia and Tranquility"), little Guido, we do not read of his birth and nothing indicates that he ever is born. (I could be mistaken, but I believe that Schlegel never had any children.) There is, covertly, something like the avowal that literature could not be born, at least according to the concept of birth which is ultimately the conception of self-conception. Which, Schlegel knows quite well, one cannot simply confuse with self-formation.

We can put it this way: if humanity self-conceives, it is by virtue of an irreducible, natural (or physical) dividing up, that no *technē* can overcome unless it is in the "allegorical" mode. In one of the instances where he apologizes to Lucinde/Dorothy for the brazenness of his narrative—this moment provides for the transition from "Characteristics of Little Wilhelmina" to "The Allegory of Impudence"—Schlegel writes: "And if this little novel about my life seems too raw to you, think of it as a child, bear its capricious innocence with a mother's patience and let it caress you." But he immediately adds: "If you wanted to not be too severe with regard to the plausibility and the general meaning of an allegory, and expect to find in this narrative as much awkwardness as would be expected in the confessions of a blunderer . . . , I will tell you one of my recent waking dreams. . . ." No genius can substitute for the original awkwardness of *technē*, even if *technē* is necessary for *phusis* to come out of its reserve (or modesty). But this is no kind of childbirth. Genius, coupled with *technē*, is incapable of having any children. It reveals and elucidates—reveals and elucidates itself—which is already a lot. And literature can indeed be this revelation, this elucidation. Which is what *Lucinde* is, right down to its very title. This does not mean that it may be born, or that it has been born.—Perhaps it is because our birth is literature.

HISTORY OF THE SUBJECT, THE SUBJECTS OF HISTORY: CRITICAL UTOPIA IN DISCOURSES ON HYSTERIA

Maroussia Hajdukowski-Ahmed

In spite of its rather stormy relationship with Marxism, feminist criticism does have certain affinities with the more renegade Marxists, the Marxians, such as Ernest Bloch, Fredric Jameson, and Mikhail Bakhtin. Indeed, it was their common interest in the confluence of the subject, language, and history and their views on critical utopia which inspired the following reflections.

Critical utopia manifests both ideological critique (negative hermeneutics) and the identification of utopian urges (positive hermeneutics) conveying the vision of, and thus escape to, a better "elsewhere"—in the sense that Mannheim and Bloch gave the term (and which feminist research and writing confirms). Critical utopia, then, is a wildflower forging an obstinate path through the monolithic discourse of power it fissures. It sketches a subversive gesture, the seed of a new knowledge and an ethics of dialogical interlocution. Rooted in history, it portrays neither a telos nor an exile to paradise; rather it proceeds from an ethics of difference and crisis, not a crisis relating to the tension inhering in opposition, but a crisis connected with a form of movement inviting better possibilities and opposing the hypostasis of the moment of thought:

> For thinking means surmounting. But not going beyond what exists, not wanting to be unaware of it. Not in its distress and certainly not in the movement that enables extrication. Not in the causes of distress and certainly not in the beginnings of change that are ripening there.[1]

Our objective here is twofold: to render the theories of Bloch and Bakhtin operative and to subvert them by exposing their blind spot: sexual

15

difference as a structuring factor of discourse ("women" as a social gendered construct, but Marxism dealt only with class differences). Until recently, one could discern a certain reluctance to theorize as a specific epistemological stance within feminist criticism. A similar reluctance will be unraveled here as we trace the evolution of the discourse on hysteria with a particular emphasis on Charcot's discourse. A study of the discourse on hysteria reveals its relations with the scientific and political powers, and thus enables us to discover, beyond the history of the feminine subject, subjects of history which need and deserve to be heard. It is their voices, the traces of resistance to the discourse of power, that we will attempt to reveal, to unseal.

Theorize and Terrorize: Theory, Therapy, Power

The succession of texts on hysteria creates a historical filiation, a mimetic network of legitimization neither fortuitous nor without consequence for women and medicine. Indeed, they work as founding texts in theoretical temporality, perfectible, of course, but with unshakable foundations. From Antiquity to the present, it has been the philosophers, clergymen, and scientists who have studied hysteria.

Hysteria has merged with the ambient culture all the way along its historico-medical route. It is the migration of the uterus which causes hysterical symptoms in the *Papyrus Kahun* of ancient Egypt; the remedy consisted in "putting it back in its place" either by the inhalation of extremely repulsive smelling concoctions or by fragrant genital fumigations (exclusion/seduction strategies). Hippocrates reports hysterical symptoms in childless women and in women who abuse carnal pleasures, thus creating a pathologico-moral confusion between lack and excess. The treatment: (re)marriage. Plato's *Timeus* confirms this nosology and adds abdominal pressure as a remedy since the convulsive movements of the uterus are believed to be caused by an energy surplus coming from the heat of dissatisfied wombs. (Im)moral qualities are projected onto the organic: woman is marked by instability, unbridled desire, and an open body of weak density.[2] In the Middle Ages, the rise of mysticism carried with it the condemnation of sexuality and introduced the Cult of the Virgin Mary. Saint Augustine maintains the existence of witches and demons; Pope Innocent VII (1484) proclaims that mental—indeed even physical—illnesses are the work of the forces of evil; refusal to believe this was heresy. Early printing presses allowed for the diffusion of the *Malleus Maleficorum* (1484). Confession, exorcism, and the Inquisition constitute the many coercive means used to expulse the sickness from those recalcitant before power—as were widows, Jacquerie leaders, and authors such as those from the Lyon school. In the middle of the eighteenth century, Doctor Pomme declares a hysteric healed when, in the numerous baths prescribed (note the excessive use of purifying baths and showers in therapeutic history), he "sees" bits of detached membranes being eliminated through the natural orifices. All efforts must be made to render the interior transparent; indeed, woman must be turned inside out like a glove in order to extirpate the secret: what women "have in their wombs" literally. And so, the word coincides with the object.

The writers of witches' confessions or of hysterics' accounts, representatives of clerical or medical power, thus established an ideological referential system that sustained a theoretical intertextual complicity. Women fashioned their accounts from what they knew of official discourses, or else the writers themselves would twist the narrative to fit their own beliefs. Thus, based on Matteuccia di Francesco's confession, with its profusion of precise, visual notations describing her nocturnal adventures, Carlo Ginzburg was able to establish exact correspondences with the sermons of Saint Bernard who was passing through Todi in 1426, two years before Matteuccia's trial. According to him, "for the next two hundred years, all witches' confessions will bear a strange resemblance."[3] This is the case also in the account of the Loudun witches' trials (1635), annotated and published in 1886 by Drs. Gabriel Légué and Gilles de la Tourette, at the time when Charcot reigned over the "court of miracles" at the Salpêtrière.

At this point, hysteria moves towards the heart, Rush considering it a pathology of excessive affect in women. Pinel, however, defines it as an insanity which also affects men. He has the chains removed from the women in the Salpêtrière and so contributes to the dissociation of hysteria with the uterus. In the transition from genital to mental affliction, hysteria is ennobled and includes men. But let it be known that hysteria, when it affects men, is caused by accidents at work (hence the soldier's "shell shock," the railroad worker's "railway spine").

Charcot, The Power of Discourse, the Discourse of Power

Francois-Marie Charcot was the great, undisputed master of neurology at the Salpêtrière in the second half of the nineteenth century. This Parisian hospital housed around 5,000 physically and mentally ill women from disadvantaged groups, a pool of patients Charcot found invaluable for his research on hysteria and epilepsy and the links between them. Charcot referred to the founding texts on hysteria in the (self-legitimizing) process of his clinical analyses. From 1845 to 1883, the number of hysterics at the Salpêtrière grew from 10 percent to 17 percent, causing Charcot to declare that:

> It seems that hysterio-epilepsy exists only in France, and I could even say, as it has sometimes been said, only at the Salpêtrière, as though I had forged it with the strength of my own will. It would be a wonderful thing if I could thus create illnesses according to my whim and fantasy. But truthfully, I am nothing but the photographer; I record what I see and it is only too easy for me to prove that it is not only at the Salpêtrière that these things happen. First of all, the accounts of those possessed by the devil in the Middle Ages are full of such events. In his book, M. Richer shows us that in the fifteenth century, it was exactly as it is today.[4]

Charcot's entire theory is subject to a scopic and positivist economy. The same positivism was later denounced by Bakhtin and by feminist criticism. As Bakhtin wrote:

> It is oriented towards the mastery of the reified, mute object which does not reveal itself in speech and which does not inform itself about anything. Here, knowledge is not tied to the reception and interpretation of the words or signs of the knowable object itself.[5]

A return to the concrete situation, however, subverts the scopic and makes the subject and history visible. During his lectures Charcot has his "patients" undress, sometimes several at one time, in order to compare them. He examines from the full height of his (large) stature and gaze; indeed, power and the gaze go hand in hand. By subscribing to a belief in the transparency of the sign, he obliterates the social process of transformation (the reading of the "look") by a historically situated subjectivity. This gaze as language is public/published in order that power be confirmed, knowledge validated and made profitable. This language makes the visible readable, rendering it significant by the universality of a language codified by increasingly refining the perceived until it creates the illusion of truth, a process which enables the phenomena to be visualized.

Thus, Charcot is excessive in his use of measurements, accumulates a plethora of facts, establishes analogies, and constructs classifications. He sets himself up as the ideal observer; "See!" he enjoys repeating to his disciples—and they see. Ultimately an archetype emerges, subsuming differences which, in another time and place, would have been significant. Passionate about numbers, Charcot went so far as to time the stages of hysteria; numerous sketches, schemas, and systems of classification were based on those minute "observations." Perception obeys his belief in the binary nature of the subject, in oppositional symmetry:

it is surface/depth, external/internal, and left/right which maps the body and divides it. He concludes that:

> ... these facts, which will contribute to establishing the history of hystero-traumatic paralyses, multiply as we look closer ... [that] all these facts, when studied methodically, come to testify in the same way. Don't talk to us about the elusive protean hysteria.[6]

It is this "elusive Proteus" — which takes the form of the Blochian "novum" here and which germinates theoretically in psychoanalysis — that Charcot's discourse aborts. Charcot, famous for the considerable use he made of photography in collaboration with Albert Londe, the hospital's appointed photographer, "borrows" his methods of investigation, classification, and photographical assemblage from the judiciary police of Paris, methods supported by a belief in the adequacy of identity and image. Indeed, it was necessary to isolate, pin, fix, and name the elusive Proteus. The positivist approach and intertextual filiation guarantee a form of scientific truth dependent on the scopic (and seeing already mortgaged by believing) and create a network legitimizing patriarchal power.

Countervoices

Where can we find hints of resistance, of a hybrid double-voice discourse, moments of critical utopia in those blocks of monological writing? First of all, they can be found in certain colleagues' repudiations which great time, catalyst of critical utopia, has often rehabilitated. Hypermimetism constitutes a second form of hybridization in critical utopia. Indeed, what could the hysteric do, caught in this discursive vice, apart from going beyond what was required and shouting even louder in order to distinguish herself from the model presented for her imitation — thereby creating a margin of liberty in which she could fit as subject. Let us remember that Bakhtin defined hybridization as

> the mixing of two social languages, of two points of view within a single enunciation, the encounter, in the arena of the enunciation of two linguistic consciousnesses separated by era, social difference, or both.[7]

And, we will add, by sexual difference. The hybrid nature of an enunciation often reveals itself late since

> the phenomena of meaning can exist in a dissimulated form, as potential, and only reveal themselves in a context which will favor their discovery embedded in culture at a later time. The plenitude of meaning only reveals itself in great time.[8]

Hybridization, which takes on the function and value of critical utopia, can appear as "preconscious surplus, exceeding the simple ideology tied to the situation itself," according to Ernest Bloch.[9] This critical utopia, deliberate or preconscious, thus exposes the mechanisms of power and unmasks their claim to truth by uncovering its ideologies and the complicity which links its institutions and its discourses.

Numerical excess (the collective possession of Loudun or the epidemic of hysteria at the Salpêtrière) creates doubt and enables one to perceive, just below the surface, a collective rejection of the norm, the negative of a solidarity that power rendered impossible. In *La Mystérique*, Luce Irigaray has already noted excess in mimetic intensity: it reproduces symptoms of possession to the point of abjection. Indeed, excess of the exhibited corporal grotesque subverts the specular body and transforms it into a spectacular body, open and reaching toward an expression of desire, the painful negative of the utopian body celebrated now in feminist texts (Dora in Hélène Cixous' *Portrait de Dora* for example). Power has travestied this excess into a black, pathological carnival via the converging scrutiny of voyeuristic practitioners and their strategies of isolation and interpretive monopoly—in consulting rooms and in discourses.

We are also interested in the dissident voices of colleagues which critical utopia revalorizes. Charcot rejected Briquet's thesis which re-examined Sydenham's seventeenth century thesis—according to which the hysteric seizes hold of known pathologies parasitically in order to translate her prohibited desires. Others, such as Hippolyte Bernheim in *Le Temps* in 1891, called into question the authenticity of photographs featuring hysterics at the Salpêtrière; patients were said to have learned hysterical contortions under the guidance of zealous assistants in order to please the ".Master." Moreover, Charcot's passion for theater and circus was not without influence on his lectures-performances. Could these grimacing faces and contorted, arched bodies in the photographs illustrating the stages of hysteria be signs of hybridization? At whom are the hysterics sticking out their tongues or making faces? What if they were like messages in bottles thrown into the sea, into the flux of great time, making us searchers of shipwrecks? The hysteric's grotesque body has already been interpreted as carnivalesque, in the work of Allon White and Peter Stallybrass, Mary Russo or Clair Willis, for example; Hélène Cixous, Catherine Clément, Luce Irigaray recognized its subversive value; and Mike Gardiner has analyzed carnival as critical utopia. In their view, the lower half of the body acquires a topological value as birth's beginnings, transformation, communicative openings. The mask, the game, and their derivatives (grimaces, excess) give shape to this open and utopian negativity, like Bloch's "dying and being born." It is, however, towards a Lenten body that the ideal female body leans: silent, closed, isolated from others, draped and camouflaged in an amplitude of veils and euphemisms. The body in transition (adolescence, gestation) or the desiring body are struck with sociocultural prohibitions and enter the category of pathology. The carnivalesque body, on the other hand, occupies an essential place in critical thought for it is thought to function epistemologically, signaling the reappropriation of desire and of the agency of the subject; it is not a produced sign. The corporality of language (voice) and verbal prohibitions (insults) subvert the norms and good manners which have constrained women in particular.

The hysterical crisis presents itself as a carnivalesque spectacle. One notices the great distension of the stomach; Charcot (and later Freud) interpret this as the hysteric's desire for motherhood, whereas, from a non-Oedipal perspective, this could be perceived as a desire for the return of/to nurturing, or a desire for self-generation. Oddly, Charcot (and also Freud, for whom Dora's swollen foot will be the sign of a faux pas) mentions the existence of a "varus equinus" deforming his patients' feet; treatment, therefore, aims to get the patient back on her feet and on the right path. The cure is rectification: making her accept the cultural regulations of her instinctual needs and leaving unruly hysterics no alternative than that of committing *oedipus interruptus* by fleeing (Augustine, Dora). Hysteria's carnivalesque figure is marked by an arc propelling the stomach upwards and bringing the head toward the feet, indicating a topological reversal of values. It is in the margins of discourse that critical utopia lies coiled; but if a theoretical intuition crosses his mind, Charcot relegates it to a footnote or to a parenthetical aside. Bourneville, who transcribed the lectures, throws the employer-landlord's rape of thirteen-year-old Augustine—a rape triggering her first fit—into the discursive refuse bin of "complementary information." Here Charcot might have recognized the importance of early sexual trauma (the theoretical novum) of which he had only a vague intuition. It is also pertinent to ask whether the fact that the majority of Charcot's hysterics were destitute did not influence their doctors' willingness to listen to them and thus mask the severity of their traumas? If the menacing strength of subversion is a function of the prohibited, what was the situation for women at the end of the nineteenth century, during Charcot's time? In the 1880s, Republican legitimacy had been established, setting women and minors apart. Above all, the universality of the people means the universality of men; women's equality is a utopian dream, their freedom a non-event. Studies aiming to determine how women were able to tear away from the confinement of the private sphere, how they made use of contradictions, systems, and discourses to escape from their status as object and weaken the dominant discourse[10]

show that women's relation to madness "is a historically constituted relationship." It seems that "exceptional" women were classed as a subspecies of hybrid monsters and that their aspirations trangressed the norms imposed by a patriarchal bourgeoisie whose power belonged to the dawn of the industrial era. Charcot belonged to this imposing bourgeoisie and, in 1872, on Gambetta's initiative, was endowed by Parliament with a clinical chair in diseases of the nervous system. In this context, then, the hysterical body becomes the outlet for a rebellion otherwise impossible to articulate.

What is the function of the hysteric's grotesque body? The hysteric, especially Charcot's, imitates to excess the example of an outlet offered by power yet it simultaneously subverts this model and the interpretation that the Master offers it. The excess becomes a blind spot breaking the mimetic symmetry, an expression of the resistance (even unconscious) she exhibits before the eyes of the Master, perhaps replaying the incestuous act of which she was the victim—but Charcot was blind to it.

This discursive hybridization jams the theoretical machine, "suspends its pretention to the production of a much too univocal truth and meaning" in a much too monological discourse. But this margin of liberating excess, "this friction between two extremely close neighbors which creates a dynamic,"[11] risks creating a pure loss of heat, consuming only the suffering subject, for we are far from the joyous body bursting with liberty, a carnival body, "triumph of a temporary freeing from the dominant truth" as Bakhtin would have put it.[12] Like Allon White and Peter Stallybrass, we recognize hysterical carnival's subversive potential but we disavow the essentialist interpretation which makes it an expression of the feminine. Instead we see in it the historical inscription of a rebellion, an attempt by woman to affirm her position as subject: "We can avoid the return to the lost realm's sentimentalism by drawing the articulation of the domains and places of discourse in the historical formation of subject classes. We thus avoid the sublimation (regressive utopia) inseparable from the strategies of domination."[13] Nonetheless, intimations of critical utopia can be seen beneath the surface of Charcot's discourse; they can also be seen in the hysteric's reported discourse.

In the following case, a mother accompanies her daughter and re-

sponds to Charcot's questions; the girl has only three brief replies of a
biographical nature (p. 111–114). A rhetoric of authority (the informal
form of address, "tu"; the use of the imperative; and insults) firmly
establishes a power relationship: "Come now, move your fingers, come
along, don't show your nasty disposition!" The process of embedding
the other's discourse, either by annexing it to a theory or by integrating
the expected response into a question ("Does your daughter stiffen when
bending backwards?"), orients the interpretation by contamination of
meaning. When an answer contains a new element (the novum) that
will not fit with Charcot's theory, he treats it as residual, ignoring it,
rejecting it, or classifying it as a mystery. Later, he asks an assistant to
apply pressure on a hysterogenous spot near the ovaries in order to
provoke an attack: "(The sick girl all of a sudden cries out: Mummy,
I'm afraid!)." No quotation marks introduce the other's words, only
parentheses which reify them into a didascaly. It is Charcot's diagnos-
tic which is emphasized and falls like a cleaver before his audiences:
"You see how hysterics scream. One could say it's a lot of noise over
nothing. Epilepsy is more serious and much quieter." A socio-ideologi-
cal discourse (the valorization of feminine silence) permeates and con-
taminates science, indeed, becomes its substitute. The hysteric's words,
which could have constituted the embryo of an interlocutional ethic
and of a new knowledge, ends up distanced and thrown into discursive
scoria by the Master.

What can we learn from this brief voyage to the depths of hysteria?
First of all, it confirms the necessity and importance of a metadisciplinary
hermeneutics which can lead us to a circumspect lucidity when dealing
with theory. In our research on hysteria, we have paid particular attention to the representation that exceeds the discourse of power in its
function as critical utopia (carnivalesque body, margins of discourse,
theoretical dissidences, hysterics' words), all the traces/*pharmakon* that
the discourse of medical power has left us in spite of itself. But for
these weak bubbles, which burst at the surface of official discourse,
how many muffled voices are there, how many blocked research trails?
In backtracking along theory's path, we have made the epistemological
choice of returning to the concrete historical origin of knowledge; we
have therefore touched a limit of human science, that of personalization, of dialogical interlocution preoccupied with an ethics of difference; it is in this direction that some sciences which later received the
name of human sciences have recently evolved. They have progressively
differentiated themselves from the other limit set by Charcot, that is to
say, from a positivist discourse serving patriarchal power. It is therefore not a question of rejecting psychoanalysis but of showing its limits

and, in the same relativizing stride, of creating receptive space for psychoanalysis which takes into consideration the sociosexual conditioning of women. Moreover, the term "human sciences" can seem like an oxymoron, emphasizing the double stumbling block its theorization is watching out for: the reification of the subject and its extreme personalization, the tyranny of science and its impossibility.

Backtracking along the path of theory has also made us complicitous voyeurs of these grotesque female bodies, an unbearable complicity to which we could not submit without exposing it critically. Indeed, seeking the critical utopian instant was our own way of refusing to enter the voyeur's game, of wanting to give a form of speech back to a human subject from a position of critical ethics. The theoretical approach in human sciences asks another ethical question; indeed, the human sciences evolve in great time, but it is a life's brief time that they affect, whence its necessary relativization and the caution it imposes. Entering into the history of the subject led us to the recovery of the lives of the subjects of history. We recognize that this approach is now possible only because we have access to academic discourse and to an interpretive community. Critical utopia teaches us how to listen to difference, not in order to marginalize it, but to welcome it as a potential; it invites us to hear dissonance as it becomes an antidote to hegemony. Further it gives feminist criticism insights into its own dialogical diffraction so that it can deconstruct its own strayings into the temptations of hegemony. However, the ethical question cannot be independent of the political question, since gratuitous interlocution without access to the possibility of change—that is, to power—can only be a simulacrum of interlocution which participates in a simulacrum of democracy. The stakes exceed the verbal interplay as any occurrence of violence reminds us.

Notes

An expanded article using this example of hysteria analyzed from a different angle has been published by the same author in *Critical Studies*, special issue on "Bakhtin, Carnival and Other Subjects" ed. David Shepherd, Vol. 3/2–Vol. 4 1/2, 1993, entitled "The Framing of the Shrew: Discourses on Hysteria and its Resisting Voices," 177–196.

1. Ernest Bloch, *Le Principe espérance* (Paris: Gallimard, 1959), p. 10.
2. Michel Foucault, *Histoire de la folie l'âge classique* (Paris: Gallimard, 1972), p. 307.
3. Carlo Ginzburg, *"Présomptions sur le sabbat"* in *Annales*, 1984, p. 346.

4. François-Marie Charcot, *L'Hystérie*, selected texts presented by E. Trillat (Paris: Privat, 1971), p. 121.
5. Mikhail Bakhtin, *Esthétique et théorie du roman* (Paris: Gallimard, 1978), p. 383.
6. François-Marie Charcot, *L'Hystérie*, selected texts presented by E. Trillat (Paris: Privat, 1971), p. 110.
7. Mikhail Bakhtin, *Esthétique et théorie du roman* (Paris: Gallimard, 1978), p. 175.
8. Mikhail Bakhtin, *Esthétique de la création verbale* (Paris: Gallimard, 1979), p. 345.
9. Ernest Bloch, *Le principe espérance* (Paris: Gallimard, 1959), p. 191.
10. Christiane Planté, "Femmes exceptionnelles: des exceptions pour quelle règle?", *Les Cahiers du GRIF*, nos. 37–38, 1988, p. 22.
11. Luce Irigaray, *Ce sexe qui n'en est pas un* (Paris: Editions de Minuit, 1977), p. 76.
12. Mikhail Bakhtin, *L'Oeuvre de François Rabelais et la culture populaire au Moyen Age* (Paris: Gallimard, 1970), p. 18.
13. Allon White and Peter Stallybrass, *The Politics and Poetics of Transgression* (Ithaca: Cornell University Press, 1986), p. 196–197.

REGARDING THE NEUTER

Eberhard Gruber

Equivalence or Incomparability?
Upstream from Gender Duality

Why tackle the problems of feminine-masculine, man-women via the "neuter"? For two reasons, essentially: on the one hand, because theses dealing with "equality" or the "equivalence of the sexes" are based upon a logic of equation which makes an abstraction of otherness. Asking that one's share be "equivalent" to the other sex's requires one to become "comparable," erasing otherness for the benefit of comparability. Here "neuter" represents the undesirable "neutralization" of which "paradigm" is the commercial measure. In this sense, therefore, "neuter" is to be avoided; to be avoided particularly when it manifests itself within the very discourse of "equality" or "equivalence." On the other hand, "neuter" is interesting because in taking up the opposing view on all argumentation based on "value," it leads to the consideration of the supposed incomparability and, indeed, the irreducibility of gender which constitute the difficulty in speaking about "sexual difference." What does the following expression proffered by Luce Irigaray mean?:[1] "[woman and man] are irreducible one to the other." What signifies "difference" here is not the word "masculine" or "feminine" but the preposition "to." The same would be found in expressions like "woman and man are different *from* each other" or "one *with* the other" ["l'un d'avec l'autre"]. In other words, the prepositions *to, from,* and *with* do not belong to those that belong to *themselves* ["s'" appartiennent], differentiate themselves ["se" différencient], connect themselves ["se" relient]. (Here we can see how much the reflexive particle *se* gives rise to ideology.) These pre-positions refer to an *other,* logically placed first, as a preposition. "Neuter" has at least the function then of pointing out that "(sexual) difference" is not in accordance with either the "feminine" or the "masculine."

The expediency of *neuter* is therefore the attempt to escape from this double impasse, to speak about "(sexual) difference" without giving in to the standardization or separation of the sexes. Which, on the grounds of the "equivalence of the sexes," leads us to undertake this *step backwards*, following the Heideggerian *step-in-retreat* [*Schritt-zurück*] that Philippe Lacoue-Labarthe requires for ethics, sketching an "archi-ethics" (or founding preethics) *upstream* from any decision as to Good and Evil and their division.[2] Whence the double methodological usage of "neuter" in what follows: as the designation of a third, a symbol of uniforming measure; as a preventative remedy (*pharmakon*). On the one hand, the "neuter" is related to *solipsism* or *tautology* and, on the other hand, to the salutary *counter-measure*.

The scope of this approach is significant: because what leaves metaphysics-in-the-masculine so open to criticism is precisely this confusion which leads to the appropriation and neglect of "difference" for the benefit of the one.[3] And to forget "difference," which is neither one nor the other of its props, is to forget the "neuter."

The Ambiguity of Ne-uter

Let us remember the etymology of the term "neuter" without which it could end up meaning anything whatsoever: *ne-uter* is "neither one nor the other." Neither one nor the other of these *words* which delimit this term; neither one nor the other of their *referents*: "feminine" and "masculine." Nor anything else referred to by a sign, whatever it may be. Defined in dictionaries as "floating, uncertain, indecisive, obscure, enigmatic, equivocal," indeed as "doubtful" or "suspicious," "neuter," in its ambiguity, aims at *neither* ambiguity *nor* precision. Rather it is a question of what is *in-between*. In all cases.

Is it necessary, then, to conclude that "neuter" means "in between"? Thus translated positively, this referent must again fall under *neuter*'s cup/cut ["sous la coupe"]: neither presence nor absence of "in-between." In other words, the *word* "neuter" has no substitute which would be its "own." It does not have its own meaning, and if it does not speak of either one or the other except to repudiate them, it speaks even less of itself. *Ne-uter is a way of avoiding the Same.* "Neuter" is in-appropriate ["im-propre"] for the designation of what a sign usually says of its referent.

The question of "neuter" therefore seems linked, from the beginning, to the unnameable, to the elusive, and its ambiguity is to be taken seriously.

Paradoxically, the difficulty in grasping or naming the "in-between" stems less from its being too *far* than from being *too close*. Language no longer has its characteristic function: to speak in the absence of "things." As if the word had no effect on the thing, the "in-between" is there, not distanced, unnamed pre-sense, yet nameable as well as having emerged in the form of a sign. A *dividing up* is thus sketched upon which the "neuter" rests while making a sign.

Now, to say that *ne-uter*, in its double negation (neither . . . nor), dismisses all effects of the Same is to state that "neuter" purports *nothing* which could take the place of the one and the other; it maintains *nothing* and thereby assures the coming of one and the other, *their* pursuit. Just as the interruption allows one to envisage the resumption of the interrupted, so "neuter" neither reifies nor annuls one and the other: it sets them in *rhythm*, rhythmic ek-sistence of one and the other. In this sense, "neuter" carries with it an opening, a *free place* (by dis-location of Sameness), a *displacement* (with regard to this opening) and an *iterativity* (the dis-placements of otherness, their intersected existence). Nothing is lost in this sectioning *except for the benefit of the other*. The "neuter" is the mark of the inevitable displacement of the two; the "in-between," an element of intermittence, ab-senses which come through recognition and interruption of its referent. Through the presentation of its present or interrupted referent.

Ne-uter also indicates a *liberated* place: liberated from *Sameness* which could have been or which has been. Against this solipsistic, tautological referent, *ne-uter* enunciates its ambivalent promise, *neither-nor*. It thus leads to a flawless *monolithic* element at the same time as it indicates the flaw of a *rift* as soon as differentiation appears. "Neuter," then, does not silence the menace of alienation's possible *return*. Between the threat of solipsistic uniformization and the opening of a differential rift, *ne-uter* emits, in a broken manner, its messages: that is to say, the peril of neutralization as well as displacement and iterativity. We are thus obliged to *sew them back together*, that is, to tell a story.

Ne-uter *on Stage*

In itself, the term *ne-uter* is already an entire staging: the direct designation by a name usually reduces effort, and therefore virtual understanding, to binary acts such as "known/unknown," "understood/not understood." Understanding is simply either acquired or lacking, no transition is possible. The "neuter," on the contrary, following the path of negations, erects scaffolding all around the unbuilt, thereby constraining *intelligence* to study the undefined areas of "looking" and "choosing between" (as in the Latin root *inter-legere*). The *ne-uter*, therefore, leads like an oracle to the edge of understanding and then demands that the task be accomplished. It thereby sketches the field of a present(ed) and doubly repudiated duality which allows us to see that the "One" must *remain absent* or *dislocate itself* so that the dual may appear. *Neuter* thus reveals itself disassociated, sign of an ex-plication (in the Heideggerian sense of *Auseinandersetzung*) which sets up the stage of a *differend* (Lyotard). (And it is not by chance that the German word for "neuter," *sächlich*, come from *Sache* in its original sense of "pursuit, conflict, war, trial [judicial]" or of "quarrels," and, precisely, "differend" [Grimm'sches *Wörterbuch*].) This conflict or *polemos* is that of a *passage* which engages One and the dual and where "neuter" simultaneously constitutes a *call* to an understanding of the "in-between" and a *reminder* of the absent or dis-appeared Sameness. In other words, *neuter*'s "free" place reads right-side up as "opening," upside down as "sacrifice," and the transition must pass by the *blow* which makes it such that One divides itself in favor of the dual, of the multiple.

What conclusion can be drawn from this heavy metaphorical baggage?

Opening and Sacrifice

Let us remember that the problem posed here is that of *belonging* and *lineage*. Heidegger, in the step-in-retreat of his thought, gives "neuter" (in its sense of the "neutrality of *Dasein*," of "being-there") the status of an "inherent positivity"[4] to which Derrida justifiedly objects that this "positive neutrality" finds itself "on the *same* side" as "binary" sexuality and thus proves to be inappropriate for the conception of a "pre-differential sexuality, or rather pre-dual."[5] As we have shown elsewhere,[6] these two positions lead to the opposition between human gender (*Geschlecht*) and the ab-ject: *Geschlecht* understood here not so much in the sense of "mark" or "stamp" as in the sense of "those who have taken the same direction" (Kluge); *ab-ject* understood in the sense of pre-ceding gender, upstream and against the flow of dual (sexual) division in the sense of a root which appears *de*generated *after* the fact, even though engendering passed through it. Which leads us to ask how the two "genders," dual and ab-ject, are just as much one *to* the other as they are one *of* the other, belonging *and* lineage. And to understand that the necessary "blow" passes through the question of the liaison between "opening" *and* "sacrifice." *Which blow* will assure the appearance of the dual without eliminating the ab-ject—thus responding to the ambivalence required by *ne-uter*. It is a blow which *connects* dis-place-ment's *violence* to the donative nature of this event by which the "ab-ject" accepts its dis-location—and we here rejoin a "etiotopotomology," that is, a questioning which reflects upon the place and reason for an original separation. Derrida develops these thoughts on etiotopotomology in his recent work entitled *Circonfession*,[7] and his approach leads in particular to criticism on circumcision, this violent blow against the male body that is to symbolize, according to the Old Testament, the Abrahamman covenant with Iahvé. Derrida asks for *"another* etiotopotomology" which would place the blow's violence differently (paragraph 26). But how can we conceive another strategem for the heteronomic covenant?

Let us go back a bit. The pecularity of the Abrahamman covenant consists in situating the sacrificial act of circumcision inside the relationship between Iahvé-Abraham—and not outside of it. The other ritual method, to which the fifteenth chapter of Genesis still refers, goes back at least as far as the second millenium B.C. to the Babylonian city of Mari and tells us this: in order to conclude a solemn alliance, an animal (if not several) was cut in two and, after arranging the halves on each side of the altar, each contracting party would pass between the bloody pieces while pronouncing a curse which, in the case of a breach of contract, would bring the fate of the victim upon himself. Let us take note of the distinctive characteristic of these two versions of the rite: according to the Abrahamman rewriting, man does not escape the sacrifice which, however, only virtually and subsequently affects the contracting party in the other version.

This, obviously, changes everything: whereas the heterosacrificial rite presupposes a protective, *donative* order (inasmuch as there is no personal error), the Abrahamman covenant knows no prior gift or help. The first depends upon a preceding element which promises protection due to lineage; the second can only rely upon a membership where he risks his skin (now is the time to say it). Leaving aside all other issues, particularly the difference of the rite in Judaism and Christianity, let us consider the precise question: *who or what is the victim?* It is evidently the sacrifice of the animal rather than the human sacrifice which meets "neuter's" criteria.

This brings us immediately from *Genesis* to *Greek* tragedy. I would suggest, however, that everything revolves around what we could call the "matter of the goat"—goat sacrificed here and there, sometimes according to the rites of the Old Testament (*Leviticus* 16), sometimes according to those of ancient Greece.

It is the goat, in Greek, *tragos*, which, as we know, lends its name to tragedy: *tragōdos* is a member of the tragic choir, a tragic actor or poet, and the plural *tragodoi* designates the tragic performance itself (Chantraine). Together (as the altar in the Greek theater still indicates) they are reminiscent of an earlier *sacrificial* scene where the *tragōdos* dances and sings for the *tragos*: *in order to* win the goat as "prize" of a competition (*agōn*) and *in order to* surround it at the place of its sacrifice. The rite unfolds in two stages: the execution of the goat and the distribution of the "prize"; distribution of a sacred meal made up of the edible parts of the animal while what is inedible (bones and fat) rises to the heavens in fire and flames (Pauly-Wissowa). I see in this an original scene by which the human explains (to itself) its lineage.

What does the death of the *tragos* signify? A living animal is cut in the middle so as to delineate the space of an interval in which the human passes and affirms an alliance. A vital unity disappears and the blow which kills the animal opens the way to the human and to a fruitful alliance in this term's multiple meanings. Nutritional "alliance," certainly, but why marked by the sacred? Let us remember that the goat was a privileged sacrificial animal because of its lustfulness and its procreative powers, and that, etymologically, *tragos* is linked to *tragizō* (in the sense of "having a voice which changes" during puberty) as well as to *tragaō* which designates "vines giving off lush and sterile shoots" (Chantraine). Here we are in full *rupture* between sterility and fertility and, according to the rite, fertility passes by the blow delivered to sterility which, then, bears fruit. The little basket (*kaneon*) where the sacrificial knife (*machaira*) is kept, completely covered with grain, with barley, it seems, resumes everything in its own way: the seeds of fertility are stronger than the violence (of the knife). Fertility passes *between* the grain and the knife: sterile unity, opened by a symbolic gesture, renders the virtual fertility ready for use. Thus occurs the *conjuction*, by the blow; to which correspond the handfuls of grain thrown by the participants into the air so that they fall around the altar and upon the animal. Violence liberates the fertilizing gesture: blow which kills and/is blow which seminates. We are only one step from believing that the cutting up of the goat symbolizes the dis-location of a preceding totality, thereby creating an obstacle to all genesis. Dis-sociating the original uniformity, the blow provokes the passage from the ab-ject mono- or dif-formity to the multiple life which benefits the human species. What is to be done when one assumes that the ancestral ab-ject "dies" for the good? It is eaten and the sacred meal reminds the multitude (the *khoros*) of its lineage. A sort of Eucharist before its (biblical) time. There is movement and singing: there is no keeping still in the *same* place, nor making the *same* sound (such is indeed the dis-location of Sameness); legs are stretched, voices vibrate: ambivalent song and dance. For not one of the Greek songs that can be historically associated to these distant times of sacrifice coincide in form and content. *Paian* ("pean"), *nomos*, and *dithurambos* move from a plaintive and funereal tone to one of jubilation in an arhythmical mode full of improvisations. This is before the rule appears. But only *these irregularities* can simultaneously evoke what pre-cedes and what follows afterward, condition and result, without passing over the impotence of the sign in silence. It is not knowing which makes the sign tremble and renders it iterative. The satyrs (*saturoi*), men who participated in sacrifices disguised as goats, sum it up rather well: after having gutted the goat with a blow of the knife, they are the ones, the satyrs, who *mime* the profitable "inversion": putting themselves in the goat's place, in its skin, they gather the fruit of their commemoration—sing, dance, revel, in a word: ek-sist. Their name, from the Indo-European root *sè (is), meaning "to send away, throw into the air or onto the ground" (used especially for the agricultural act of *sowing* [Kluge; Pokorny]) announces their role: to be the good demons of a fertility overflowing with crops. And it is by following their own logic, which consists of gathering the effects of an original Sameness' dislocation that one can associate the satyrs with Greek mythology's *Burst God* ["*Dieu éclaté*"]: with Dionysus in his double form of *Zagreus*, the "first" Dionysus who was torn apart by the Titans, and of *Bacchus* who, born of the Dionysian heart swallowed by his mother Semele, is identified with nocturnal revelries and the theater (Grimal). The tetralogy of Greek theater reflects this double origin by a mixed form, always completing the cycle of three tragedies by a "satyric" comedy—one that bodes well.

Tackling the question of the tragic from its background allows us to keep to the essential: the tragic, it is said, represents the *inevitable blow* which leads (human) life to death. Now, it is precisely that which is no longer justified: the sacrifice of the *tragos* does not affect life but deals symbolically with *its birth*. "Birth" which explains the appearance of the dual, of the multiple arising from an "ancestral" root which de-generates, giving up its place and which is only conceivable by its beneficiaries in terms of de-formation, ab-ject, of "revolting" ["dégueulasse"] as Lacan says of the misunderstood anamorphosis.[8] By means of the sacrificed goat, processions, song, and dance, the participants, the *khoros*, stage the history of their ab-ject ancestor (role to which the male symbol lends itself better than the feminine, for it is not the male who gives birth). And this staging clearly indicates its importance: the "One ab-ject" "divides itself" only under the condition that the *division* he is advocating is respected by the beneficiaries: specifically, the distancing-dismembering in favor of the dual. The sacrificial rite does not constitute just any slaughter or murder but rather the *mimesis* of a preceding act. We know that the very gesture that *makes the animal's blood flow* is never performed in ancient Greece: the murder bows down before ritual reasons. On the other hand, if the rite moves *beyond* the symbolic to meet with a supposed "original," it is a disaster. It is in this perspective that one must understand, I believe, Lacoue-Labarthe's notion of "original *mimēsis*."[9] The essential is in Art, and its intersection with ethics is indisputable: the staging of the monstrous entails the ethical decision to limit oneself to the performance. *Tragedy is the commemorative staging of ab-ject's "neutralization" which, from pre-positional thus becomes generative.* Art answers abject's immense gift. Any other act would lead to the calculation of exchange or to an ideological inversion of the events. This is why one cannot judge Antigone on a psychological level, whether she be "haughty" or "intractable," guilty of *hubris* like Sophocles' choir suggests. Only the *inhuman* can show where we come from: from the dividing up of the "Ab-ject." This act is the necessary turning point which "turns the distress" (in the literal German sense of *not-wendig*) of all that nonexists. When Antigone turns away from life, she symbolically designates the "birth" of all. And that which can be read as the moving history of a cursed dynasty, arousing pity and fear, represents, beyond the necessary compassion, the limits of an *anthropocentrism* from which we all still suffer. Perhaps one can understand this better from the *tragos* than from the human tragedy: we can be content with a simulacrum of the sacrifice. The ethics of Art are very clear on this point.

Aside from the inhuman Antigone, where are the *women* situated? With the bacchantes who ecstatically tear apart living beings, men and animals? Most unexpectedly, these actions place them on the *good* side. Because a God who has survived being torn apart perceives those who resist him as only a bad copy: Pentheus, whose name indicates his connection to "mourning" (*penthos*) and to "being bound" (Indo-European root *bhendh-) *neither unties himself nor bursts* before Dionysus. And Dionysus marks the strength of his own original tearing: he orders the bacchantes to tear Pentheus apart so that it will be clear that he should have let himself go without fear, with enthusiastic vitality. In spite of all appearances, women here play the role of *those who know* that enthusiasm without a victim is legitimate and necessary. They situate themselves, rather, in the logic of the *ololugē*: the ritual cries which *accompany* sadness and joy, sacrifice and celebration.

Is this to say that women find themselves distanced from the principal action? It matters little. All that precedes the real possibility of giving birth—this "birthing power" which is, indeed, *their* point of view in the symbolic system—is only *pre*history. They place themselves afterwards. If the satyrs want to procreate without being able to give birth, one lends them, and rightfully so, a sterile excitation, lechery to the point of being ridiculous—whereas the women benefit from the serenity given by the knowledge-of-being-fertile.

Radiance with Shadow

Will we be ending up with a *natural superiority in women* with masculine cultural predominance as counterpart? Certain viewpoints with regard to the mythological Great Mother's glory or of historical matriarchy presuppose this superiority and at the same time refute cultural phallocracy. It seems to me that this confrontation between supposed superiorities on the natural and social levels replay what Hegel said about the master/servant relationship: it is through work that the male not only catches up with woman's procreative lead but surpasses their power by instating cultural dominance. Which is no proof of legitimacy. And the *ne-uter* states this by its double negation: on the one hand, it designates that which, before the dual (and the sexual), deconstructs itself in the direction of both sexes and arrives there like a gift. (The greatest "value" called "natural" marks therefore the One-Deconstructer and not the dual or the sexes.) On the other hand, *ne-uter* opposes what Marx calls *leveller*[10] and which summarizes the essence of masculine domination well. "Neuter" goes *against capital* which, situated after otherness, is supposed to represent what comes before as a uniform constraint having priority weighing upon the real. All of our gestures and acts are in fact worked on *from below* by a differential that requires both displacement and an increase in productive competence, stipulating an active diversity in everyone financed by personally accumulated plus-value. The liberation of women (and of men) occurs, as we know, through the *deconstruction of the dualism* between "dwelling place = woman" and "place of work = man."

One can therefore read the notion of "value" both ways: capital is to plus-value what the "ab-ject" is to the "in-between." And if deconstructing capital is bringing plus-value back down to its proper dimension (rhythmic indicator for the increasing variety of personal competence), all the while keeping the notion of "capital" as a negative delineation, the "ab-ject" and the "in-between" similarly acknowledge their participation in the general order of division. It is for us to decide upon our relationship to these elements: in sign-sign logic, this relationship will be a commemorative staging of the "Monstrous"; in the logic of the sign-real transgression, this relationship will be a return of the catastrophic. Taking the "ab-ject" into consideration in a symbolic manner is to assign it its position of presence-pre-cedence. The ab-ject, on the threshold of division, is only waiting for a sign.

Looking again at the problem of the "equivalence of the sexes," we must now situate it in terms other than impasse: by taking it up in a *transitional* perspective. "The neuter-child does not exist," Irigaray tells us;[11] no more than the "human genus," I would add. They are nothing but abstractions, yet necessary ones, since inducing a parallel feminine-masculine order obviates any encounter. The "ne-uter," on the contrary, marks the interruption of parallels and prepares crossroads. The terms "child" or "human genus" are *the very condition to enable speaking to each other in "sexual difference."* In fact, we speak to each other directly by using the personal pronouns *I, you, we*, leaving the indicator of sex to *he, she* and their plural forms. Without "ne-uter," there is no dialogue or understanding, and *ne-uter* adds, moreover, that all that is said, is said *in passing*. Derrida refers to this in his manner: "my sole desire remains *to give the interruption to be read* which will, in any case, decide upon the figure itself" (*Circonfession*, paragraph 10). Dialogue as writing would then be situated between two incommensurable Samenesses to be disarticulated: silence and noise; the whiteness of the page and the blackness of the ink. In deconstructing these two extremes, the artifice of oral and written dialogue is formed. The alliance is made through *rhythm*. And Hélène Cixous does this, in *Neutre*, for example: by metamorphosizing extremes, their conflicts, their losses, their placated encounters as well as their being put back into play. She thus sketches a perpetual staging which strives to interpret an initial crossroads in succession, in pro-cession.[12]

Where do we come from? From our anni-versary: something turns, has turned. The relief of the delivery is also called "afterbirth" ["arrière-faix"] from the Latin *fascis*, a bundle of sticks ["fagot"], which takes on the meaning of "burden," and "foetus"; *fascis* bears similarities to the Greek "fagot," *phakelos*, and subsequently to "torch" (Greek *phanos*, Latin *fax*). Just as the newborn is the "burden" by which the "light" of life arrives, so the "arrière-faix" is the *placentiary* "fagot" which is lost at birth, this "revolting" thing whence we come. Ab-ject thing through which begetting passes. Indissociable right and wrong side of a vital irruption. In this respect, the greatest objection that one might make to Heidegger's famous *Lichtung* is that a glade can only exist where there is sterility: "natural" or created by slaughter and stubble-burning. Does this mean that there is *gift* because there has been *fire*, burn of a disappearance? That there is no appearance without loss? No *it is/it gives* [*es gibt*] without *it burns* [*es brennt*]?[13] In its immolation of the goat, the Greek rite tells us that it is something *else* that is consumed "by fire" and gives up its place.

In the Greek theater there was an altar (*thumelē*) in the middle of the *orkhēstra*, and, further behind, separate, the *skēnē* delimited by a barrier with three passages, the portico. Did tragedy revolve around openings and sacrifices? Does the tragic put on stage the place of a necessary and de-cisive passage? Antigone replies with the appropriateness of her *hubris*, a liberating insolence because she is returning to *her* place which is death; and the entire play responds by staging such a passage.

Dionysus' tomb, which the Ancients located at Delphi, had the form of a small altar (*bōmos*), also called a "step" or "support" or "embankment" (or, for Heideggerians, *Gestell*) and which was situated at the very foot of the altar dedicated to Apollo. "Step" of a being torn apart in the service of a "luminous" God? Antigone had no doubt about the relationship between the "tomb" (*bothros*) and the "step" (*bōmos*): in sprinkling earth upon Polynices' inert body, she creates an "embankment," and in giving him funereal honors, she buries her brother as he should be. Funereal embankment and trench, the sacred and death converge. Indeed, *bōmos* and *bothros* are the two distinct places of veneration: one for the Olympian gods; the other for the chtonian gods.

Ne-uter is what indicates the deconstruction of One, the start of *katharsis*, purification of a monstrous beginning; it thus traces the way for the *kharis*, the joy of all, the choir: commemorative song, dance, enthusiasm.

What is given and what remains is therefore, in the best case, the best . . . possible. Inscribed in this sublime distancing, joy needs terrible, although symbolic, memories—needs the radiance of Art *with* shadow.

Notes

1. Luce Irigaray, *L'Éthique de la différence sexuelle* (Paris: Éditions de Minuit, 1984), p. 19 *sq.*
2. Philippe Lacoue-Labarthe, "De l'éthique: à propos d'Antigone," in *Lacan avec les philosophes* (Paris: Albin Michel, 1991), p. 21–36.
3. Jean-François Lyotard indicates a similar danger on the feminine side in *Les Fins de l'homme. A partir du travail de Jacques Derrida* (Paris: Galilée, 1981), p. 393.
4. Martin Heidegger, *Metaphysische Anfangsgründe der Logik im Ausgang von Leibniz* (1928) (Frankfurt am Main: Klostermann, 1978), 10.1, 2.
5. Jacques Derrida, "Geschlecht. Différence sexuelle, différence ontologique" (1983) in *Psyché, Inventions de l'autre* (Paris: Galilée, 1987), p. 403 (emphasis added).
6. Eberhard Gruber, "L'Humain partagé ou Comment (s') emanciper sans exclure" in *Lectures de la différence sexuelle*, Anne E. Berger, ed., vol. 2.

7. Jacques Derrida, "Circonfession" in Geoffrey Bennington and Jacques Derrida, *Jacques Derrida* (Paris: Seuil, 1991).

8. Jacques Lacan, *L'Éthique de la psychanalyse. Le séminaire* (Paris: Seuil, 1986), p. 162 *sq.*

9. Eberhard Gruber, "Mimésis de quoi? En discussion avec Philippe Lacoue-Labarthe," *Cahiers de l'École des sciences philosophiques et religieuses*, Brussels, 8 (1990), p. 67–88.

10. [In English in the original.]

11. Luce Irigaray, *Sexes et genres à travers les langues* (Paris: Grasset, 1990), p. 19.

12. Hélène Cixous, *Neutre* (Paris: Grasset, 1972).

13. Eberhard Gruber, "Du droit de blesser. In(ter)ventions à propos de Jacques Derrida. *Circonfession*," *Cahiers de l'École des Sciences Philosophiques et Religieuses*, Brussels 13 (1993): pp. 121–153.

THE FEMININE
AND ECOLOGY
Verena Andermatt Conley

The social can no longer be thought of as separate from natural problems. Natural problems are tied to the social. This will have perhaps
been one of the important lessons of the twentieth century and upon
which, according to some, will depend the twenty-first century's very
existence. If we decide to count by centuries, we must turn back to the
nineteenth to find the origin of important social discourses. It is from
this point on that women, Blacks, and other minorities — as well as those
who hold power — must think of their claims as "subject," in the singular or collectively, in connection with nature. The subject is to be re-
thought in a world that may sometimes appear foreign to it but which,
in any case, can no longer serve as simple decor. For today, as Michel
Serres points out, "nature enters history, history enters nature. This is
what is unprecedented in philosophy.[1]

It is following the first landing on the moon, from where the Earth
could be seen in its entirety, that the term "ecology," in its everyday
meaning of the protection of nature, was coined. Paradoxically, the
term "ecology" remains tied to the visibility and division between subject and object, to the division, therefore, that in the span of a few
hundred years contributed to the earth's deterioration. This division
resulted in the birth of *homo faber* who, valorizing existence in terms
of "production," set himself up as master of himself as well as of the
universe and worked to appropriate the world by technique in its sense
of instrumentality. The new rational subject tried to extend its domination over the world, other peoples, and women. Now, the majority of
social theories prolong the dialectic of master and slave without taking the world into consideration. In their attempts to appropriate
the world through the domination of nature, capitalism and commu-
nism converge.

However, some theoreticians and cultural critics have recently drawn
attention to the fact that a simple displacement of power will not suffice. If social theories were the prerogative of the nineteenth century, in

the twentieth century, they will have to be rendered more complex by ecological concerns. In a talk on liberty delivered before the National Assembly, Claude Lévi-Strauss invokes cultural pluralism and suggests replacing the term "man" with the term "living being." He accuses our technological society of having contributed to the deterioration of the world and of lacking respect for other cultures and other species.[2] Michel de Certeau acerbically criticizes Western society which, in its drive to dominate and by its techniques, destroys the common man's habitat. In praising the South American Indians' politics of resistance, he emphasizes what he calls Western man's hatred of a nature that he wants only to dominate or eliminate.[3] Nearer to contemporary ecological movements, Michel Serres insists on the necessity of a new bond with nature. The natural contract which has, up until now, guaranteed the inalienable rights of man must include the world and its entities. Other ties must be woven with the world, other means of attaching ourselves to it and detaching ourselves from it. And it is especially necessary to learn how to listen to the language of things.[4]

Ecology is therefore not simply the "protection of nature" and of what we mistakenly call the "environment." Ecological problems result from an ideology that has contributed to the deterioration of our habitat and nature. Furthermore, not only have ecological problems not been prevented, they have been produced by technology at the service of an ideology with its inherent idea of progress. The birth of this ideology of integrated global capitalism where divisions between left and right are less and less clear can be historically dated. It coincides with the second scientific revolution which went hand in hand with the birth of the rational subject which will dominate and enlighten the world by expansionism and colonialism. Now, given current ecological problems, social demands can no longer be content with a simple overturning of power but must at the same time challenge the ideology underlying a technocratic world with its politics of speed and profit. Henceforth, all discourses of emancipation—feminist, pluralist, cultural—must let themselves be crossed—and not crowned—by ecological concerns.

Some women have discerned the connection between the single subject and the subjugation not only of women but also of indigenous peoples and other species. Their artistic practices portray how women's claims must pass through the world and, of course, through language. Indeed, expansionist ideology goes hand in hand with grammar, syntax, and especially with the reduction of the world to two-dimensions, that is, to an object that can be studied. For women, it will be a question of inventing new relationships with the world through language. All pluralism is also—or above all—linguistic, and it is necessary to (re)invent a language that allows the other to speak and which speaks (about) the other.

We can think of Marguerite Duras who, in all her texts, criticizes Western white man's rational language and invents other languages that are often transmitted through feminine voices. Rejecting the contemporary, technological world, she seeks to write other relationships between humans and objects. These concerns can be seen in *Le Camion* where she alternately presents visions of a postmodern and a mystical world. It is with a certain irony that she shows images of a mock progress, dehumanized zones or so-called "new" cities and alludes to historical cases of technological destruction as in concentration camps and the atomic bomb. She establishes a tension between these images and the hitchhiker's mystical vision. The invisible woman in the truck exists only in transition. She clears herself a path by narration and brushes against the world without possessing it. As opposed to the technological world which compresses space-time, she opens a space by movement and narration.

In this context, we think especially of Hélène Cixous who has always strongly criticized technological reduction by means of her textual cosmologies. In her use of the adjective "feminine," which circulates in some of her more theoretical texts as an attribute of both *writing* and *economy*, she emphasizes the exchange between other subjects and the world. In choosing the adjective rather than the noun, she anticipates all that is reductive about the latter. If writing, in Cixous' sense of the word, is not of the technological sort which has supplanted the voice, but is rather that which, like a spacing out, is already in the voice and traces the path, it is always in relation with the other.[5] As an attribute of *economy*, "feminine" opens onto the gift. The opposite of masculine retention and appropriation, "feminine" functions as that which exceeds, crosses, burrows through time and space, and gives without holding back.

"Feminine" can be associated with "ecology" by an implicit critique of the habitat and nature's deterioration and of technological reduction. The way in which this critique is fashioned at the level of language can be seen in one of the texts written when Hélène Cixous met Clarice Lispector and Heidegger.

Writing in the country of the Amazon, Lispector was also brimming with Eastern ideas, particularly Indian ones. In the Western era of the "I" which coincides with the habitat's deterioration, she meditates upon the oriental concepts of casting off the "I" and of spiritual richness in poverty. Texts like *Agua viva* focus on decentering the human being in a world which is equally animal and vegetal. *La Passion selon G.H.*

tells of an experience of oriental renunciation and concludes with the narrator and the world's interdependence.

In his analyses of technique, particularly in "The Question of Technique," Heidegger clearly distinguishes between an instrumental technology which dominates and destroys the world and a poetic technique which is open to movement and where the human is thought of within the world.

Reading with—or as she prefers to say, "letting herself be read by"—Lispector and Heidegger, Hélène Cixous writes being in the world. In *Illa*, we find a heavenly garden that the writing "I" finds within "she." I (she) seek to enter into a relationship with various entities that would not be one of domination. It is a matter of learning how to listen to the language of these things and to let them happen. In a passage calling itself the "calm school of approaches," Hélène Cixous writes a new apprenticeship. To the dehumanization of the modern world she condemns, she opposes a world where the human being is not cut off from its body. She replaces a world of domination with a world of love and unrestrained exchange.

> In our days of stupid fatigue, we go years without opening the windows, we don't think about it anymore, we forget them one by one, first, those of the house, then those of the heart, then we no longer read the letters that love, we no longer descend into the book, neither into the garden, we no longer touch the earth with our hand. We are of a modern distraction.[6]

This transformation of the "technologized" subject into a loving subject is achieved by the feminine. Some women are able to remember a childhood where they were at one with the world: "But there are some childhoods which remember themselves. And certain women are all childhood." A hellish technological world is opposed to the memory of a childhood paradise at one with the world through another language:

> I have an Oranian childhood which remembers the plants at the foot of the hill inside the Jardin d'essais ["Garden of Endeavors"]. From it I learned what I can still understand of the plants' words. It was a childhood absolutely faithful to the world: naturally . . . It did not think about the plants, it lived among them, and, in an obscure way, felt itself grow, swell, expand underground, felt breathing, breathing. That which was mysteriously happening in the garden happened within it in the same mystery. It did not pay attention, it was all attention. It is still that within me which knows how to stay in a garden without moving away, without excluding, without losing itself: without seeking to win it; how to live as a garden, remain in its milieu, to be naturally in its reign and to keep it.

This harmony with the world refuses the appropriation which passes through language and reduces the world to an object: "Without trying to appropriate it, making an inventory of it, uprooting it from its soil, treating it like a municipal park, far from plants, denaturing it, contemptuous of its immense living culture." A new knowledge, lost and found again—other—is the opposite of a schoolish knowledge with its technologies: "This childhood knew how to tend a true garden of endeavors: it knew it without having to learn. It undoubtedly knew it from the garden itself, in time, before beginning the studies of forgetfulness." The woman writer must work to find a language of immediacy, body and soul, soil and sky:

> And I must strive to find what it was given before learning everything, at the same time it lived the earth, plant to plant, what was known about it since the soil and sky, immediately. Our modern faithfulness is not natural. It is not given. We can no longer listen to things speak in their languages, go to listen to the languages of things before any translation, we no longer know how, we forget to do so.

This passage puts into play the opposition between a technological, destructive, rational, white man's world with his language that forgets, projects, and names, and another world with a secret language, nameless, that knows how to find certain women, closer to the body, who have a memory of their childhood:

> We have been taught the language that speaks from on high, from afar, which listens to itself, which has ears only for itself, deaf language, deafening, that speaks to us ahead of time. We have been taught the language which translates everything into itself—understands nothing other than in translation; speaks only in its own language, listens only to its own grammar; and we are separated from things by its order.
>
> To hear the song of a fig from the Barbary Coast, I must first leave the language that speaks to me before I have had the time to remember it. Speaks very loud, throws about names so noisily and I no longer hear the beloved call of the eucalyptus.

And the feminine "I" proposes—and writes—in the place of the language that separates and distances the body and the world, one which produces the book as object, another language, close to the living, to the instant, where writing and living are not separated, a language before the division into subject and object.

> But I have a childhood which knew. It lives in the Jardin d'essais. It still knows what I know no longer. I have so much to unlearn before I can re-know what it knows. Language distracts us. We let our-

selves be diverted by grammar, distanced from objects by sentences, we let language dub us, slyly throw itself in front of things just before we are able to reach them. Language tells about the promenade before we have been able to accomplish it in life: and we walk around in language, following its instructions, we have walked to its head, we don't know what we are doing, what we are living is intercepted, undone, put back into place, and the promenade is given back to us, all awry, on the plane of language, we descend according to its slopes, it is what guides us, far from ourselves, makes us walk in the missteps of its languages steps, staggering.

This new language is that of immediacy and pleasure. "The financial market" with its restrained exchange is replaced by the "movement of the market" so as to live with its colors, perfumes, and animated voices:

> To enjoy a promenade from the path along the ridge to the soil of the Jardin d'essais, to follow the path faithfully, according to life, according to the body, we must leave surreptitiously, give every sentence of recommendation the slip, and now live, simply live, live entirely there where we live, begin as it begins, let things happen the way they happen their way, let the rose be smelled in the way of the rose, go down toward the garden, enticed, drawn by the call of its freshness, go down trusting the body, like my childhood went down, before knowing the names of the streets, but the senses know their way, before proper names and common names, all the way along the perfume, walking with feet in sandals, among heavy odors, in the movement of the market.

The habitat's deterioration is treated here at the level of language. The text denounces contemporary technological hell with its masculine economy and creates a feminine cosmology or a new "ecological" paradise. Contrary to technological acceleration which kills things—or relegates them to oblivion—it is a question of slowing down and allowing things to appear in their own manner and time. It is about slowly approaching the other, letting it be, and not taking it by its name. The modern world where everything is calculated and appropriated according to precise techniques signifies the loss of paradise. To find what has been lost in oneself is another feminine gesture. This passage contrasts the adult world and childhood, nature and culture, the lived and the book (grammar, language of translation, rules), being-in-the-world and that which dominates and possesses the world.

It is about the loss of a paradise. The garden has been lost, repressed by culture and schooling which prevent us from living in harmony with the animal, human, and vegetal world. In the contemporary world, we live in projection. We have a linear relationship with the world and do not live it like paradise, according to its rhythms, its breath, that is to say, in harmony with it, in the moment, before all language that cuts and replaces.

It is about finding the lost world of childhood *in* the adult. Paradise is lost and found otherwise. Hélène Cixous proposes substituting a culture cut off from the world with a living culture. She wants to find a language before any translation or "uprooting" which would allow the book to be written as it would be lived and where she could walk among things without having to dominate them from above.

It is not, however, a simple paradox of replacement. Paradise is lost but it is still the "I" coming into play ["il est encore en 'je'"], such that she may write it. It is the memory of childhood as "I" that permits her to write it. The long sentences mime the movement of the promenade, the time that burrows into the walk. Text of presence, unfragmented. Everything is connected. Verbs give movement to a text punctuated by commas, colons, but without abrupt stops. So as to let things speak, Hélène invents a language that is not cut off from the world: "She no longer thought about the plants, she lived among them." "She," the little girl in "I," feels before thinking. Thought separates, leads to the subject and to domination. In the Jardin d'essais, writing does not weigh or think as it does in the essay. She fruit: *and it is*. The world is there, everything begins with a place, "and." Our contemporary culture blocks access with its insistence on acceleration and domination.

To the postmodern world she condemns, Hélène Cixous opposes a (linguistic) paradise that "she" carries within herself and to which "I" must gain access. In order to get there, it is necessary to undo all that burdens, camouflages, translates, and go so far as to cast off the "I," achieve the infinite weightlessness where thinking and being—or living—are scarcely distinguishable. The endeavor is close to being. The garden of endeavors ["jardin d'essais"] or of "and is" ["et c'est"] or "and knows" ["et sait"], of a swarm of life. She has a knowledge always already there, connected to the world (everything begins by and . . .) without severing, without separation, without a body subjected to the multiple technologies of schooling. If it is necessary, by definition, to lose paradise and go through a first death, the emphasis is on life and harmony with the world which works through the body. Paradise is lost, but it is still a game of "I." Hélène Cixous substitutes intellectual, technical knowledge with the body's knowledge. The language founded upon the loss of innocence and the mother's body is substituted by a language of (corporal) pleasure and of immediacy. But being is always in movement and in becoming.

It is not simply about a lost paradise which one weeps over in writing, like in Proust. It is not a question of the remembrance of things past ["retrouver du temps perdu"]. On the contrary. It is necessary to find (again) the other in oneself or that which has been suffocated, forgotten, by acculturation and technologies which have transformed the body into a social subject. It is a matter of finding the spontaneity of a corporal knowledge which respects the other and which, always in movement, approaches without taking. Hélène Cixous' cosmogony rejects the world of technological construction.

Recently, turning toward cultural pluralism, Hélène Cixous shifted her writing toward what is called the "human." In her writings on theater, she meditates upon man's quest for truth, upon his desire to become human. Now, being human is to live in the world—in the Eastern manner. It is to live in our era of the ego, the "I", and paranoia, by casting oneself off, abandoning false values, and asking the question: how to become human, that is, how to respect the world? In her play on Cambodia, *L'Histoire terrible mais inachevée de Norodom Sihanouk roi du Cambodge* which, in the light of recent events, takes on a new topicality, Hélène Cixous opposes a country, a "garden" where everyone lives in harmony, to the world of capitalist ideology, especially American, with its destructive technology. Again the East giving lessons to the West.

In her writing, Hélène Cixous makes the human being a living being among the animal and vegetal species. She opens the space by movement and voice. Lets things speak. Ecology cannot be thought of in its restricted sense of protecting the environment, which has something military in the vocabulary and keeps man in the center and nature subordinate. In Hélène Cixous' texts, it is a question of love—not of defense—and of how to write the world, be part of it, without dominating it.

Notes

1. Michel Serres, *Le Contrat naturel* (Paris: François Bourin, 1990), p. 18.
2. Claude Lévi-Strauss, "Réflexions sur la liberté," *Le Regard éloigné* (Paris: Plon, 1983), p. 371–382. This article is cited by Catherine Clément in her recent book, *La Syncope, philosophie du ravissement* (Paris: Grasset), 1990.
3. Michel de Certeau, *L'Invention du quotidien*, re-edition (Paris: Bourgois), 1990, and "Politics of Silence," translated by Brian Massoumi in *Heterologies* (Minneapolis: University of Minnesota Press), 1980.
4. Michel Serres, *op. cit.*
5. Hélène Cixous est proche ici des méditations de Jacques Derrida sur l'écriture.
6. Hélène Cixous, *Illa* (Paris: des femmes, 1980), p. 135–137. All citations are taken from this passage.

CIXOUS WITHOUT BORDERS

Gayatri Chakravorty Spivak

It was about fifteen years ago that I had the chance to meet Hélène Cixous, and once I attended one of her seminars. In other words, I know her mostly as text, in the strongest sense of the term. A text that I read, teach, and write (about).

Without being a Cixous specialist, I am aware of her remarkably varied route as well as changes en route. Specialists like Verena Conley have taught us about her journey.[1] The title—"Cixous Without Borders"—could lead one to think that I am going to be dealing with *L'Indiade* or *La Prise de l'école de Madubai* in particular. No. As an Indian who remains interested in a certain type of women's politics in India, I do not think that it is there that borders give way. Rather, I am going to read Hélène Cixous' very first text, a classic text belonging to a certain Cixous who is not necessarily the one who is with us today: I am referring to "[R]ire de la méduse."[2]

My work has recently led me to the theme of feminism in decolonization. It revolves around Algeria, Bangladesh, and India. To start with, I was particularly fascinated by the question of how the work of the women's movement in the excolonies could ally itself with that of the metropolis, this latter work being theoretical. I quote Chafika Marouf, professor at the University of Oran, addressing an audience of Maghrebian sociologists:

> Current research on the family in Algeria and the Maghreb cannot be evaluated without a retrospective view, however brief, of the movement of ideas that have emerged in Europe, and in Anglo-Saxon and transatlantic countries. . . . This imperative necessity does not arise from a subjective choice, but precisely from the fact that the paradigms of academic intelligibility of feminism in Algeria and in the Maghreb have, for the most part, been modulated in the intellectual configurations of Western thought: They have offered the frame and the genesis. . . .[3]

This intelligent passage defines my charge: to see that the view is retrospective, and that the requirements are of academic intelligibility, in the service of which we write for publication.

In its first stage, my work especially strived, therefore, to supplement social sciences with philosophy and literature. I thus created an allegory *(allegory of reading)*,[4] of crossed borders, crossed out.

It is in the light of this allegory of reading that I read the moments of writing, history, and the mother in "The Laugh of the Medusa"; and in conjunction with Law, History, and the Family as they are presented in the work of the Algerian feminist Marie-Aimée Hélie-Lucas. I know that the word "feminist" is problematic in the French context and in today's Cixousian context. But I know only too well that once we jump over boundaries, we are not following the rules established either by the metropolis or by subjects-supposed-to-know. The Cixous-Hélie-Lucas encounter is what I will share with you today.

It is simultaneously odd and unnerving to offer a reading rather than a (simple) homage of a text whose author is present. But is that not perhaps what writing is, if writing is anything at all? A sort of structure which works in the absence of the expeditor, stolen from its addressee. I know that Cixous is generous enough to allow me to be a thief of her writing(s).

* * *

I will not, however, begin with my reading. We were at the first stage of my tentative steps toward feminism in decolonization, a title that I substituted for the alibi-expression: Women in development. I will also remind you that my other two spaces are called India and Bangladesh.

For me, India and Bangladesh are literary spaces unto themselves. I can manage a little broken Algerian Arabic, and I do not read classical Arabic at all. I did not know Algeria as a literary space. And I would like to thank my friend, Mireille Calle-Gruber, for having helped me make my uncertain step over *this* hurdle. She is the one who introduced me to the texts of Assia Djebar.

In the strictest manner possible, I would like to frame my reading of Cixous—a reading in the first stage of the work—with an attempt to inscribe my voice as an *aphonia* by following certain texts of Assia Djebar's.

With *L'Amour, la fantasia*, Assia Djebar situates herself in the long line of great autobiographers such as St. Augustine, Le Berbère who wrote not only his theology but also his *Confessions* in the language of Rome; and Ibn Khaldun, son of a family who fled southern Arabia and who writes not only his story but also his *Ta'arif* ("Identity") in Arabic.[5] In staging herself as an Islamic Algerian woman, Assia Djebar

provides a fragmented version of the graft-graph of her bio in French.
I quote the following passages:

> Lamination of my oral culture in distress. . . . Writing the most harmless
> childhood memories refers, therefore, to the body stripped of its voice.
> Attempting an autobiography only in French is to show more than
> one's skin under the live autopsy's slow scalpel. In speaking about a
> childhood that is no longer written, it seems that one's flesh desquamates
> in shreds. Wounds open, veins cry, one's own blood flows with that
> of others, which has never dried. (p. 177–178)

Identity: A wound exposed by historically hegemonic languages for those
women who have learned the double-binding "practice" "of [their] writing"
(p. 181). I accept this difficult definition so as to present a series of
quotes from "myself" engaged in an *identity talk*—"speaker of identity."[6]

One of the main motifs of *L'Amour, la fantasia* is a meditation on
this possibility: to carry off an autobiography in the double-bind of
this practice of the conqueror's writing is to learn to be taken seriously
by the "other woman" who has not mastered this skill. Which is why,
hidden in the third part of the book which is divided into several seg-
ments, there is a single episode where the autobiographer [*use*] speaks
in the ethical peculiarity of *tu-toi* to Zohra, a *mujahida* (liberation
fighter), an eighty-year-old peasant ravaged both by her participation
in the nationalist struggle and by her negligence of a woman's demands
in decolonized Algeria. (I will point out such a moment of ethical peculiarity in Cixous.) The uncertain end for the autobiographer-in-fiction
is to be an accomplished soothsayer for this intimate interlocutor. To
tell not one's own story, but to animate, give life to the story of two
nineteenth-century Algerian prostitutes found in Eugène Fromentin's
Un été au Sahara. And to succeed, because Zohra's curiosity burns:
"'And Fatma? And Mériem?' interrupts Lla Zohra, surprised at herself for following this story as if it were a bard's legend—'Where
did you hear that?' she continues impatiently." The "I" finally articulated to the "you," since related and responsible, can now reply:
"'I read it!' I retorted. 'A witness told it to a friend who wrote it
down'" (p. 166).

The relationship between the conqueror's and the autobiographer's
texts are part of *L'Amour, la fantasia*'s spectacular "arabesques." This
understated section concludes with these words: "I translate the relationship in the mother tongue and I bring it to you, I, your cousin.
Thus I try, as a clairvoyant, close to you, little mother in front of your
vegetable garden" (p. 167). She shares her mother tongue, instrument
of translation, with the other woman.

In the chiasma of this divided field, shared history in the mother tongue is forever present (in each reading act), and forever absent, being in the mother tongue. The authority of "now" inaugurates this absent autobiography of every "here" in the book: framed fugitive moment dismantles the "memory's blank" of its own personal childhood, giving over only the image of an old woman whose muttered curses from the Koran cannot be understood (p. 10).

The final movement of *L'Amour, la fantasia* is executed in three short pieces: what remains of an autobiography after it has been emptied thread by thread. First in an homage to Pauline Rolland, the French revolutionary of 1848 exiled to Algeria, the *mujahidat*'s true ancestor. For women, revolutionary discourse cannot count upon indigenous cultural production. If the story told to Zohra is a divided moment in the access to autobiography as a narrative of absent history, here autobiography represents the possibility to write or to give writing to the other, identifiable solely as "metonymy" of violence, mutilated metonymy, partly object. The source, once again, is Eugène Fromentin. In the following passage, an Arabic word remains untranslated: the last word in the quotation which, incidentally, means "pen":

> Eugène Fromentin holds out to me an unexpected hand, a stranger's hand that he has never been able to draw ... He then evokes a disquieting detail: at the edge of the oasis which, six months afterwards, reeked of the massacre, Fromentin picks up from the dust the hand of an anonymous Algerian woman. He then throws it onto his path. Later, I snatch up this living hand, hand of mutilation and memory, and I try to make it hold the "qalam." (p. 226)

It is with Assia Djebar's *qalam*, in this hand so distant from North Africa and France, that I will broach the mother figure and its plural staging in "The Laugh of the Medusa." I have explained myself elsewhere regarding this embrace.[7] This essay falls into two modes of address—one where, addressing one woman intimately as "*tu*," Cixous gives advice about writing and publishing on the then current French scene. By using the second-person *style indirect libre*, Cixous characterizes this person fairly elaborately. The bit about mothering is still in the "*tu-toi*" form, but it seems to dissolve the lineaments of the character of the addressee. By the time the talk moves on to the historical plurality of woman, the mode of "address," if one can even use such a term for this part of the essay, is the implicit and impersonal one of expository prose. Let us consider the two moments without ignoring their mode of presentation.

Strictly speaking, an ethical relationship with the other entails universalizing the singular. And there is no room for an ethicotheological I-thou in the space where the mother is in species-life [*Gattungsleben*] rather than species-being [*Gattungswesen*], as the prepropriative figure. In the first part of the I-thou situation of "The Laugh of the Medusa," by contrast, it is the extreme specificity of the situation—the Parisan publishing scene in the mid-1970s—that will not allow a transposition into a too-easy ethical exchange.

But what of the moment when the Parisian literary scene unobtrusively fades out and, although the "*tu*" is retained, the usefulness of the addressee's characterization is also dissolved by an entry into a strange injunction? "It is necessary and sufficient," Cixous writes first, "that the best be given to woman by another woman for her to be able to love herself and return in love the body that was 'born' to her" (p. 44). And "Mother" is the name of this "giving." Then she moves to the injunction: "You [*toi*], if you wish, touch me, caress me, give me you the living no-name, even me as myself." I would like to suggest that by thus framing the moment, Cixous releases the peculiar threshold of an ethical "I-thou" which has nothing to do with the theological. Such devices of foregrounding are not uncommon in practice that is recognizably "literary and is routinely noticed in minimally efficient literary criticism. By releasing this threshold, Cixous might be bringing into the feminine familiar that space described by Heidegger as a space of prior interrogation, "a vague average understanding of Being . . . [which] up close, we cannot grasp at all."[8]

We know that Derrida has reread such Heideggerian passages as the effaced/disclosed trace (not a past present), and the differed/deferred end (not a future present), inscribing what we must stage as our present, here and now, here only insofar as it is also away, elsewhere. Cixous's genius is to take these ways of thinking and straining to turn them into something doable. I think she is helped in this by her somewhat unexamined belief in the power of poetry and art in general which she has never lost. To be sure, in the hands of essentialist enthusiasm, this doability can turn into precious posturing. But, then, in the hands of rationalist convictions, attempts to bring the aesthetic into the *Lebenswelt* can lead to interminable systems talk bent on the simple task of proving that the aesthetic is coherent. And, in the grip of *anti*essentialist enthusiasm, the Derridean maneuvers can *also* turn into precious posturing. The task here is not to suspend reading until such time as a text is out of quarantine.

All precautions taken, then, we can say that Cixous is staging the thought that, even as we are determined in all kinds of other ways—

academics, philosophers, feminists, blacks, homeowners, menstruating women, for example—we *are* also *always* in the peculiar being-determination that sustains these. She is staging that dimension in the name of the place of mother-and-child. This is not really a space accessible to political determinations or to specific determinations of mothering in specific cultural formations. Following a chronological notion of human psychobiography, this is where, at the same *time* as we mature into adulthood and responsibility, we continue to exist in a peculiar being-determination to which the name "child" can be lent:

> The relation to the "mother," in terms of intense pleasure and violence, is curtailed no more than the relation to childhood (the child that she was, that she is, that she makes, remakes, undoes, there at the point where, the same she mothers herself). (p. 44)

I have argued elsewhere that this sort of poststructuralist nominalism brings with it the burden of "paleonymy," imposed by the fact that the name belongs to the imbrication of a so-called empirical-historical account which is the condition and effect of the role of the word in the history of the language. Cixous makes a selective use of the paleonymy of the name "mother," comparable to Derrida's selective use of the paleonymy of words such as "writing" or "justice." *Not* the narrow sense: "Listen to me, it is not the overbearing clutchy 'mother' but rather, it is, touching you, the equivoice that affects you" (p. 252).

Notice that determinative essentialisms become irrelevant here. No matter if I have no children and therefore no "experience" of "giving the mother to the other woman." It is a general sense of mothering— its minimal definitive and presupposed cultural predication as *selfless* love, reinscribed in Simone de Beauvoir as the species-other passing into loved subject—that is supposedly also a defining characteristic of woman in the narrow sense—that Cixous is turning into a relationship with the other woman—who is precisely not a child of my body. If read seriously, this must be rigorously distinguished from being motherly or maternal, matronizing, et cetera. The other woman's age is not specified, only that she is other. As a formulation, it is perhaps better than what I wrote four years ago:

> [En]chanting [of] all the perils that exist in transforming a "noun" into a "referent"—in other terms, making a catechism from a catachresis—let us nonetheless name (as) "woman" this disenfranchized woman that we *cannot* strictly, historically, or geopolitically *imagine* as a literal referent.

Try to think of what Cixous is actually asking you to do and you will begin to see what an amazing formulation of responsibility this is, especially since the dimension is inaccessible and therefore the responsibility is effortful. If you want to reduce to conceptual logic some of the more obviously metaphoric passages, there are handles, such as "woman does not defend herself against these unknown women whom she's surprised at becoming, pleasuring [*jouissant*] in this gift of alterability." We must be able to read this "present tense" in that nondimensional verbal mode of which I spoke earlier: not a future present but a persistent effortfulness that makes a "present." This practice "does and will take place in areas other than those subordinated to philosophicotheoretical domination." Up close, we cannot grasp it at all. The undecidable in view of which decisions *must* be risked.

*   *   *

Should Hélie-Lucas listen to Hélène Cixous? Not necessarily. But the cultural politics of asking Hélie-Lucas to listen only to purely "traditional" Algerian things comes quite often from the most Frenchified. Since Hélie-Lucas is not a member of an Algerian minority in the United States, in decolonization, she has to negotiate actively with the trace of the French until it becomes unrecognizable as such and useful; with Hélène Cixous, or with much worse, especially when unacknowledged. And Cixous's text has put a limit to its *own* power in the field of negotiation. The ethical field of the I-thou requires that the I earn the right to *tutoyer* the interlocutor. Indeed, that felicitous *tu-toi*-ing is itself a case of what she is speaking of: "Everything will be changed once woman gives woman to the other woman" (p. 260).

In the heritage of imperialism, one of the peculiar by-products is the "emancipated" woman *in* the decolonized nation, not her sister in metropolitan space, whom we know much better. However unwilling she may be to acknowledge this, part of the historical burden of the "emancipated" postcolonial is to be in a situation of *tu-toi*-ing with the radical feminist in the metropolis. If she wants to turn away from this, to learn to "give woman to *the other woman*" in her own nation-state is certainly a way, for it is by no means certain that, by virtue of organizational and social work alone—doing good from above, itself infinitely better than doing nothing—she is in touch with the Algerian gendered subaltern in that inaccessible "I-thou".

At any rate, my agenda is not to recommend Hélène Cixous to Marie-Aimée Hélie-Lucas or to prescribe Hélène Cixous for Marie-Aimée Hélie-Lucas, but in a sense to judge Hélène Cixous's text to see if it can live in Hélie-Lucas's world, which is not the grassroots world of Algeria.

This is a particularly interesting challenge because, like Derrida, Cixous is, in the strictest sense, a Creole, a Frenchwoman born and raised in early childhood in Oran in the days before the Revolution. It is in that spirit that I have lingered on this moment in "The Laugh of the Medusa." I want now to pass on to the thought of plurality, which is lodged in one of the islands of comparatively expository prose coming immediately after the passage I have read.

As a subject for history [*sujet à l'histoire*], woman always occurs simultaneously in several places. Woman un-thinks or squanders the unifying, ordering history that homogenizes and channels forces, herding contradictions into the practice of a single battlefield. In woman, the history of all women blends together with her personal history, national and international history. *As a fighter*, woman enlists [*fait corps*] in all liberations. She must be far-sighted. Not blow for blow. She foresees that her liberation will do more than modify relations of force or toss the ball over to the other camp; she will bring about a mutation in human relations, in thought, in all practices: it is not only the question of a class struggle, which she sweeps along in fact into a much vaster movement. Not that in order to be a woman-in-struggle(s) one must leave the class struggle or deny it; but one must open it up, split it, push it, fill it with the fundamental struggle so as to prevent the class struggle, or any other struggle for the liberation of a class or people, from operating as an agent of repression, pretext for postponing the inevitable, the staggering alteration in relations of force and in the production of individualities. (p. 252–253)

In her exchange with Catherine Clément, later published as *La Jeune née*, Cixous shows herself to be somewhat ethereal in her take on "hard" politics.[9] But perhaps Catherine Clément is not her best interlocutor. Here, in "The Medusa," under the surface of an often-read passage, some surprising points are being made. Certain seeming generalizations are being advanced about woman's role as subject *for* history. Remember the ordinary-language double charge of the word "histoire" in French. It is almost as if Cixous is speaking of a narrativization or figuration of woman that would be appropriate *for* this new story. This is not, in other words, an account of woman as world-historical subject or, in a humbler vein, subject of history.

The "is," "will," and "must" of the passage are articulated within *this* framework. Thus these straightforward lines do not necessarily mark a forgetfulness of the deconstructive lesson of timing that Cixous seems to know elsewhere. The general point is that the appropriate subject *for* such a new story is the one that makes visible all the plural arenas that are suppressed when history is written with the representative man as its subject. This temporality operates within the task of producing a subject *for* a story—at the other end from ethical intimacy. Within this peculiar time, then, woman as subject *for* history will not merely modify but mutate and alter relations of force. If the manifold, irreducibly plural, and incessantly shifting strategic exclusions required by a coherent systematic account of history are incessantly attended to, power/ knowledge [*pouvoir/savoir*] relations are thoroughly displaced and productively disrupted, framing in undecidability the sure ground of decision. This feminism is a persistent critique of history.

Cixous finesses the question of agency delicately. Not for her the Derridean unfleshed figuration/nomination, but rather the task of conceiving an agent of pluralization, alteration. This is unusual in metropolitan feminism, yet may be a requirement in decolonized feminism. Thus Cixous *opposes* single-issue feminism. *If* and *when* woman as subject *for* storying or history is conceived as militant, she must be faithful to the subversive logic or graphic of plurality and thus become part of the body of all struggles (*faire corps* in French is more charged, especially in military metaphors, than the English "integrate"). Like most French radicals, Cixous sees the class struggle as the only *struggle* that operates out of a coherent narrative. Therefore it presupposes exclusions and invites supplementation by repression. Yet the fundamental struggle as such is not woman's struggle alone. It is to split, open, and fill all generalized, unified struggles with plurality. Within the framing of the putting together of a subject for a new story, the status of the last phrase "production of individualities" is rhetorically charged. An "individuality" here is not merely an exclusionist repressive construction, but a necessary underived fiction, the agent's springboard for a decision in the face of radical undecidability, affirmative deconstruction performed in the way of a writer rather than a philosopher.

Is Cixous able to become part of the body of the struggle for national liberation, or against imperialism? That struggle too is pluralized— travelling up and down, and in a discontinuous way—from the familiar to the aggregative and out, from the epistemic to the legal and away. The way in which Cixous attaches to this moving base is, inevitably, interpretable. When she writes her Indian and Indonesian plays, her take on the complexity and hybridity of so-called postcolonial nations is shaky. If one understands the serviceability of underived fictions, one is obliged to know more intimately the contaminated fictions of the empirical, and for this we must turn to Marie-Aimée Hélie-Lucas.

I will not speak about Hélie-Lucas in detail: I will only touch upon the area where, for me, their convergence is the strongest.

Defending women's rights "now" (this "now" being any historical moment) is always a betrayal—of the people, of the nation, of the revolution, of Islam, of national identity, of cultural-roots, of the Third World . . . according to the terminologies in use *hic et nunc*. . . .[10]

What Hélie-Lucas is speaking of is, clearly, the *postponement* of the production of individualities. "There is a constant ideological confusion," she reminds us, "between religion, culture and nationality." But if Cixous's individuality is short of the "real individual" because it is posited *in* the possibility of fiction, Hélie-Lucas is beyond the "real individual" because posited *as* the possibility of collectivity. Each should presuppose the other, as each leaves the space of the "real individual" negotiable. When Cixous imagines collectivity, Hélie-Lucas must thicken it. When Hélie-Lucas naturalizes individuality, Cixous can stand as a warning. The enabling violation of imperialism laid the line for a woman's alliance in decolonization. Hélie-Lucas can only ever animate that line with the implicit metaphor of sisterhood. Cixous's impossible dimension of giving woman to the other woman can split up and fill that thought of sisterhood so that it does not become the repressive hegemony of the old colonial subject.

Hélie-Lucas calls for a "true internationalism" of women. The antagonist here is clearly the strained Marxist ideal of internationalism-after-national-liberation. It is only when we see that we can begin further to see that the word being really put into question here is "nation." Everyone who gets embroiled in the real politics and history of nationalism begins to get the uneasy sense that the nation-state, spring and source of nationalisms, is not altogether a good thing. This is not really an unease for the North Atlantic radical when it comes to the history and development of nationalism in that part of the world. When it comes to the development of national identity in the Third World, it is harder to acknowledge the mysterious anonymity of space, to acknowledge that all nationalism is, in the last instance, a mere inscription on the earth's body. Yet this is where, to use two of the formulas I use most, the persistently critical voice must be raised at the same time as a strategic use of essentialism—in other words this is the crucial scene of the usefulness of catachresis. Hélie-Lucas is using the historical empirical definitive predication of women in exogamous societies: a woman's home is radical exile, fixed by her male owner. A woman's *norm* of *pouvoir/savoir* is a persistent passive *critique* of the idea of the *miraculating* agency or identity produced by a home. Thus the simple conviction of exchangeability, bred in the little girl in sorrow and joy, is the internalized critique that *can* be mobilized against all essentialist notions of the home as base of identity. This is a particularly important practical resource because the rational aggregative consolidation of this notion *is* the apparatus of the nation, presupposed by the great aggregative teleological system of internationalism. And this is the telos that Hélie-Lucas shakes up through the *pouvoir/savoir* of the feminine. This is a perspective that is almost always lacking in North Atlantic calls for female solidarity, whether metropolitan or migrant. This is an internationalism that takes a distance from the project of national identity when it interferes with the production of female individualities. And the *critique* of individualities, not merely individualism, will bring us back to Cixous.

I will stop here, half-way. Political theorization, politicalization of the theoretical are vast, assymetric aggregatives; the hardest lesson at the heart of these enterprises is the impossibility to imitate the ethical. It is within this lesson that Hélène Cixous tries time and time again to embrace us.

As for myself, who for thirty-four years have studied and taught English and have since then looked for answers in English to the questions asked, I would like to conclude with the words of Assia Djebar: "To attempt an answer in only English words is to show more than the skin of a voiceless body under the autopsy's slow scalpel."

Notes

The sections of this text on Hélène Cixous and Marie-Aimée Hélie-Lucas have been reproduced in the original English with the author's permission from her book entitled *Outside in the Teaching Machine* (New York and London: Routledge, 1992), from the chapter "French Feminism Revisited."

1. Verena Andermatt Conley, *Hélène Cixous: Writing the Feminine*, Expanded edition (Lincoln: University of Nebraska Press, 1984).
2. Hélène Cixous, "Le rire de la méduse," *L'Arc*, 61 (1975), p. 39–54.
3. Chafika Marouf, "État de la recherche sur le monde féminin et la famille en Algérie et au Maghreb," *Femme, famille et société en Algérie* (Oran: URASC, 1988), p. 5.
4. In English in the original.
5. Assia Djebar, *L'Amour, la fantasia* (Paris: Lattès, 1985).
6. In English in the original.
7. Gayatri Spivak, "Acting Bits/Identity Talk," *Critical Inquiry*, Summer 1992.
8. Martin Heidegger, *L'Etre et le temps*, trans. Rudolph Boehm et Alphonse de Waelhens (Paris, Gallimard, 1964), p. 21.
9. Hélène Cixous and Catherine Clément, *La Jeune nee* (Paris: UGE, 1975).
10. Marie-Aimée Hélie-Lucas, "Bound and Gagged by the Family Code," in Miranda Davies (ed.), *Third World, Second Sex* (London: Zed Books, 1987) p. 13.

HÉLÈNE CIXOUS: INITIATORY READINGS, CENTRIFUGAL READINGS

Lynn Kettler Penrod

> With the help of memory and forgetting, I could reread the book. Begin it again. From another point of view, from another, from another. In reading I discovered that writing is the infinite. The everlasting. The eternal. . . . Flesh is writing, and writing is never read: it is always still to be read, to be studied, to be sought, to be invented.
>
> Hélène Cixous, *La Venue à l'écriture*

> Through reading this story-that-ends-well, she learns the paths that lead her to "loss" which is her fate. A little stroll and then off. A kiss; and he goes away. His fragile desire, supported by lack, maintains . absence: the man pursues. As if he never manages to get what he has. Where is she, the woman, in all these spaces he surveys, all the scenes he sets up inside the literary enclosure?
>
> Hélène Cixous, *La Jeune née*

By way of an introduction, I would like to start with an anecdote. This happened in the month of February 1978. I was then already at the University of Alberta but not yet professor of French. I was only a lecturer in the department of Romance languages and was at the same time studying in the Faculty of Law. The winter in Edmonton that year was very hard: it was always cold, there was a lot of snow, a sky always overcast and gray, and I couldn't bear the nights that seemed to start every day around four in the afternoon. In short, it was a time of personal anguish for me. One day, however, as is my habit when things aren't going well, I went to the Rutherford library to look at the recently received books. All of a sudden I saw a little red book bearing on the back in white letters: "H. Cixous, ANGST." This is perhaps a message for me, I said to myself. I opened the book and, as I am always a little superstitious as far as dates are concerned, I turned immediately to page 25 (the 25th is the date of my birthday) to try to

57

find a message there. And here, indeed, is the message I received, that cold, gray morning now almost fourteen years ago:

> If you were called, it is because there must have been a little ground for you to stand on. It was time! For her, it was a certitude. So, I was going to arrive? Sometimes extraordinary things happen deep in your flesh without your being aware of it. Time passes, being passes, possible people, letters that would not be addressed if it were necessary that they be read; and answers to the next presences. While we were not there. As if we had yielded to the call of a name. The mother was preparing the first nappy, folding it into a V, she was announcing me. So, I was going to be born! Myself my mother, my child. Shyness. First news.

It was an extraordinary moment for me. I heard a voice, a voice that I didn't understand at all, but a voice that urged me to respond. It was, in a sense, my personal initiation to Cixousian writing. And as you can imagine, every time I pick up a new book by Hélène Cixous, I open at page 25.

My intention is to present a quasi-pedagogical approach to the work of a woman, Hélène Cixous, writing in a society (France, Europe), by another woman, me, who teaches these texts in a very different society, that is, in Canada, North America. I would particularly like to address two important questions which, in my opinion, distinguish Cixous's textual practice and production, especially during the period of her first writings in the 1960s (*Le Prénom de Dieu, Les Commencements, Le Troisième Corps, Dedans*) up to the publication of the *Livre de Promethea* in 1983. The first question deals with the profoundly initiatory role played by the twin processes of reading and writing in Cixous's texts. The second, stemming from the first, deals with the represented movement at the heart of this initiatory experience and which I call *centrifugal*, in the scientific and anthropological sense of the word. The ideas of initiation and centrifugal movement are closely connected to the idea of a simutaneously liberating and feminist pedagogy.

What do I mean by initiation and initiatory rites? In their anthropological signification, initiatory rites, or rites of passage, refer to a magic or religious ceremony which serves to mark the transition from infancy to adulthood. Circumcision, for example, is a very common initiatory rite for boys; for girls, clitoridectomies are practiced even today in various Third World cultures. Even in so-called civilized cultures, initiatory rites exist in order to mark cultural and social transitions within a group. Among the most technologically advanced civilizations, these rites are rarely based on magic experiences, but they are still a sign of movement from one stage to another in an individual's life. Initiation can perhaps be the action of revealing or receiving knowledge of certain practices; or the action of giving first rudiments of a discipline. Anthropologically, initiation refers to a ceremony which gives an individual access to a new group of belonging. In any case, initiation is always defined by the sharing of a common knowledge, often tied to a bodily process.

It is important to note that in primitive as well as in modern and technological societies, the theme for any discussion of initiatory rites is the constant and consistent differentiation between the rites associated with men and those associated with women.

In matters of initiation, gender differences are important.

Speaking about initiatory rites in primitive societies, Michel Tournier has pointed out the basic differences between masculine and feminine initiation:

> For [girls], initiation cannot have the meaning it does for boys. Brought up like their brothers by women, they obviously do not have to break from this milieu and integrate into another group, as do the boys. They are normally destined to remain in the gynaeceum.[1]

According to Tournier, initiation certainly exists for females, but the nature of this initiation is profoundly different from that undergone by the boys:

> It is a question of a sort of inverted initiation, centrifugal instead of centripetal. . . . An adolescent boy leaves the feminine group to integrate into the masculine group. What can a girl do? Prisoner in the gynaeceum, she can try to leave it. To go where? This is the entire problem of women's liberation. Between the gynaeceum and male society, there does not yet exist a unisex society to receive her. There remains then the revolt-initiation. . . . For the adolescent girl, initiation can only be permanent flight. (p. 340)

Three terms of this passage are of interest to us: *centrifugal, centripetal,* and *permanent flight.*

Tournier uses the two terms *centrifugal* and *centripetal* in a very general way but, in my opinion, this metaphorical presentation serves to indicate important distinctions between the initiatory experience of boys and girls. When Sir Isaac Newton invented the term "centrifugal" around 1700 (from the Latin *centrum,* "center" and *fugere,* "to flee"), he wanted to describe a physical force which tends to push away from the center. The *Petit Robert* explains that the centrifugal force is "the force of inertia that must be introduced in addition to the centripetal force to describe a uniform, circular movement in the non-Galilean referential linked to the mobile." In botany, the term is used to describe (definite) inflorescences when flowers blossom first in the center of the inflorescence, then slowly toward the periphery; in physiology, the term refers to afferent matter which transports something away from a body's center. Centrifugal force, then, is simply the natural force that distances from the center. Here, such a physical movement is always the result of inertia.

The term *centripetal*, on the other hand (from the Latin *centrum* "center" et *petere* "tend toward" or "seek to gain"), also a lexical invention of Newton, is used especially with regard to the acceleration of a uniform, circular movement and the force that produces it. Centripetal force is the physical force directed toward the center. In botany, "centripetal" is used to describe (indefinite) inflorescences when flowers first open at the periphery, and then slowly toward the center; in physiology, it refers to afferent material always transported toward the body's center.

If we accept the idea that patriarchal society—based on the hierarchization of the *phallus* and the *logos* and their privileged position—inevitably tries, one way or another, to draw men, metaphorically speaking at least, toward the center (of power, authority, voice, language), we must admit that *centripetal* seems to be the right word to describe cultural initiatory rites like certain literary texts (*Bildungsroman*, chansons de geste, etc.). For women, the centrifugal movement, far from the center (far from power, authority, voice, language) is just as suggestive, at least metaphorically. I repeat that centrifugal movement has its origin in inertia.

If we now try to qualify Hélène Cixous's texts, we will say that her writing is always a writing of discovery—discovery (Verena Conley says *uncovery*) of language and textual voice for the transmitter of the text (the writing subject) and for the addressee (the reading subject).

This reading and writing, this rewriting of discovery and initiation find their origin in three represented movements. Curiously, two of them are contradictory: first, the whole metaphorical network of the act to dig, to excavate; then the opposite metaphorical network, constructed upon images where acts of flying, soaring upwards into the sky predominate. The third metaphorical structure—which, in my opinion, serves as an intermediary between the first two—is made up of an oscillating movement which becomes spiral, reuniting the images of a circle (cycles of time, movement, transition) and a vertical axis (principles of duration, the unchanging, the invariable): in other words, a simplified scheme of the snake and the pole.

It is perhaps in her first published text, the collection of novella entitled *Le Prénom de Dieu*,[2] that one can most easily discover these metaphorical networks of excavation and flight, and participate in the discovery and recuperation of the narrative voice. In the story "Le Lac," the protagonist goes after the discovery of her voice: "The girl set off

without delay, moves away heavily at first, without help, without ambition, her mind harassed by all the questions, deprived of all responses,
the imagination limp" (p. 143). Every evening,

> she bored out her body toward that knowledge to which her con-
> science was slowly descending. Somewhere at the end of the tunnel
> in the mirror of her flesh she would find *it*. She would throw herself
> against its intact white body, thus she would enter into its dream. . . .
> (p. 146)

The narrator "becomes a snake" and continues her speleological ex-
ploration: "And here, in descending, she had no more limits; inside she
found herself larger than the men whose bodies she saw, larger than
the room in which she was looking about . . . (p. 147–148). The quest
here becomes more and more urgent: "Little by little she retreated from
the cage. From silence to silence, she descended toward the interior."
Finally, she arrives at her "promised place"—the lake in the title:

> The snake had to descend through a passage narrower than she was.
> The young girl saw herself at the edge of the promised and forbid-
> den lake. Had she descended at such great cost only to be stopped at
> the end? Was it there, the secret place? (p. 149).

Following all these images of excavation (dig, wind, plunge, descend,
excavate) and this progressive yet terribly slow movement toward knowledge, comes the moment of recognition:

> There, all knowledge was immediate, she was night, black envelope,
> in the center of the white, pulpy lake. She was boundless and the
> disk was edged in silver. A delicious liquidity where fire and ice
> embraced, sketching a venomous vegetation into its infinite mem-
> bers. (p. 151)

Other of Cixous's texts would lend themselves easily to a detailed
reading which would bring out more examples of these first two tropes,
especially *Dedans, Angst,* or in the twin texts *Les Commencements* and
Le Troisième Corps.

One of the richest sources of this phenomenon is found in *Le Livre
de Promethea,* published in 1983. There we encounter the fusion of the
three metaphorical movements: figures of excavation and flight as well
as of the spiral's oscillating movements gradually blend as readers share
the narrative dilemma of "H," "I," and Promethea. Especially notable
are the efforts of this triple narrative voice to construct a textual genesis, create a textual birth or rebirth; at the same time, the parts of the
text which seem the most rigid and interwoven are constantly in the
process of fraying. From the Lascaux caves that we, like Ariadne, ex-
plore ("the layout of the interior book is astonishingly similar to that

of the Lascaux site"),[3] to Promethea's feminine flight toward creation and love, this text bears witness to feminine initiation, strictly speaking, as well as to centrifugal and spiral movements. In other words, it is an inversion of the feminine initiation described by Tournier.

> It has sometimes happened that our two whirlwinds coincide to such a degree that, one being incapable of securing the other to the ground, neither one being able to press down nor the other to restrain itself, one in the other we have rolled into the abyss, it was perhaps a sky, it was perhaps a sea, love turned upside down, neither one nor the other capable of desiring, even if it meant being saved, to move away from the other's bosom, intertwined, we flow while turning under the great silvered blades of time, eternally, until one of us feels like watching us die. (p. 77)

For most Anglo-American feminist criticism, the most well-known of Cixous's texts is *La Jeune née*, published in collaboration with Catherine Clément in 1975.[4] In the section entitled "Sorties," we discover the theoretical basis of the commentaries we just made with regard to the metaphorical and centrifugal structures in her textual production.

In *La Jeune née*, Cixous points out that the masculine, libidinal economy, based on conservation, is always defined by appropriation of the Other; feminine libidinal economy, however, is defined by the spontaneous gift. So-called feminine writing is never simple, linear, objectified, or generalized. Feminine writing resonates with voice, with the song before the Law which finds its origin in the sea/mother ["mer/mère"], that is, in the presymbolic imaginary, the no-name ["non-nom"] of Lacanian Imagination.

> She [the woman] has never stayed "in place"; explosion, diffusion, effervescence, abundance, she revels in being limitless, outside of me, outside of the same, far from a "center," from a capital of her "dark continent," so far from this "home" to which man brings her back so that she may maintain *his* fire always menaced by extinction. (p. 168)

Similarly, *La Venue à l'écriture*[5] traces the author's personal, spiral, and impressionistic progression toward writing; the book, which comes across as an injunction to write addressed to women, is constructed by stages that seem necessary for this "feminine" writing. First, one must have a deep understanding of women's condition; the constraining forces and the social repression which make the feminine culturally inferior; but also the understanding that the two activities of reading and writing are determined by the priorities of this same cultural repression. Moreover, one must know how to recognize the object of the struggle and, finally, with what one must break, because these are negative and monolithic forces. Only this rupture can liberate the multiple, polyphonic voices that exist in the reader/writer. Finally, it is necessary to discover within oneself the path toward desire, toward the passion for writing that Cixous defines as a fusion, "a practice of the greatest passivity." For Cixous, the absolute impossibility of separating writing from love, from the expression of the gift, from the word of the flesh, reveals a writing in the future—which will be "infinite, tireless, eternal."

> All I can say about it is that the "coming" to language is a fusion, a flow in fusion, if there is "intervention" on my part it is in a sort of "position," an activity—passive as if I were urging myself: "let yourself do it, let the writing in, let yourself be soaked; wash, relax, become the river, let go of everything, open, unbuckle, open the floodgates, roll, let yourself roll.... A practice of the greatest passivity. Both a vocation and a technique. This passivity is our way—an active one, really—of knowing things by letting ourselves be known by them. (p. 68)

It is time to come back to Tournier's term "permanent flight." Flight, for an adolescent, means to leave without warning, wander for hours or entire days. Or else a momentary departure, an inconsequential escapade, to be free from constraints, distract oneself from daily activities. For the child, flight is escape from the milieu of the family, school, from a collectivity. It occurs more frequently when the familial milieu is dissociated. Occasionally, it is a matter of returning to a place that had positive value in the past.

In the context described by Tournier, the specter of a permanent, feminine flight presents us with a world where women would be condemned by society to flee the center—eternally exiled, repulsed, rejected, marginalized—excluded from the power of the voice, of the logos. The texts of Cixous which present the oscillation between center and margin, this represented centrifugal movement, give us, on the contrary, a very powerful image of the liberating force of writing and the creative force of reading. The term permanent flight is completely revalorized. If "permanent flight" has a special sense in Hélène Cixous's work, it is because it stems from the musical—a fugue defined as a textual voice, its successive imitations forming several parts which follow each other.

The importance of initiation and of centrifugal movement can also be measured in the context of a different pedagogy called "feminine." In 1989, the University of Liverpool devoted a conference to feminine studies and to Hélène Cixous's work; a Norwegian professor, Sissel Lie, had this to say about her students in French literature:

My students are mostly very young women, often coming straight from secondary school. They don't have any knowledge of the theories of the 1970s and 1980s. They are mostly used to realistic novels when they read fiction at all. They don't read poetry if they don't have to and some have to be lured into the world of literature because they have two years to learn French language with me and never beforehand believed they had to read fiction. If I start with theories, they will write down all I say and be impressed, but not touched, not changed. They will be taking notes, not making notes. If they read Hélène Cixous's texts, most of them will find them too different from what they already know and therefore too difficult. They will give up even before having tried.[6]

In Edmonton, the situation is analagous. Our students are, for the most part, anglophone Canadians born in western Canada. They are not terribly interested in literature. Our teaching is generally very conservative. Introductory courses on the important periods of French literature and on French culture present an authoritative interpretation: the process is entirely linear and hierarchical between the professor, who represents the institution, and the students, who are an echo. Obviously, this system that always goes toward the center, toward mastery of the text, cannot function with Hélène Cixous's texts.

Sissel Lie exposes a method that she calls *process-oriented writing* (p. 199) which aims at encouraging an emotional engagement on the part of the reader: "[The students] should meet the novel not only with their heads but also with their bodies and with the openness that Cixous' books require" (p. 199). Like my Norwegian colleague, I feel strongly about encouraging an emotional engagement. There are no lecture courses; there is no exam. We try to conduct an open reading without any formalist interpretation. The written work can take many forms: diary, poem, short story, English translation of Cixous' texts—the whole scale of personal expression for initiation into feminine reading. In short, if feminist studies have an importance for us here in Canada—especially in anglophone Canada—it is in the area of university pedagogy. As Toril Moi says, for Hélène Cixous, the act of writing is always a libidinal gesture, "a linking of sexuality and textuality [which] opens up a whole new field of feminist investigation of the articulations of desire in language. . . .[7]

Reading Cixous always puts us in the presence of what Moi calls "intricate webs of contradiction and conflict" (p. 126). And I am convinced that these textual networks of contradictions and conflicts can be deciphered by the metaphorical structures of centrifuge and the initiatory process. This is what Hélène Cixous says when speaking about

Clarice Lispector: "There are fifty possible ways of entering this text ["Sunday, before falling asleep"], and it is up to the reader to find them. In terms of a quest, we can set out in many different directions. What counts is to find ourselves in the process."

* * *

Today, I am a French professor, lawyer, and associate dean of the Faculty of Arts at the University of Manitoba. My initiation into feminine reading is now far in the past and I am in the process of writing an introductory book on Hélène Cixous's work. When I am discouraged by the difficulty of gathering my thoughts, of finding words, I open the most recent of Hélène Cixous's texts, *L'Ange au secret*, and, still superstitious, I look for my secret message on page 25: "The world, in front of me, so great, is inner, it is immense life hidden behind restrained life, it is the first forest which spreads under the bed, the marsh of women and poets."

Notes

1. Michel Tournier, *Le Coq de cruyère* (Paris: Gallimard, 1978), p. 339–340.
2. Hélène Cixous, *Le Prénom de Dieu* (Paris: Grasset, 1967).
3. Hélène Cixous, *Le Livre de Promethea* (Paris: Gallimard, 1983), p. 25.
4. Hélène Cixous, *La Jeune née* (with Catherine Clément) (Paris: UGE, Collection 10/18, 1975).
5. Hélène Cixous, *La Venue à l'écriture* (with Annie Le Clerc and Madeleine Gagnon) (Paris: UGE, Collection 10/18, 1977).
6. Helen Wilcox, Keith McWatters, Ann Thompson and Linda R. Williams, (dir.), *The Body and the Text. Hélène Cixous, Reading and Teaching* (Hemel Hempstead: Harvester Wheatsheaf, 1990), p. 197–198.
7. Toril Moi, *Sexual/Textual Politics: Feminist Literary Theory* (London and New York: Methun, 1985), p. 126.

HÉLÈNE CIXOUS'S
WRITING-THINKING

Mireille Calle

One *must* go beyond
the possibilities of the instrument.
But unconsciously.
We are there to lose.

L'Ange au secret, p. 237.

Until now.

I have never spoken about Hélène Cixous's books until now.

Once formulated, the statement shatters into interrogations, brings back the indecision at work, dismantles its apparent platitude and splits it, indicating a crossing of paths and that it may have to do with an undecidable. Or rather, with a relationship of incertitude which slips away from what would be the nature of the grasp; which still struggles with the work that requires it—at the price of saying nothing. Medusa's reading. In short, it is not an acknowledgment: a choice, a fact, a fixed frontier—no. "I have never spoken about Hélène Cixous's books": this calls out, *puts everything into questions*. Notably these:

Is it a matter of speaking *about*, feigning that the books are objectivized according to a repertoire of ideas, themes, images, a reunion with the eternal human's catalogue of characteristics? It is then a *forceful topical blow*, attempting to classify the unclassifiable.

Or is it a matter of speaking *with*, maintaining, by mimetic and identificatory words, the illusion that the author of the work exchanges a look with her reader? Then it would be a *heartfelt blow* which makes one forget that writing holds forth *in absentia*, out of sight, and that the reader becomes blinded by the image in the mirror.

Or again, is it a question of speaking *on*, the pen running along on top, re-covering, pre-texting Cixous's text so as to gloss the dreams,

66

rewrite the cry? It would then be a *stylistic blow* of tropic discourse which strikes out, erases, speaks between the words and languages.

Such are the questions asked *at* the origin (addressed to the origin), and there is no doubt that Cixous's writing solicits and stages the triple modality of these three blows. Questions of distance which divide the origin, make the gesture of literary criticism an always already divided gesture. Ruinous reading obsessed by these words: from what distance to speak of it, write of it? Words grafted onto the words of the other, the writer, echoing them: at what distance does the work of fiction speak? It speaks *to me*—speaks about me. It speaks *itself*—to itself about itself, about the other itselves, about others. And at what distance does writing's stream emerge, interrupt itself, leave again?

In fact, the critical approach is undecided about the call of works which present the ruinous and runiform writing of texts which leak everywhere.[1] The cost is exorbitant: no point of view which does not immediately overflow, no role-play not displaced, no narrative which is not eccentric; no beginning that is not disconnected between Auctor and Actor, between *the author*-she who eternally casts ink,[2] from book to book, and a winged-I[3] who pursues a thousand me's ["moi(s)"].[4] It is what we discern in the title *Jours de l'an* where the plural of "jour" alters the usual meaning, no longer designates the first day of a newborn year but every day as so many birthdays of a dead and reborn "I":

> The person we have been is now an "I was," the character from our past. She follows us, but at a distance. And sometimes she can even become the character of one of our books.
>
> This is how I have behind me one, two, three, four defunct women (and maybe others whose bones and dust are all that remain)....
>
> Is left today the one who will have followed us till here. And who passes with me into the present. We cherish this one, the one who has traversed decades whereas others have fallen: she cannot be, we believe, but the strongest and the best of ourselves. This is but a belief....
>
> At sixty years of age we are still baby chicks in the limestone. I will reveal myself in my own time. My already thin shell will explode into bits. I sense that this birth is imminent. Already a part of me is future: everything I've just thought is what I am going to think about in the next hour. (*F*, p. 27–28)[5]

In short, an entire theatricality goes to work on the ruins of the origin: *theater of writing* which is an effect of distance, that is, of passage, simultaneously from mechanism and representation, from place to illusion, where doing and being interpolate. Writing's representations are what they make themselves, they do what they say, say what they do,

make true and false—but the true and the false scarcely matter; it is
the question of doing that prevails. And for this doing, which is always
"on the point, between already and not yet" (*F*, p. 28), it is necessary
that the staging, in setting off all its fireworks, reduces writing to ashes.
Only one rule now seems to drive Cixous's pen: to come back to the
greatest incertitude, to let speech speak, let it phrase the phrase, making the tongue slip, without some predestination of a previous thought—
since by virtue of the infinite displacement of significations, "death is
not what we think" (*F*, 49), "crime is not what we think" (p. 65),
"thinking is not what we think" (p. 30–35). The rule is to choose dis-
persion, diversion, surprise, to invent a "state before God," that is, to
lose "the secret of Genesis" (*F*, p. 35) so that writing *comes* from before History and all stories, from before society's narratives, common
language, references; so that, *in extremis*, at the delivery, it delivers us
a *bookish blow*.

> Author, have you ever written the book you wanted to write? What
> is an author? wonders the author. The shipwrecked, the vanquished
> survivor of a thousand books.
> All I had to do was not want? That's impossible. We want. This is
> how it always starts. I wanted. I bore the brunt of a thousand storms
> and saved thirty shells.
> Have I ever wanted to write a book and believed I am writing it?
> I tried. In the end, a book is left. And I adopt it. (*F*, p. 32)

Deliver a bookish blow means: between aban-don[6] ("defeated") and
adoption, to give chance all the room. At *the end*, unhoped for and
despairing, desired and undesirable, fallen and saved, there is: a book.
A book happens: like a miracle and like an intrusion. It is delivered
(like a postal delivery) and does not render itself: lost and found object, unseemly, non-corresponding, there against all expectations, sur-
reptitiously, the Cixousian book is grief and gift. Grief for the "thousand"
lost works it excludes. Gift without an address: which was not wanted,
was not believed in, was not owed. A remainder.—I'll take it, thank
you.—It's nothing. A gift of nothing unless of the insatiable desire to
write the book that is not written:

> And for thirty years I have been writing, borne by writing, this book
> that book; and now, suddenly, I sense it: among all these books is
> the book I haven't written; haven't ceased not to not write. And it's
> now that I sense it, today, one day after February twelfth, now I
> learn this and not before, there is the book I've missed. . . .
> And behold what can befall us: for thirty years we never think
> about the book we do not write. (*F*, p. 2)

What is affirmed here is a writing in the negative which strives to make heard the unheardof, to think the unthinkable, to read and write there where it is not done, in the negatives which, in Cixous's text, take existence, ek-sist, and become an abutment of significations.

There follows an upheaval of concepts and values which normally organize the relationship to literature. Most notably, the concept of the author. *The author*, who is written in her books in foreign italic letters, as in a quotation, or mentioned in passing in the disconnection of the interpolated "asks/thinks/says the author," the author is *a so-called voice*, she so-calls herself, a way of saying a very relative authority—an instance constrained to relations with a winged-I which escapes, the book-wreck that arrives, every me, all the dead and characters who file out of the library. In short, the book is not the author's own, it gives itself there where, by definition, there is no "own"—but disowning, endless dispossession. Consequently, the author never stops spying on her author–character who then assumes a specious, equivocal genre: "*the* shipwrecked" ["*le* naufragé"], *the* survivor ["*la* survivante"]; and a double voice, one being smuggled past the other.

As for the book: it is an unidentifiable object; not a product but *the trace*, the deposit of something that happened, that is past: place of a passage, a place of passages. It is not an object because it cannot be reified: not a program but a trajectory: pro-ject, tra-ject; incompletion; always book desire-to-be-book; a beach of time and space opened to/ by writing. It is the *scene of writing*: where it enters, grows, shows itself. It is also *the* scene of writing: primitive, first, fundamental, and therefore, by definition, unbearable—upheld by no antecedent.[7] Hélène Cixous does not write the "book about nothing,"[8] but a "*book from nothing.*" At mercy.

Writing thus becomes a place of the sublime: exasperating tensions and contrasts, it works on the right and wrong sides, reversibility against meaning, adoption against option, basting line against the straight line of the narrative, twisted line against logical sequence. Writing approaches significations obliquely, by tangents. From wanting, it retains volition; from power, the potential; from strength, the possible. In short, it is a writing of faculties and of the facultative—not a writing of rules and prerogatives.[9] To this, Hélène opposes a writing which is a *weak force*: which exercises no mastery; which, at the very most, exercises in attempts.

In the beginning of this under-taking was the fissure and the fallible—not the Word. A weak force writing is what is poised to falter and goes together with the thought of failure. Declension and decline of significations: the book falls to me, founders, fails.

The storm passes. We are run aground, swirling around, having
wrenched a few atoms from the wind, and that's already immense.
And yet it was really I who unleashed it. I press a button and there
is the explanation of the world, but all I command is the button.
Thinking: running aground. Running aground: thinking. (*F*, p. 32)

"To think?: to fail. To fail: to think." The aphorism's turn here is
exemplary of what occurs *during the course* of the sentence, hand holding
pen, now on the page: writing always does and says more; repetition,
inversion overflow the pure reciprocity of coming and going, symmetry
is dissymmetry, changing the place of two elements brought together
by invention. In sum, any intervention in the text entails a significant
displacement; in this case, that which is not only the author's stance
but the ethics of the written: pre-posed, thinking is doomed to failure;
agreed to at the origin, to fail *leads to* thinking. Moreover: to fail *is* to
think (the failure). Because by unfolding the triple construction (active, passive, reflexive) of the verb "to fail/to founder" ["(s')échouer"],
Hélène Cixous emphasizes with acuity that thinking extends beyond all
finality, the thought never ends up (never thinks) there where it thought
to arrive (to think). And by the same token, the origin also comes
undone: writing is endless end, beginningless beginning. At the antipo-
des of divine creation: without alpha or omega. In the beginning, it is
always already in the middle:

> It is always like this when it is a question of beginning a book. We
> are in the middle.... God begins—not us. We, it's in the middle.
> Thus we have begun to exist, thus we write: begun, and in the mid-
> dle. And: without knowing it. (*A*, p. 11)

In other words, for Hélène Cixous it is a matter of not bolting the door
of meaning, of giving it/herself over to the chance of linguistic and
textual crossroads, of working a non-form. Not so much saying this or
that than listening to the language speak. Not writing a novel but *fiction*—and we will see that the term here accepts all consequences, making
the book a vast scene of invention. It is also a matter of disarming
thought; consciously striving to see that all writing is a trouble factor,
that one must lose meaning so that more is discovered, *un*think in order to think, go blindly ahead so that thought rises up step by step,
"page to page in a book" (*F*, p. 55), according to its weight by the
words it bends.[10]

This is what I call Hélène Cixous's writing-thinking: nothing is conceived outside the process of writing, but even so, there is no textual
diktat; it is always a writing that *almost failed to make it* and which
fails at its task.

... the impossibility of ever painting Fuji-Yama authorized the painter to paint and to attempt to paint his entire life. For if it ever came to pass that one succeeded in painting what one had dreamed of painting since the very first paint-brush, everything would perish on the spot: art, nature, the painter, hope, everything would have come to pass, the painted mountain would fade into a picture, the picture would lose the desperate trembling of that which delicately tore at its canvas. A stony completion would seize the universe. (*F*, p. 9)

This comparison with the "mad truth" of painting invariably reminds us of Edgar Allan Poe's *Oval Portrait*—where reality, that is, the young female model, from whom is pulled the painting's *very Life*, literally dies from the metaphor—and signifies the agonizing contradiction constitutive of art. Hélène Cixous's writing-thinking is the undoing which seizes self-inflective writing at work. Or reflecting itself in the mirror of its others: Hokusai, Rembrandt, Clarice Lispector, Marina Tsvetaeva, Thomas Bernhard. In short, with Hélène Cixous's books comes the end of the world: *our* imagined world—thinkable, presentable, representable.

Under the auspices of "axe and knife," (*A*, p. 37), writing-thinking inaugurates a space which is *combat* (see the metaphorical matador, *J*);[11] made *pulsation* by the game of rupture-suture, detaching writing from the tale; which is a place of toppling over because this end of the world does not end ending in its successive scenes of *remake*.

It remains to be asked, of course, how: how does writing proceed when it seeks to undermine a terrain reputed to be its own? What maneuvers, what know-how, or what unknowing of art allows the regulation of the "writing's magic progression" (*A*, p. 236–237)? allows the intolerable discourse which dreams of being *natural*, speaking *like* the wind, the storm, the sea? What mechanisms enable one to invent a writing before the invention of writing, before Thot, when, as is said in Plato's *Phèdre, the tree spoke*? In short, it is a book which proceeds by blows of writing, unaddressed.[12]

I will consider only one aspect, in my opinion an essential one: the writing in the first person "I."

Hélène Cixous's writing necessarily goes through the I: the pronoun. In fact, in her books there is not one but thousands of persons, and no first one among them. No order. All is cardinal. Or rather, what is cardinal is the use of this pronoun—which is put in the noun's place—it is the finite and indefinite displacement of the "own," the subject. From then on, active/passive, subject *of*, subject *to* slippage. Less a possessor than a possessed—by the writing demon.

This use of I is opposed to the in-itself. There where the in-itself points to substance density and coincidence, the Cixousian "I" is accident, phenomenon, alteration, other. It is a mobile, a non-presence to itself, a non-figure. The "I" is the place of intuitions, roles, representations as the only possibility of knowledge: it leads to a writing of interruption and separation; it leads the writer to make "self-portraits of a blind woman"—title of one of the sections in *Jours de l'an*. It begins as follows:

> During this time the author . . . the author hasn't returned. She is completely given over to her drama, always. . . . Whereas I, since February 12 of this year, have been trying with all my might to seize some brief glimmers of truth, or at least I do everything I can to lie as little as possible, all the author is taken up with is this story. To tell. An ideal story. She goes for it . . . So slowly that in the meantime I could tell ten stories. I write underground, she says, like a beast, burrowing into the silence of my breast. . . .
> One difference between the author and me: the author is the daughter of the dead-fathers. Me, I'm on the side of the living mother. Between us everything is different, unequal, rending. (*F*, p. 94–95)

Putting the I into play is inherent in the very course of the writing it establishes which is necessarily dis-course; a revelation of the double requirement which puts Hélène's writing under extreme pressure: between scription and diction; between fiction (coherent, completed, a story) and fraction; between the effects of the text and the affects whose violence makes the writer "a reading body with its head cut off" (*A*, p. 91); tension too between the slowness of the written which organizes the page and the telegraphic surprise of meaning "by flashes" (*F*, p. 96), illumination. The nascent work nourished by a handicap which is the very essence of the writer's gesture: "we toil for months to recopy the flash," we who "are made of a star on the end of a stick" (*A*, p. 70).

Writing, consequently, is proceeding to the necessary liaison between contraries, internal liaison of the text which constitutes its presupposition (non-writing writing), its essential structure; because here—as Walter Benjamin points out in Hölderlin—"one cannot seize the elements in their pure state, only the relational structure where the identity of the singular essence is a function of an infinite serial chain."[13] In other words, an order of writing takes shape where the plurality of relationships is not without a lyrical and emotional seizure and where thought has a textual place, becomes substance with the letter, grows "fully into the earth of this text" (*F*, p. 96). This is what we must understand by the text's "truth": an *aesthethic* with two "h"s so one reads "aesthetic" with "ethic." This way, the contradictory knot is reinscribed in infinite constellations there where significations stumble.

This narrative is not a novel, does not seek to create an illusion; it is a place of confrontations where "I" never stops making (itself) scenes.

In these fictions, it is a question of life or death; vital question—that is, suicidal because "playing with fire" is Promethean: "To write a book is a suicide one can begin again. A book has everything about suicide, except the end" (*A*, p. 254).

Everything, therefore, will be played out on the page: word, error, surprise. The work will be gripping or will not be. Nothing will be hidden offstage. It is before my staring eyes that it overflows and not in a secret or allusive elsewhere. Fiction founds reality, invention is the basis of truth, theatricality underpins life. Without a literary, moral, or ideological way out. As always in Hélène Cixous's books, language makes profit *from* and *for* thought: prevents thought from being established but thought still finds derivative consequences and unexpected rebounds. When "*I*" ["la mise *en je*"] indicates the fundamental differend, the subject's drama, we are watching the struggle with the *angel* ["ange"], and this is precisely what is *at stake* ["enjeu"] in literature, keeps an eye on the win-lose of its non-mastery, permitting, at this price, to "transfer literally."

> I read: "There was nothing more on the earth save nothing," Cello said. I read Celan....
>
> A God had provided for her need to weep by inventing Celan, the poet with the name in reverse, the poet who began by being called Ancel, then ceased to be called Ancel, then called himself: Celan, and thus had emerged from the forgetting into which we had slipped him, *by calling himself contrarily*, and behold him standing on the silent soil, his chest full of cello boughs. Only in this way are we able to advance, by beginning at the end, death first, life next, next celative life, so celative, so elative, so celantive.
>
> Mused she, the author, trembling.... (*F*, p. 14, author's emphasis)

In this writing which renders thought divisible then multiplies the intersections, we can read the stakes of literature which outline a decisive division between novel and poem. Hélène Cixous rejects the novel that "forgets its debris" (*A*, p. 225) and its "people with passions," unlike in Dostoyevsky where (*A*, p. 224):

> Angels prey on us, but as our angels are always troublemakers, we never know what kind of good they will inflict upon us. They preach for the high, we bend for the low.... I want what is not given, not ready, not finished, I want lava, I want the era which boils before the work, with countless seeds, irritations, angers..., nothing is played, no one has won, I want life before the deluge and before the ark, because afterward, everything is put in order.... Hundreds of characters will be chased from the work. The novel forgets its debris. (*A*, p. 225)

On the horizon of the work there is the novel-foil on the one hand, the paradigm-poem on the other, which is the name of the "distant existence of the book, its starry wandering about" (*F*, p. 3), of its "cardiac certainty" (*ibid.*), rhythms, rhymes, passages—from another temporality, that of the plural *Jours de l'an*, for example. But for all that, "with words, music, images, with desire and pain—we nonetheless do not have what it takes to make a whole book" (p. 4). Cixousian writing elaborates between two impossibles, two erasures: neither novel nor poem but bearing the unbearable division; the position of the gap. Giving *poietic* body back to the narrative; making the book an illusion of an illusion of the tale ["un retard sur fable"]—Like Marcel Duchamp in painting "Retard sur verre," reflecting the process of loss.

Writing-thinking has no measure except its errors (written "by mistake: by definition" [*F*, p. 35]) and no progression except its corrective brushstrokes. The book works to maintain the gap: "L'Ange au secret" announces this in its title, going back to the etymology of *secretus*— separated, apart, promising an obstacle to saying, to communicating. In short, there is no reason to stop, nor to conclude. Without end, rather: go back over the lines.

* * *

Hélène Cixous writes in *Jours de l'an*:

> Yes what we could give of most loving to a person, that is to say of most giving, I imagine this would be her portrait *in truth*. (p. 70, italics in the text)

Quickly going back a little, I would like to try to sketch this writer's portrait *in truth*, that is, *in trouble*, here, on the page. And to do that, I will refer to Picasso's drawing: *The Ironer (La Repasseuse)*, that she herself chose from the Musée Picasso's collection (Paris) in order to comment upon it in a collective volume.[14]

To me, this drawing appears to inscribe "the truth" of the writer as an ironer. Two-headed figure, she is not at all the two faces of Janus both looking at us, but is torn, rather, between low and high, bent over in the meticulousness of her task, bent backwards in a curse to the heavens or in an apostrophe; she who does, she who thinks; body's head, soul's head.

There is more: emotion's meaning is added to the figure's meaning. For the corrective brushstrokes say also that the head does not fit the body. *Between* the two heads there is *headless* space. An ironing, a writing, "with one's head cut off." With emotion. Between writing and thinking, the emotional pulsation—syncope. ("I prefer to keep my head cut off," *A*, p. 92).

I do not want to draw the idea, I do not want to write being, I want what is happening in the Ironer, I want the nerve, I want the revelation of the broken Ironer. (*Repentirs*, p. 60)

However, it is not exactly the portrait of a writer-ironer's decapitation. Writing-thinking certainly does not go without breakage. Without losing: one's head. But there is more. In the debris of the stroke, the work of corrections. Hélène Cixous's writing-thinking is, in every case, *holding one's own (head) against the other (head)* [*tenir tête à la tête*].

Notes

1. [The author is playing on the French "faire voie"—"to leak"—and "faire voix"—"to make voices." Trans.]
2. [The word-play stems from "encre," "ink," and "ancre," "anchor." Trans.]
3. [Je-elle" ("I-she") is heard in "je-aile" ("I-wing"). Trans.]
4. ["Moi" = "me"; "mois" = "months." Trans.]
5. The quotations in this article refer to: the translation of Hélène Cixous' *Jours de l'an* by Catherine A. F. MacGillivray, entitled *Firstdays of the Year* abbreviated *F*; and Hélène Cixous, *L'Ange au secret* (Paris: des femmes, 1991), abbreviated *A*.
6. ["Don" = "gift." Trans.]
7. Jean-Luc Nancy, *Le Discours de la syncope. I. Logodoaedalus* (Paris: Flammarion, 1976), p. 13: "That which founds, that which supports, must it not be 'itself' unbearable?"
8. [Reference here is made to Gustave Flaubert's qualification of *Madame Bovary* as "un livre sur rien." Trans.]
9. " . . . one can want, and approach and remain on the point of no-will. It is the most difficult: to want without will," *L'Ange au secret*, p. 16.
10. Jean-Luc Nancy, *Le poids d'une pensée*, (Grenoble, Québec: Presses Universitaires de Grenoble, Éditions Le Griffon d'argile, Collection Trait d'union, 1991).
11. "The way I fight with myself is akin to that of the matador and the bull.
    In the arena, am I the matador who deep down doesn't dare charge unreservedly at the bull, but who calls him from a ways away, or else am I the bull who doesn't respond, who doesn't attack the matador . . .?
    There was between the matador and the bull such a mysterious mix of peace and war and resignation.
    Nothing is served by struggling in love. One of us must lose her head. Whoever we may be and whatever we may do, in the arena it is written that the beast will die. . . .
    As bull and matador I am condemned to death." *F*, p. 14–15 and 17.
12. [In the French text, this sentence concludes with the idiomatic expression "il ne l'envoie pas dire" which the author uses not in its usual sense of

"addressing someone harshly without an intermediary" but literally, as "natural self-diffusion." Trans.]

13. Walter Benjamin, *Mythe et violence*, p. 61.

14. Hélène Cixous, "Sans Arrêt non État de Dessination non, plutôt: Le Décollage du Bourreau," *Repentirs* (Paris: Louvre, Édition da la réunion des musées nationaux, 1991), p. 55–64.

IN OCTOBER 1991 . . .
Hélène Cixous

In October 1991 . . . When I submitted the title of this talk, it was in 1990. Which is to say that the talk to come was without a title. That I didn't know what would be essential. Which meant: I don't know what the face of the world will be, nor mine, in October 1991, nor whether I will still have face. Which meant: blindness, not-clearsightedness, unpredictability. And then also: *will I be* in October 1991? Who knows? I like to be in the present, am interested in what is in the process: of passing, of happening. The instant—the eternity of the instant.

I am not coming to you tonight with *tomorrows* ["demains"]; with *two hands* ["deux mains"] of course, but with *nows* ["maintenants"].

I like to be in the present. You will say to me: dream on! That's exactly what I'm trying to do. And then, I also have a special affection for the present because it's theatrical time. It's something I discovered in working for the theater: the peculiarity of this genre which invents, which invents for us, ceaselessly, a time without time.

The present is also always a just afterwards. But for us, October—for us in other times—it was the beginning of the new school year, the tenth month which was the first, the beginning at the end of an era. It was the first day, a menace, and a maturing.

So, in October 1991 and just afterwards, what has been, what remains? What makes this October and what runs off? What has passed?

To answer quickly, in a scene which remains for me the scene of writing: one of my lives, for example, is also: the USSR. Through the different readings that had been proposed from what I have been able to write—from what *Cixous*, as they say, has been able to write—it appeared that I am—well, *she* is—often preoccupied, perhaps principally, with loss and its paradoxes. This one, for example: I can only save from perdition that which I have already lost. Obviously, I am not going to try to save the USSR.

But on the other hand, my path through perdition is traversed, or crossed, by our century's catastrophes and cataclysms. And I was thinking, around October, in these parts, I was thinking about witnesses; about the fact that we are distant witnesses, strangers, inadequate for those

77

without witnesses. We are the strange, privileged unprivileged witnesses for those without witnesses. It seemed to me that we have the writing task of echoing the history of this century's sorrows. This history pro- duces a number of signs and metaphors, and one of them appears quite familiar to me—it is to everybody, I know that it was inaugural for me, in a subjective manner: it is that of the *wall*. Within us. Of the wall within us, outside of us. And followed by the question: and if our wall were to be taken away? History of walls, history of annihilations: this is what we will have had to deal with in this October 1991.

I use the word *us*—it's true, I have problems with pronouns, always. When I say the word *us*, I am aware of the double value in its use. On the one hand, I admit that it's violent: I say "us" as if I were you and you me. But it is also a form of humility.

The disappearance of the USSR. I am not going to give a political talk. I am still staying with the theater, our theater. Theater of us, subjected to the winds of History. Here: outside of France. And I will make a few remarks precisely because of the journey. I am going to report to you one among a thousand effects of the disappearance of the USSR as it can be observed in France, one feature, typical of our times, written on the French scene. The kind of flash effect that events have on ideology, discourse, and desire: for example, in France, on something that belongs to our little memory and which is the fall of what has been called the PC.[1]

There were immediately articles in the newspapers that I will call badly-intentioned or in bad faith—as always: therefore normal—on the "PC" . . . but the American "PC"! That is to say, and I won't be the first to tell you, on the notion of the Politically Correct. There was, typically, confusion in much French opinion, an amalgam between PC and "PC": what was PC was in any case loathsome, since it was the PC. Inscription, therefore, of a phobia in France. France manufactures and sells phobia and phobigenic objects. You have to be in Paris to smell the daily odor of the hunt, this desire to kill, this desire to set up in order to decapitate. The smell of newspaper. But in October, it was the French PC *and* the American Politically Correct that found themselves both rejected and blacklisted!

Why do I mention these incidents? Because it's true that when I write in flight, in fleeing, I am of course always pursued and caught by the echoes of the big scene. There, for example, in this moment, by the intensity of contradictory struggles, the question of identity, nationalisms, the sad phobia of nonidentity appearing in Berlin for example, and in general the phobia of difference. Each time, I say to myself: fortunately there is this voice, this poetry-philosophy, so as to think or, in any case, sing; so as to write, play, to make contradictions and the world as tragedy vibrate.

With regard to this, I will speak about the theme of betrayal. Like me, you must have seen scenes lifted out of the historico-political scene and visibly played as theater: I'm thinking of Gorbachev's face in particular, it was a Shakespearean face. All of a sudden we saw a defeated, humiliated Gorbachev, reintroducing tragedy onto the political screen. I am not at all in the process of crying over Gorbachev. On the other hand, I observed with great interest the exposing, stripping, deposing of the statesman. All the more so because, it has to be said, statesmen fiercely resist being deposed. I haven't yet seen in France a statesman of our time undergo, accept to undergo, and not resist divestment, deposition. The last tragic "act" we saw was de Gaulle's back. But the unmasking, the wrenching of the character and the projection, the haste made toward human nudity, that we had never seen.

What we saw was uncontrollable suffering, whatever its cause or quality. And it's true that a statesman doesn't show, doesn't suffer. I will speak then of betrayal, ours; the betrayal to which we are always given over. Of abandonment. Of the childish situation produced by abandonment. For as soon as we are betrayed, we are little children. I will speak of persecution: of the subject which becomes object, the thing that falls between one's hands. Of the brusque, dazzling, terrible, magnificent admission of blindness. Gorbachev's admission of blindness. Of having been blind. Of being blind. We saw him being blind. Blindness beheld is constitutive of theater.

What else did I think about this summer that was moving toward October, that was in the process of making October? *About viewpoint.* About the expression "point of view." An expression that I wouldn't be able to exploit as I would like in a language other than French. For thanks to our language—languages give us gifts—, "point de vue" in English is *viewpoint*, but also the point of nonview. There where there is no view. Point of view always goes with: no view.

Point of view: a story, for example, that I borrow from Thomas Bernhard's *Imitator*. A story of a beautiful view, belvedere. It's the one about two university professors who climb Grossglockner; and Thomas Bernhard tells us that these characters are bonded by friendship; that they have reached a place where there is a telescope; and that, necessarily, having arrived and in spite of all academic resistance to the idea of believing what they had always been told, they were going to behold a countryside of extraordinary beauty, and each wonders who will first take hold of the telescope. There, a new viewpoint circle: it is very complicated to know which one of the two, decently and without feeling guilty, has the right to the telescope. So, our two academics discuss and at the end of their conference, finally agree. It's the oldest,—and, says Thomas Bernhard, the most learned, and naturally the most considerate—who is the first to look through the telescope. He is filled with wonder. Then, it's his colleague's turn; he takes the telescope, looks, gives a great cry, and falls dead. After which they are only one who can ask himself what exactly, from this point of view, occasioned such a great consequential difference. What was it that? But as they are now only one, we will never know. Since it takes two for viewpoint to function.

That is why I always liked Plutarch when I was little. He's the one who taught me that, when telling a story, you must say: "according to this version," "according to that version," "according to this version." That is what the newspapers don't do, of course. We neither.

The most important point of view for all of us is, I think, this one: only Brutus can kill us. Only the person who can't kill us can kill us. Ah! but that's Caesar's viewpoint. Brutus' point of view is, obviously, that only Caesar can kill us. That is, only prekilled Brutus, only Brutus seeing Caesar's dagger coming down upon him, can kill the first. The question being precisely who is going to kill first? According to the point of view.

What did I think about this summer? About love full of non-love. About the quantity of non-love in love. And especially about the complicity of executioner and victim.

(Nota Bene. This is a correction: I'll say right away that I am not talking about the executioner and victim of the greatest stage and before which I feel humble: the Holocaust. I remain on the domestic stage.)

How, in the private scene, the executioner—you or me—feels victimized by the victim. How the victim is the executioner's executioner. Which makes our persecutory love relations very difficult. I thought about the victim's misdeed. I thought about the real tragedy which is that the victim is guilty of being a victim. About the danger incurred by being the cause of a feeling of executioner, of guilt, in you, in the other.

But careful, I'm taking the victim's point of view. So, I change.

We are all guilty innocents. We are guilty of being innocent. That is, guilty of innocence. Or, of guilt. That is, the innocent guilty. That is what renders dense and difficult the mystery of . . .: there, I don't know if I can use the word "innocence" or the word "guilt" separately. So, let's talk instead about the mystery of forgiveness. To forgive is urgent. It's just that: it's extremely difficult to forgive. I don't even know if it exists. I don't know if there is any forgiving. In general, our practice of forgiving is vengeance. To forgive . . . If I forgive, I signify that there is fault. To forgive is to offend.

How to go about forgiving, be forgiven? We need forgiveness. Every day. Every day, we need forgiveness. Every day we need to be forgiven and to forgive. We who are guilty of all the wrongs in the world. What to do when instead of forgiveness there is, in general, repression, or flight? I don't know. It seems to me that one would have to find forgiveness beyond forgiveness. Neutral, absolute, unspoken forgiveness. *Forgiveness ahead of time*. It is already much more difficult to express forgiveness afterwards. Therefore, forgiveness ahead of time, yes.

Likewise, since I'm moving around in these intensities, in these difficulties: what to do so that love, our main activity—even if we don't believe it—*loves*? I have come to the point of telling myself that only love without confidence, love which does without confidence, is *love*. Love without confidence is greater than love with confidence. To love is to love without confidence. Similarly: the greatest proof of love is to not speak the greatest proof of love.

Often we say to ourselves: how short life will have been. But I was saying to myself: how short death will have been. It's also a point of view. The point of view on time is always the most subjective point of view.

That is the text, I believe, that will never manage to be written: a text which takes into consideration the dilation and contraction of time. All things we know perfectly well. The fact that all of a sudden, a day has the duration of a year; or that all of a sudden, a terrible thing, time stops. How to write that? I don't know. I have had the experience, but I still don't know how it would be expressed.

I thought about the challenge that life and death present to writing. For writing goes at the speed of the hand. Life, and death, flash by. A fire takes us, by surprise. Writing is way behind. How to seize the burning moments? How to take fire by the hand? By the way, we would be well advised to take the fire with our hands very quickly. Because if you take the fire with your hands fast enough, you don't burn yourself. Fire seized at the speed of fire: that's what would have to be done. In order to write.

What made me laugh this summer? Ah! I really laughed. I have difficulty laughing, especially at performances, but this time I really did laugh. It was Stendhal who was telling me a wonderful story. From the age of thirteen to fifty-three, with the greatest steadfastness, the greatest fidelity, he had two passions. A passion for Shakespeare and a passion for spinach. You too, you laugh like me. You laugh because it's true. Strangely, it's what I like that makes me laugh. What gives me satisfaction, exultation. I too, from thirteen to fifty-three, I liked Shakespeare and spinach. I

am not Stendhal. I liked Shakespeare, it's true. What made me laugh
about Stendhal: the beauty of his text, obviously, its veracity. "My only
pleasure in reading was Shakespeare, a passion which lasted like the
physical one for spinach and is at least as strong at fifty-three as it was
at thirteen." He says it three or four times. It seemed to me a marvelous
definition of writing. That writing is made of Shakespeare and spinach.
That Shakespeare is to reading what spinach is to the physical: that
the large is small, depending on one's point of view. That to see the
large small and the small large is true, and that is what makes us
laugh. It is a transmutation of values, but on-the-spot, concretely. And
providing that the large and small mix together, as in Shakespeare, all
that is ordinary is endowed with a supernatural quality.

When I say that the large and small mix together, the difference is,
of course, there. There is *some* difference. In the tangle of large and
small: the gardeners and Richard II; of the porter and Macbeth; and in
the exchange or collision of good and evil.

I was therefore overjoyed as I followed Stendhal in these places of
correction: in the sense, precisely, of *pentimento*, of corrective brushstrokes
in drawing and painting. Not in his novels but in his *Journals* and in
his *Memories of egoism*; in *The Life of Henry Brulard* that seems to me
to be the youngest text, the most eternally young that I have ever seen.

What did Stendhal bring us? Permanently? The viewpoint—for
example—of he who does not see the battle. And not only in *The
Charterhouse of Parma*. Just to savor it, here is this little wonder: how
Stendhal saw the Revolution in Grenoble. He was at his window, he
hears a charge, gunshots, soldiers, and he sees in the street an old
woman running as fast as she can, waving her shoes and yelling: I
revort! I revort! And I, at Stendhal's window, I said to myself: who in
the world could summarize the French revolution better than Stendhal
and his old woman with the shoes? I revort!

And still with Stendhal—who, when it comes down to it, had writing's
taste of good and evil—a story of taste, the sensation of evil's meaty
taste. There too, something that he saw up close, so close that, after
the condemned man's execution, he saw drops of blood form along the
knife's edge before falling. "And that," he says, "was so loathsome that
I wasn't able to eat boiled meat for I don't know how long afterwards."

And what made me cry? What made me cry, and think a lot, was
the *Nibelungen*. I reread the *Nibelungen* and experienced extremely strong
emotions. For me, it's one of the most powerful texts in the world
because of its narrative process. It is the story of betrayal. It's a single
book, but there are several books in the *Nibelungen*. The first book is
a book of joy, of conquests. It ends with marriages and everybody is

very happy. At that moment, obviously, everybody is going to be very unhappy. In the second book—which stays with us, which hurts us the most, which leaves a scar in our memory,—we are told of Siegfried's death, a traitorous assassination. In the third book, we go through a very long period of time which allows Kriemhild, Siegfried's wife, to plan her revenge. She lives only for that, to staunch her sorrow by some kind of equivalent. The text, by the way, tells us that Kriemhild cried for thirteen unbroken years. At some time in my life, perhaps, I would have said to myself: crying for thirteen years straight, that can't be. Now I know that one can cry for thirteen years.

The *Nibelungen* is a text that cries and makes one cry like no other text. And it's the narrative's fault. The narrative which knows everything beforehand and which ceaselessly cautions us. It's a narrative that warns us. We go to the wedding and the narrative says, while we are going there: "and at the end of this joyous ceremony never will we have been so unhappy." And we go to the marriage, torn between the joy we want to feel and the horrible despair that has been promised us and which will be carried out. We? We the readers. And we don't know very well who we are. Because as a result of being forewarned, we are in a process of divided identification. We die, we don't die. We know that he is going to die, that she is going to die, and we are finally powerless accomplices in this series of tragedies.

And then, in the *Nibelungen*, "all have left, no one comes back." In saying that, I quote Akhmatova. All the Russian poets have left, no one has come back. It's exceptional. The *Illiad*: everyone left, a few came back. The *Nibelungen*: everyone left, not a soul came back. And they are innumerable, we know them all, each will successively go to spill all his blood, whereas we, we shed all our tears, and they too. Such a shedding of tears, we can't even imagine it. Who would have thought we had so many tears?

However, the tears are not alone. In the saddle, still from the viewpoint of mourning, this prior mourning that follows us everywhere, precedes us, envelopes us, while we follow this cavalcade, saying to ourselves that we are going to cry—and we cry for them, alive they are already dead, these alive-dead men—during this time, flowers grow, the prairie is beautiful, it's spring, soon blood will flow. I don't know whether it's the flowers that create the beauty of the blood or the blood that creates the beauty of the flowers, but not one without the other. As in *The Song of Roland*. As soon as there are flowers, there is blood.

The *Nibelungen* is not the first book to make all the tears and all the blood flow. The oldest, the one most familiar to us, is the *Book of Job*, whose motto—if we can call it that—is that everything we fear is granted.

There is nothing more terrible. And I wonder why I read the *Nibelungen*, why I drink this blood. Why I shed these tears and why I need to be in mourning. You and I. Why do we read these books that make us cry? Undoubtedly because, in reality, we never have enough lamentations. We need to play with fire, with blood, with mourning, not because we are players but because we need to almost die. We need to mourn ourselves. Yet we remain alive. That is what a text like the *Nibelungen* is for. Everyone cries, everyone is cried for. All drink and all tears are drunk.

There are some texts, though, that make me neither laugh nor cry. And which, however, give me joy. There aren't many of them.

However, I will say in homage that the only one that has this effect on me—makes me neither laugh, cry, nor tremble, but still gives me joy—is Clarice Lispector's text. But that's a mystery. I can only say it quickly. *She* is beyond good and evil. How? Because she writes posthumously. She writes after. After dying. Indeed, one experiences at this moment a feeling of acute joy which hurts but which remains silent. This is a text without pity or mourning. The only one.

Let's leave the book and come back to the room, to bed, to us. And to the point of view. And to our personal tragedy. One thing that I have always found beautiful and terrible and intransposable is the degree to which tragic characters make us laugh—that is, us—when they are without an audience.

Since I was going to evoke my October 1991, I remembered: I must say something as a *woman*. One day, when I will be 250 years old, I won't have to do it anymore. And I will be relieved. Because it's the greatest, most fabulous, most marvelous trap of our era.

I won't get into theorizing, nor will I try to bring out things I have often tried to write. Let's say that, as a woman, if I am a woman—and I believe that I can say to myself that I am a woman only because, from time to time, I have experiences that belong to this universe—the idea comes to me that, perhaps, the two great intimate and strange experiences of life have to do with childbirth (I use an uninterpretable [French][2] word on purpose); it would be childbirth, and then: unchildbirth ["désenfantement"]. It happens that we are born. It's the experience of grieving. I believe that in mourning, whomever the person may be that we're losing, our grandfather, our old schoolteacher, our friend, we always lose the child.

And the love of women? A worrying subject, worried. I hasten to say: we don't know much about it. That is what experience has whispered to me. To what point we haven't yet thought—we have lived but not thought, inscribed—the difference within women, or within one woman.

The fact, for example, that a woman exists who is not a woman and who is, however, a woman. The difficulty of thinking, for example, that according to the Greek tragedians, Clytemnestra has a virile force; she is described as having a virile force in assassinating Agamemnon. If I take my great Greek tragedian's unconscious literally, I am obliged to ask myself who, in Clytemnestra, kills Agamemnon. For Clytemnestra is going to be condemned as a woman, but it's as a man that she puts Agamemnon to death. . . . Now, here are our daily experiences: vacillation, difficulty, indefinition. Where, in fact, one could glimpse, inside, within, behind appearances, this unclear emergence of identity. But it's true that the social scene and all our investments, our speculations, prevent us from really looking.

Sometimes—for example in what Philippe Lacoue-Labarthe was saying this morning—, woman and mother go together. I have a tendency to think that. I have a tendency to maternalize woman. To feel that a woman is more woman when a mother. But it's a question to be asked. I prefer to speak about myself because it's not as dangerous as generalizing; if I'm mistaken, I'm only betraying myself.

I very often catch myself in the act of being a son's mother. For example, when I saw Gorbachev, I pitied someone for whom I have no pity. And I felt this bizarre "son's mother" person in me being carried away by pity. What's worse—it's a burning confession—, I'll tell you that I even felt pity for someone whom I find despicable: Judge Thomas. In spite of myself, I thought: there it is, she's moving, this person who must restrain herself so as to not forgive the unforgivable. I think that threatens many women as mothers-of-all-men. It may be good but it's also very dangerous.

I am also a daughter's mother. It's an extremely complicated but particularly rich and pleasant situation. The one, perhaps, on which we work the least since, in fact, we are always summoned to be mother-of-a-son. It is in this space that one can find, in certain cases, the greatest hate but also the greatest love. A love which would be sublime friendship.

I was heading toward October 1991 when I said to myself, all of a sudden: but afterwards, there will be October 1992; for once, then, here are completely perishable words.

Everything passes, as Montaigne, our master, everyone's grandfather, says to us all. In writing, I have the feeling—Mireille Calle spoke about me better than I will ever be able to do—I have the feeling I'm always writing at the side of what's passing. Which, as she showed, is problematic. I also perceive writing in a differential: I am not a painter, I am not a musician. For it seems to me that painters and musicians paint, write, under the deluge, that which doesn't pass. That their effort, even in inscribing what passes, is to reach that which doesn't pass. I apologize to painters and musicians if I've said something foolish. It seems to me that there is a striving toward *permanence*. On the other hand, for those of us who write, what is important is the process. It's the storm, the rough copy. "I wander." (That isn't me, it's Stendhal.) It's love, that which passes. It is difference that passes, that is what escapes us.

Which is why I have always been passionate about a certain type of book: *books that slip away*. To be understood by making the language resonate: that run away, escape books' fate at every page. That don't close, let us fall, don't finish. There are some that are extremely violent toward us. For example Thomas Bernhard's, that slam the door in our face, throw us out. That say to us: now that's enough. Those ones are of a somewhat artificial type.

There are innumerable texts—for me the most beautiful—that don't know how to finish. Exactly as in life. That don't finish or that force themselves to finish. Dostoyevsky's *The Idiot*. One puts an end to it, muzzles it, cuts off its breath—even though the book continues, elsewhere and differently.

We pass. We all want to forget that we pass. Yet—yet, we are more true when we admit that we never do anything but try. The dinosaurs lived for three hundred million years and then, all of a sudden, they disappeared. We are all future dinosaurs. We live 300,000,000 years and, all of a sudden, we disappear entirely. Entirely. That is how we pass.

We can believe or not believe that three hundred million years is soon. It's a thought I find very necessary, very beautiful, precisely because we do not live that knowledge. We would certainly want to laugh more often and we would certainly be more humble if we knew that in 300,000,000 years we will have disappeared in any case.

Who would know how, who could be humble? I would think—but it's a thought I form cautiously—that some women could be on the side of humility to the extent that they would have had the experience of "starting over again at zero." This journey which goes from zero to zero, from the child to death.

I don't know. I have difficulty speaking in terms of "gender" as is said here. Remembering vividly that one must not forget, Clarice Lispector sometimes says: and the tortoises? I haven't thought about tortoises for at least ten years! It's not that I'm comparing them to tortoises, but I must exclaim: and the men? Obviously, they are unforgettable. But the problem, for us who are supposed to be women, is: how to talk about them? I shouldn't talk about them. I shouldn't talk about men. I can write, love. But that's a different matter.

I shouldn't talk about power either, that is, about assassination. I should not talk about that which I am not nor that with which I do not form an integral part. And at the same time, I would like to talk about it because I am afraid of being taken for a "feminist." I'm not saying that "women" are "better." Simply that they do not have "the" *Power.* Why? (1) "They" ["Ils"] are there so that they don't have It. (2) But when they ["elles] have It, there so often occurs a drift in their sufficiently masculine desire, a moment of distraction, hunger, love, that "the" *Power* escapes them . . .

A few words about the mother. I sometimes think that, "at the bottom," of a human being, what makes the difference, *his* or *her* difference, is the mother. What the mother was, how she inscribed herself. Sometimes I think to myself that one should do away with the invisible meridian of difference, not between men and women but between vengeance and patience, between insatiable and nurturing nurturer, male or female.

I feel like using "mother" as I would a metaphor, but at the same time it's not a metaphor. It is this secret and decisive figure that one can feel living and writing in those who write. One could say, for example, that men and women who have had a good mother are not big eaters of steak, are not big eaters. Those who have the mother in them approach the other with circumspection. Or else with circonfession. The mother is a quality.

Careful: I just said something completely disputable. I speak as though the mother were good. I believe it, absolutely: a good mother, that's good. But that is from my point of view. And the question about point of view relentlessly comes to interrogate an enunciation of this sort. It's that a good mother can be seen in a bad light. She can be very bad being good. Et cetera.

I'm going to tell you an October memory. A mother's memory. My first October memory is of having cried, cried, cried for my mother on my way to school. At that time, it was during the war—as is said in the time of: "during-the-war"; and there was no school. In my native village, therefore, the school was in a small room in an apartment where a woman taught bunches of Jewish children of all ages. So when I went to school—which happened very rarely—I was in a very beautiful little "class" because there was a first row, a second row and so on, and you went down from the first row where they were already learning conjugations, to the back, where they made lines and circles. That was me. But I rarely made it there. And at the same time, I learned everything because while I made dashes and circles, I listened: "qualifying adjective."

Upon arriving at this sort of school, I cried. I couldn't stop myself from crying. The entire world was nothing but tears. My only memory of the first day is to have cried endlessly, completely given over to a flood of tears. Upon arriving the second day, there we go, it's coming, I start again! . . .

I had therefore developed the habit of saying, just before entering the class, "Madam, I am going to cry." And she would say to me: "Well cry! You will come in when you have finished crying." Sometimes I ended up coming in. And I would hear "qualifying adjective," and I was in paradise. I would finish crying and come in. Sometimes I didn't finish crying. I cried for my mother. Sometimes I finished up with my mother, other times not. And it didn't depend on me. It was stronger than anything else. It was an all-powerful magic that set itself off like a beam, as soon as I arrived at the school.

That was how I spent my entire first school year. I thought that it was a destiny, a stroke come from outside, a sort of arrow that had pierced me. I didn't think I was the one who was crying but that it was unhappiness crying within me. The second year: no tears. I concluded that my pain had a regular rhythm and that I would cry every second year. So, I said to myself, next year I will cry.

Come the following October, I expected tears. Nothing. I sometimes wonder whether this magic is still not at work within me.

About my mother, who just had her eighty-first birthday—I cannot talk about her but I can say one thing: I always called her my mother, and one day I saw her: as a young girl. I was already thirty years old. And it was in writing that I understood all of a sudden that my father was a bird and my mother a young girl. I said to myself: thus, all my life I haven't understood to what degree I was overdetermined by the fact that my mother was a young girl, even younger than I. Some twelve years later, I said to myself: but I've been mistaken all my life. My mother has always been a young boy. I could talk to you about her, but in a way it's terrifying because she is so young. I have written about my mother—in an extremely succinct manner. What I did was nothing, really. It seems that we cannot write about our mothers. I'm sure of it. It's one of the limits of writing.

Thus, my first memory associates my mother's imagined death and school. And since then, I have never stopped crying, going to school, learning, crying, exchanging. Shedding of tears and absorption. Forgetting, overcoming the loss of my mother's body. Or on the contrary: not overcoming it. Inventing. Representing to myself the horror of this loss. All the while wondering who is crying.

Curiously, I know that it's not my mother I lost; it's my father who died and for whom I didn't cry, my father whom I loved. I obviously cried for him differently, but I didn't shed any tears. There is a horrible happiness in tears, in certain tears, which is tied to performance, representation, to the fact that there are witnesses. One cries before witnesses, in company. In a way, it's happiness. One isn't aware of it because of the suffering. But even so, it is happiness. Unhappiness is having no one to cry with. No one to remember with, no one to tell. But I stray.

How did I "write" this? I took notes. I thought: I'm going to do the portrait of October which comes and which passes. It was in a notebook, on detachable sheets. This is not a diary that follows the course of the days. October presented itself in breaths, fragments, emotions, sorrows, and I think that that is how one writes: in a discontinuous fashion. Then you have to cheat in a way: gather together, attach, make order. The order doesn't only come from outside, of course. What is order? It is a form hidden in the disorder.

Actually, I noted or wrote this sitting up in bed at the end of the summer, around October, at the school of mourning, I wrote it in my bed. Which never happens. Except for dreams. That is, I write in the dream and I write my dreams while sleeping. But daytime writing, never. But this time, yes. It was a little before October. It was already October. And I very quickly noted the summer as it was finishing, life, death in the process of finishing.

There is this question of speed in things that happen at the heart's peak which concerns me. To escape the predator, a lion, the deer runs faster than itself. It runs harder than itself. This is a zoological truth: it goes into overcapacity. It goes beyond its forces to survive. And it survives the predator but does not survive the effort. The deer has left the lion behind but then it dies. It survives, it dies from it.

I think that to escape death you have to go through death. Obviously, it's intolerable. I was in the process of writing in my bed, tired from running errands. And there came to me, or there remained with me, a speed, a lightness that I was not successful in keeping.

In October 1991, where am I going? Who goes, who speaks, who is in the process of going, in the process of speaking to you, who is passing? Who still lives and answers to my name? I don't know. If my name wasn't there, my famous unpronounceable name, to which I have finally reconciled myself, if there was not my name to go ahead of me and replace me, make me in my absence, fill in my gaps, if there was not a you/roof ["toi(t)"] when I'm not there, and if there was not my shadow, it would be a fine catastrophe. It's possible—I fear—that these days, instead of me, there will be an interval, a meanwhile, as it happens . . .

I would have liked to have inscribed a state, probably impossible to write, a state, an instance of discontinuity. Discontinuity, the rupture of continuity, interruption, to go through it, it's necessary to have a palpitating heart. Invent something to pass death.

These are not confidences, never mind confessions. But I am giving, in a certain way, my address, position, where my boat is, my plane, on what meridian. I am in the process of turning my attention, your attention, to our fundamental, simple, and naive duplicity, we act and think and move forward while supporting ourselves on continuity. Positing continuity. As if we were (1) all immortal, (2) all dead. When I think of the academic programs we elaborate! We are asked, one year, two years in advance, to promise to be present, that is to say, alive, at such and such a place. And we do it. Even better: we are asked, we ask ourselves, to say what we will think in two years. We ask ourselves to be prophets or dead; to already think, to be simultaneously past and future. It's a mad vision of human time. But we do it. We all feign immortality.

Sometimes, when I go away to write, friends ask me: "about what?" What is the subject? Myself, I never know of course. It knows it, however, I know that it knows it. I mean: *that knows.* Otherwise, I wouldn't go to write. It's a mystery: there where *that* gels, where it grows, where it builds up like rain. Fortunately. I count on it. *That must know.* Not *me.*

It's that I am still of the time—it too in the process of passing—when a woman didn't know whether she was pregnant with a girl or a boy right up until the last minute. I want the last minute. I don't want to know before the last minute. Even if *that* knows. The problem: when is the last minute? The last minute is in the other world. Afterwards.

Stendhal goes away to the other world, he tells us. "When I go into the other world, I will, if possible, go to see Montesquieu. And I will say to him: well, what do you think? Did I write well or did I not write well?—Hmph—Well, if he does that. . . ." This is the scene of Stendhal and Montesquieu. It's beautiful; it's courage.

It's not by chance that I feel close to those who wrote on the edge, in transit, just after or just before. Very quickly, especially. And in dying. And am I going to die? I think about it, why not? Because if it's not me, it's my other, if it's not my other, it's me. One of us is going to die. I could say that it's good, and at the same time I cry over it, nostalgically live it.

I say to myself: If it's not me, it's you, you who are me. How you are going to miss me! I mean: how I'm going to miss you. That is: how you miss me. That is: how we miss each other. I refuse mourning and nostalgia.

And now, after such reflections, I'm going to be born. That's not a sentence from Hélène Cixous, it's a sentence from Stendhal. Quick, let's live, let's think about it.

When I have finished something—when I stop, or when that stops—I wonder: what have I forgotten? I have, obviously, always forgotten. (It's true, that's what the end is: work of memory and forgetting.) At least this: careful, when we read texts. Apart from those, very rare, like *The Life of Henry Brulard*—and again, I wouldn't swear by it—, where the principal characters of the texts, all those who are visible, are not the main characters of a life.

Notes

1. ["Parti communiste," the French Communist Party. Trans.]
2. [Hélène Cixous here uses "enfantement," an older term than "accouchement," a more common term for "childbirth." Trans.]

INSTITUTIONS AND LITERARY IMAGINARIES

THE TRAGIC WOMAN
Claire Nancy

Here we will be dealing essentially with tragedy: Greek tragedy, because that is both its original and accomplished form, accomplished from the very beginning. And therefore woman, also Greek. Greek, at least in her representation. Now, in this context, "the tragic woman" sounds like an oxymoron. If the feminine presence invariably plays an important, indeed decisive role in Greek tragedy, it is also a banality—at least to Hellenists—to note that within the confines of a civic institution, as was tragedy, in the ultimate mimetic genre where the city represents itself, one did not expect to see this "men's club," to use the notorious definition that Pierre Vidal-Naquet gives of *polis* (a city constructed upon the radical exclusion of women), enter onstage and allow women to speak. Even if women's roles are in fact played by men, the theater—this is its foremost effectiveness—will emit women's voices.

Now, it is precisely from speaking that women are most prohibited. They are confined to silence or chatting, reduced, as Pericles reminds them in the celebrated funeral oration of 430 in the second book of Thucydides, to hoping, as their only glory, to be talked about as little as possible. Speech is a citizen's instrument—and women are not citizens. As Nicole Loraux notes, the word "Athenian," which qualifies the citizen of Athens, has no feminine form [in French]. Women are called "Attic," like drachmas or vessels (I cite, as does Nicole Loraux, the entry in Chantraine's dictionary), "with an expressive or pleasant connotation" (still the same entry).

To this exclusion is added another: women, as is known, are relegated to the back of the house or palace. Now, the decor—the place of tragedy, its *skēnē*—is outside: at the front of the palace or in a military camp. Women can therefore not appear. Any feminine presence on the stage of Greek tragedy is by definition a trangression: it implies that a threshold—*the* threshold—the one which separates feminine from masculine, has been crossed. The tragic text itself often comments on this in having women excuse themselves for coming outside, in having them justify why they are there.

This is where my question begins. There are two sides to it. What is

the Greek woman doing in Greek tragedy? But conversely, if tragedy is
an institution of the *polis*, a masterpiece of the citizen's *paideia*, the
city's ritual rendezvous, how can one account for the separation between the civic and tragic stage? What is the political function of the
tragic device?

*   *   *

Aeschylus' theater, the oldest and closest to civic orthodoxy, seems at
first glance to illustrate these elements. Here I will refer to two scenes,
in the broad sense of the term: to two scenic mechanisms. First, *Seven
Against Thebes*, which will be my original scene. On one side Eteocles,
leader and savior of Thebes, sovereign and exemplary warrior. On the
other, the chorus of terrified Thebian women who spread panic throughout
the city and threaten to demobilize the citizens at the moment of
confrontation between the two armies. To the women's whimperings
and disorderly prayers, Eteocles attempts to oppose the bulwark of an
articulate harangue:

> I ask of you, unbearable creatures,
> is this a noble attitude, is it saving the city?
> is it encouraging a people under attack
> to collapse at the feet of our gods' statues,
> to cry, to yell—all these things hated by reasonable beings.
> Neither in misfortune, neither in joyful prosperity,
> do I want to share my dwelling with the species of woman.
> If she has the upper hand, her insolence prohibits any relationship
>   with her.
> If she gives in to fear, it is a plague much worse for the city than for
>   the home.
> Today, with your frantic running in all directions
> you have, for the citizens, made resonate
> the cowardly rumor of discouragement.
> Nothing will be more useful for those at our door
> than if, inside, we are bringing destruction upon ourselves.
> That is what you gain by living with women
>   . . .
> the affairs of the State are men's affairs; woman's voice must not be
>   raised.[1]
> Stay inside, so as to avoid doing us harm.

This says it all and in extremely precise terms. Eteocles' gesture, a
verbal gesture, is obviously that of *massive* repression: massive since
women here are taken as a block, as a species (*genos: gender*), and

radically opposed to the *politai*, who are not a species but unique representatives of a responsible and accomplished humanity. The repression is double.

1. It is, first of all, ethnological. Women are a species, a separate race (born with Pandora for the misery of men who have been always already there and suddenly find themselves, as a result of divine retaliation, stuck with this plague, henceforth necessary for generation but which they are incapable of integrating). According to the Hesiodian tradition and iambic poetry, they are reduced to a determined, unchanging nature which gives rise, elsewhere or in the tragic corpus, to ethnological maxims and descriptions; such that women are not capable of any *paideia*, any development. Always already encircled, they form the object of a discourse of which men—males—are the subjects, masters, therefore, of knowledge: it is the *psogos gunaïkōn*, the traditional fault of women.

2. Next, it is political, by an inevitable consequence according to Greek logic—the Greek conception of *logos*. If the *polis* is the assembly of those who are determined according to a *logos*—a reason—according to models they follow by *imitation*, women are, naturally, excluded. They know only instinct or relationships of force. No cohabitation is conceivable. It is perfectly clear that the only solution is the most rigorous demarcation: they must be granted the house so that men can have a free rein in the city. Even moreso when the city is at war—but in tragedy, the city is almost always at war—and given that the same word means the courage and virility *to andreion*. Women, in this case, are the inside enemy. The assailants' objective ally.

3. Finally, from a tragic point of view this time, that is, from a poetic genre which, as Aristotle says, is based upon the twin relationships of terror and pity, Eteocles' repression of the women is repression of the panic created by their terror—pure, passive creatures, prey to pure passion. Repressed by the military chief concerned about collective cohesion before the enemy. Eteocles purges the city of women, but if the principle of tragic *katharsis* is that of homeopathy—embracing the most threatening passion in order to heal from it—one could doubt the effectiveness of this purgation which is more a type of elimination.

The second scene is from *Orestes*, beginning with *Agamemnon*. The one which presents the figure of Clytemnestra; Clytemnestra or the other form of the menace conjured up by Eteocles: the woman who has *kratos* at her disposal, superiority, Lemnian author of what the Greeks called "the Lemnian crime," the murder of a man by a woman, by his wife; often collective: all the women of Lemnos massacred their husbands. It is the supreme transgression, the very effectuation of what Eteocles dreaded: the *destruction of the polis*—of the public man, the hero dedicated to the city's defense, the male-born-for-the-State—by the *oikos*, the being assigned to domesticity. Should there be a disruption of the equilibrium—the hero has been retained at war, for example, leaving no one in power—and should there be no institutional mechanism to contain what Aeschylus calls "the unchecked desire that drives both the human and animal female," the woman will destroy the entire civic construction and justify the radical distrust of which she is the object.

Furthermore, she openly exhibits a nature dreaded by the male: in addition to her sexual insatiability, woman is an essentially cunning creature. The perfidy of the trap set for Agamemnon in the back of the palace is compounded by a treacherous use of discourse: Clytemnestra uses it only to deceive Agamemnon. She perverts the *logos* and the entire system of persuasion, presenting arguments that are only so many pretexts. Woman is incapable of what Aeschyles, in *The Choephori*, calls "the clear speech which passes from male to male." Clytemnestra here seems to speak only to induce a tragic confirmation of this feminine *apistosunē*, women's radical inability to enter into the world of pacts and conventions by which the city holds natural anarchy at bay.

Thus it is understood that there is no other solution except to kill Clytemnestra in order to protect all heroes, all future men, and to acquit Orestes of matricide, a crime that an archaic justice, founded upon the primacy of blood lines, condemned above all others. The Erinys must be relegated to a cave under the Acropolis, leaving Athena sovereign, Athena the virgin warrior, born fully armed from the paternal thigh and who, based on her own situation, affirms that women play no role in generation. Eternal virgin, Athena confirms that autochthony is the Athenian truth, that no Athenian comes from a woman. The Athenian owes nothing to nature, he owes everything to his father and to Athens.

However, things are not that simple. On the one hand, even if Clytemnestra only says what one expects of her, even if she is the very representation of the Athenian fantasy, even if no effective subject seems to speak when she opens her mouth, she is not the pure manifestation of a consistently monstrous nature. Aeschylus endows Clytemnestra with at least a little bit of *history*: she witnessed Iphigenia's sacrifice, she knew that at Troy Agamemnon had loved Croesus, she sees him come back to the palace with Cassandra. Scorned woman and mother, she invokes a *dikē* to justify her actions: a justice in whose name she feels she has the right to punish, and a vengeful genie of whom she is the instrument. Jealousy can certainly be accounted for ethnologically: a

woman wronged in her bed, Medusa will say, is a bloodthirsty monster.
But Iphigenia's murder is an error recognized by the gods even though
it was one of their own who ordered it. State reason is not always
undivided. The rights of women and children are perhaps not illegiti-
mate. In any case, the question is raised: the city cannot ignore its
other without endangering itself.

If we look closely, the same ambiguity affects the celebrated judgment which concludes the *Eumenides*. Everything certainly seems in
order; the immediate succession of crimes is taken up by judicial debate, the first well-argued debate, the model for modern debate that
illustrates what the *logos* can, in all its glory, do henceforth: produce a
"fair judgment," as Athena puts it. And yet, everything is "rigged":
Apollo's arguments, his *loxias*, work such as to deny the mother's role
in childbirth and reduce her to a womb, as in Athena's case. The *logos*
is oblique: it serves truth less than it distorts it according to the needs
of its thesis.

Whatever it may be that Aeschylus's tragic mechanism contributes to
the civic mechanism, the fact that he replays the founding scene, represents its symbolic elements, and revives the stakes shows that he in-
terrogates it. Unlike the funeral oration and what Nicole Loraux called
his "ideological repetition," his infinitely reiterated glorification of Greek
democracy and the civilization of the *logos*, tragedy, even that which
seems to have the most legitimizing function, never stops resoliciting
the myth, measuring the meaning of the event. Calling women together
to retell the story of their eviction is also to continue repeating the
question: is the de facto state a legitimate state?

*   *   *

With Sophocles, tragedy clearly widens the gap in its representations.
In two ways. On the one hand—and I refer to the scene in *The Women
of Trachis*—it disethnologizes, if one can say, the feminine image. The
story of *The Women of Trachis* is, we remember, that of the couple
Dejanira-Hercules. Hercules of the twelve labors, exemplary hero who
comes back to the city of Trachis after a shining new victory over the
city of Chios. Dejanira, whose name means "she who kills or burns the
male," does in fact bring about the hero's death by consuming him in
the fire of a poisoned tunic that she offers him as a gift. She accomplishes her name's prophecy, proper name which is obviously a common name and immediately places Dejanira among the women capable
and guilty of the Lemnian crime.

However, according to a dramatic strategy peculiar to Sophocles, the tragedy is based on a theatrical coup. The staging of the legend delivers a decisive blow to the meaning it carried within it. It is first of all the deconstruction of a hero whose glory is deceptive, as the Messenger soon tells Dejanira: his victory over Chios masks what is nothing more than a plundering of the village, a pretext for the abduction of the king's daughter, Iolas, whom Dejanira sees pass before her, weeping and reduced to the state of a captive. It is then Dejanira's turn to speak, tragedy's first true feminine character. True in the Greek sense of *alēthēs: revealed*. If only because she addresses the chorus of women to confide in them, explain to them her reactions as well as her intentions. For the first time, tragedy endows a feminine character with an interior, reveals a reflection, authorizes some leeway. And this leeway is that of powerless innocence; Dejanira's mortal stratagem is only the fatal outcome of a displaced or exonerated story; the malevolent trap—the poisoned tunic—is not Dejanira's doing but that of the centaur, Nessos, who had, while dying from Hercules' arrows, imagined a posthumous revenge on his murderer. All he had to do was deceive Dejanira (whom he had just abducted and raped) by giving her the poison, saying it was a love philter that she might one day use to revive a failing lover. The Lemnian crime is therefore committed against the will of her heart. In the very act of living out her name, Dejanira refutes it. She frees herself, at least in intention—and the intentionality here is determinant—from the curse that weighed upon her in her sex and her name.

There is a lot at stake here. Especially because, much more than for Clytemnestra, the story in which Dejanira is caught takes over from the natural explanation. Without the denigration of Hercules and what is presented as his betrayal, Dejanira would never have used the *pharmakon*, balm-poison which is part of the feminine panoply. Here she is nothing more than a plaything of a story in which she has no role.

With Dejanira, the tragic woman swings from the side of terror to the side of pity. But this pity indicates precisely the operation's limits. Victim and murderer in spite of herself, Dejanira is discharged but she is also destitute: dependent on her love for Hercules, dispossessed by the centaur and destiny's malice, deprived of the gesture she wanted to make, she is the subject of nothing, stripped of all autonomy, all signification. Pure *pathos*: it is easy for anyone to use her.

Sophocles' second gesture is of an entirely different scope: we are speaking, of course, about *Antigone*. Unheard of gesture, if we think about it, that proposes a confrontation on the tragic stage, a veritable *agōn*, that is, a debate—a political one—between a man and a woman.

If we remember that the norm is *Seven against Thebes*, that is, the collective relegation of women inside, barred from speaking (deliberative speech and voice), we can measure the violence of the subversion that is at work here. Of course, this subversion has its limits: Sophocles did not go so far as to make Antigone a woman in the accomplished sense of the term. Neither married, nor mother, intact—in every sense of the word—better known to the dead than to the living, Antigone is more a voice than a spokeswoman for femininity, and it is perhaps this more symbolic than effectively incarnated status that lends her strength. Nonetheless, her opposition to Creon is, at least for him, perceived as coming from a woman because it is on these grounds that he challenges her, refusing to have his rules dictated by a woman who, by her sex, is allotted to submission.

In any case, the stakes this time are purely political. What is in question is nothing more than the essential: laws, the dead, gods, the tie that the city maintains with them through Creon's person. Antigone is intervening in the very heart of the Greek State. And contrary to what we have so often read, she is not challenging a tyrannical Creon's abuse of power but, as Hegel had seen, the very principle of the State—the modern State. In the sense of it having been inaugurated by the Greeks— they were acutely aware of it. She is challenging (according to the etymology of her name: she who is born to rise up against) man's unilateral institution of new laws. Challenging political self-foundation, self-legislation, the abandonment of reference to the gods, the promulgation of new laws, in short, the birth of a History. And of a History inaugurated by discrimination, by the decreed split between Eteocles and Polynices, between good and bad, patriot and antipatriot. The political *logos* slices, reslices. It makes divisions and laws without recourse to the gods, without concern for any transcendence. It subjugates the gods as it subjugates ethics.

Now, echoes of Antigone's violent protestation can be heard in the suspicions expressed in the most celebrated chorus in the play, the one that inscribes the entire human History under the auspices of the *deinon*, *deinon* that the Hellenistic tradition translates as "marvelous," whereas Hölderlin, followed by Heidegger, prefers to refer to its etymological origin of "monstrous." At the same time marvelous and monstrous, it is the progress that brought humanity from primitive life to this unheard-of accomplishment called "legislating drive." Sophocles' tragedy, in its turn, returns to this creation's principle in order to question it, admire it, and worry about it. Legislative inspiration, he says, is the daughter of *technē* which permits it to civilize nature but transgresses order by the very gesture that accomplishes its mastery.

Risk is therefore essential, and it is perhaps thus that one must understand the human *deinon*. The chorus opposes three terms to this risk: first, death, from which *technē* will never find a way out. It is therefore simultaneously human and inhuman, if the definition of human is mortality. Second, laws of nature, of which *technē* is unaware, as if man could cut himself off from his origin. And third, the gods' justice. *Technē* is atheist, this is its third weakness. With its corollary: it knows neither good nor evil since it can indiscriminately take one path or the other.

The chorus does not see any other response to this risk than to reinject (the Greek term is *pareirō*: introduce from the side) the "laws of the land" and "sworn justice to the gods." The very ones from which *technē*, following its own logic, frees itself. *The city is running the risk of becoming an aporia.*

But with regard to Sophocles, this proposition is probably excessive. The chorus' suggestion, like Antigone and Creon's symmetric excess, each as intransigent as the other, leaves the door open perhaps for a reconciliation — or at least for a better tempered city which would take nature and the gods into consideration and reconcile the sexes by having them become disenchanted with their roles; like the dialogue between Oedipus and Jocasta (but Jocasta is Oedipus's mother and it is the only example of tragic love) allows us to imagine for a moment . . .

For Euripides, on the other hand, there is no more ambiguity. A response to the anxieties formulated by the old men in *Antigone*'s chorus can be heard, ten years later, in the univocal report drawn up in the first chant in *Medea* by the women that compose this chorus. That is, women's speech:

Backwards flows the course of sacred rivers,
And justice and all things turn around.
To men, the designs of trickery,
Faith sworn to the gods no longer holds.

The "retreat of the divine," as Hölderlin would say, is from now on a fact. The text takes up the Hesiodic myth: at the end of the Golden Age, justice had left the earth. The very justice that Sophocles' chorus hoped to see reintroduced into the city to check *technē*'s irresistible progress. The "clear speech that passes from male to male" is now nothing but the modern, virile form of duplicity. And what was the very figure of the unthinkable, the rhetorical formula of the impossible — that rivers return to their source — is, however, what henceforth *takes place*. The *polis* has not kept the promises of its transparent mastery.

The consequences are immediately stated in the antistrophe which responds to the first strophe,

The rumor will return in my favor
To grant me the glory of my existence.
Now the time is coming when woman's race will be esteemed,
Never again will offensive murmurings be taken up against women.
The muses will stop their antique songs
That reiterate my treachery.

The defection of the ethico-political system obviously entails the return of what it most strongly repressed. In a contract which used to exclude women in the name of their essential treacherousness—the betrayal of masculine faith, of which Jason will set the example—speech is restored to women. They are entirely ready, incidentally, to accept it, to set themselves up as subjects of discourse, to constitute males, in their turn, according to an unheardof neologism, as a "race of males" (*gender*), as an ethnological object. But they come up against a *genre fault*: there is no feminine poetic genre.

Our way of thinking has not received from Phoibos,
guardian of lyric poems,
the gift of the lyre-inspired song.
Because then, I would have turned the hymn
against the race of men. Time, in its long course
gives much to say about them, and as much about us.

This new situation, this unveiling of a masculine nature owed to a History they themselves set in motion, leaves women facing the absence of a poetic tradition. Because the same dividing line which rigorously cleaves humanity into natural creatures and civilized men, into apolitical women and citizens, equally affects all *mousikē*, the golden order of literary and musical production. Be it a question of musical modes, as in the list Plato draws up in Book III of *The Republic*, rigorously distinguishing oriental, effeminate, plaintive modes, appropriate to demobilize the keepers of the ideal city, from articulate and energetic phrygian or dorian modes, alone capable of the tension necessary for virile development; or a question of types of instruments, privileging the lyre, Apollinian instrument of *ethos* and self-affirming individuality, suitable only for males, as opposed to Marsyas or Dionysus's flute, instrument of pathos and accompaniment of transes, delirium, and anarchic collectives. Be it a question, finally, of the mimetic function of words upon which Plato—like Aristotle in his *Poetics*—will establish a rigorously sexed typology, prohibiting men to reproduce themes or forms belonging to the feminine repertory.

At the moment of taking up speech, women have no genre. Aeschylus's women did not have this obstacle and limited themselves, mimetic of their own image, to expressions expected of their sex: fear, panic, or violence of aggression and trickery. Sophocles' women questioned this image but never gained access to the status of a feminine *ethos*: Dejanira is a woman, but she is pure *pathos*—victim—even if this *pathos* is endowed with a conscience. Antigone is an *ethos* but at the price of renouncing her femininity. Femininity replaced by both paternal filiation and—actually the same thing—by sisterhood. The original community she opposes to Creon's political discrimation is a community of the same, of "familiarity."

We can, on the other hand, say of all of Euripides' women that they are neologisms. So many women, so many, or almost, oxymorons, breaches—or bridges, if you like—so many transgressions of gender limits. Typological oxymoron: Aristophanes reproached Euripides for not only staging *pornai* and *sophai*, degenerates and intellectuals, but—even worse—this unheard of creature, the *pornē sophē*: the debauched intellectual. Ethical oxymoron: with Euripides, feminine *pathos* becomes *ethos*. Political oxymoron, finally, with the *polis* of women, since Euripides' women propose their own political version.

Pornē sophē, the ultimate unthinkable feminine being, is first of all Melanippe the Philosopher, heroine of a lost trilogy which created a scandal and thereby ensured the preservation of some of its fragments. Black mare with a name suggesting animality and obscurity, Melanippe's transgression of sexual and maternal laws is confirmed by her history (unmarried, impregnated by Poseidon, mother of two bastards). Melanippe speaks. To define herself, she pronounces this extraordinary sentence:

ego gunmen eimi, noūs d'enesti moi.
I, I am a woman, inhabited by intelligence.

It is in the name of this *noūs* that, in a discourse of a distinctly philosophical timber inspired by Protagoras, she claims the legitimacy of her exogamic practice and the dissemination of her maternity. Discourse that Aristotle will take precisely as an example of tragic aberration, mimetic error, since it has a woman speaking as only a man can and must speak.

Next it is Phaedra, another heroine so scandalous that Euripides had to correct and rewrite his play, just as he had done with Melanippe. With Phaedra, Euripides pushes the oxymoron even further, if this is possible. For the threat that weighed down Melanippe's discourse is now effective, efficient: discourse moves to action. Entirely possessed by Aphrodite who is using her to seek vengeance on a Hippolytus scornful of love, Phaedra, like Melanippe, first demonstrates a mastery that muddles all the cards—the account she gives of her passion (*pathos*) is dominated by reflection and will. Phaedra seems to have no other existence than a logical one. Her tirade closes with a denunciation of language's duplicity and of the ethical confusion it entails. But when it is a question of finding a way out of an aporetic situation—(Hippolytus is aware of and refuses her passion; in love and desirous of glory, Phaedra is presented in the manner of an Athenian man)—Phaedra, according to the very logic which animates her, perverts the principle that presides over political cleavage. *Logos* for the men, panoply of occult resources, drugs, *pharmaka*, machinations for the women. She resorts, precisely as a woman, to a trick, which is a *pharmakon*, a remedy for her pain *and* a mortal poison for Hippolytus. But this *pharmakon* is nothing other than a *logos*: she commits suicide with a tablet attached to her wrist bearing the false denunciation of Hippolytus—logical *pharmakon* which she seals with her death, transforming the *logos* into pure *pharmakon*—thus revealing, well before another Phaedra, this time masculine (I am referring to Plato's dialogue), the pharmaceutical nature of the *logos* once it becomes written text: dead discourse of a dead woman, it forever prevents verification and, inexorable, makes the entire discourse tip over into fiction. The mastery of language has become prostitution.

With Euripides, the immediacy of feminine *pathos* is finished. This can be seen most spectacularly in the treatment he reserves for Medea the barbarian, the magician she was before him and that she will become again from Seneca to Corneille; woman of machinations, philtres, and black magic, she is also a *sophē*. In a situation comparable to Clytemnestra's or Dejanira's—women scorned for nothing—she does not rejoin according to a logic of passion. With her, everything is mediated by thought and critical reflection. She does not return blow for blow, she methodically adjusts her own. She does not seek vengeance, she exercises justice. She does not blame man but through him she deliberately destroys a system that she exposes and dismantles. Every gesture is charged with meaning, makes sense, reveals the sense under the evidence. Globally, this system is first what one could call Greek ideology and which she violently contests in the great *agōn* which opposes her to Jason: repetition of a superiority which is no longer anything but a fiction, loss of heroic values for the profit of political ambition and private interests, double language and ethical degradation, betrayal of the given word. Next, it is the destiny of women and children, of women through their children in a city where one does not deal with women except to reproduce in incessantly reiterated grief for an impossible autochthony (Greek men do not cease to dream of the utopia of the pure engenderment of the same which would avoid the detour through the womb), where mothers give birth only to have their children torn away from them for the good of the State. It was the misfortune of Clytemnestra, it will be that of Hecuba: the exploitation and brutal denial of maternity.

Medea discovers that the love Jason felt for her was never anything more than *political* love. She kills her children so as to annul that benefit. Through the children, who are from him and her, from him *by* her, she can make him pay the stiff price of his error: she strikes him dead in his paternity as he had struck her in her feminity by exploiting her maternity. Whatever the cost—and the text leaves no doubt as to this point—Medea *must* kill her children. Euripides perhaps made Medea the barbarian his most heroic and most ethical character, the most heroic because he constantly lends her an epic language which makes her the feminine double of Sophocles' Ajax; the most ethical because her monstrous decision—"a Greek woman would never have done this," Jason will say—is made at the end of a long monologue, the first deliberative monologue in the tragic tradition and which, it is commonly said, attests to the emergence of Greek moral conscience. The monologue alternates between the voices of passion and will. For Medea, passion is maternity, that which wants the children's lives. And that is what she decides to sacrifice according to her duty's demands. Medea does not kill her children, she sacrifices them. Her vocabulary is, incidentally, that of sacrifice.

Now, it is essential to note that Medea returns to voluntary action, engaged in her own initiative which, for the mother, is the most serious *pathos*, the one the city inflicts upon her, Clytemnestra's as well as Hecuba's *pathos*: that is to say, precisely, to sacrifice her own children. Medea annuls in herself the city's reproductive instrument. Exemplary scandalous mother, she leaves the state in glory with her dead children on the sun's chariot, whereas on earth, the vanquished Jason bewails his powerlessness.

* * *

With Euripides, women raise a political voice. As women—this is the difference which separates them from Antigone—critical and destructive voices—it is the price of the aporia which is theirs—they can also, inasmuch as History gives them the necessary distance, propose their version of the community. Here again, Euripides' tragedy accentuates its distance from orthodoxy.

The Trojans feature a surprising Cassandra. Unlike Aeschylus's mythical Cassandra, Euripides' character is no longer the accursed instrument of Apollo. She renounces prophecy so as to borrow, she says, the language of *demonstration*. A new sort of Cassandra, therefore (she later claims to be of the Dionysian spirit), she enunciates a version of the Trojan war with perfect lucidity. An amazing version because it is a matter of proving that Troy, the defeated city, is happier than victorious Greece. For her, the Greeks lost everything in this war which was their founding gesture: Iphigenia, innumerable male victims, but most important is the fact that they died far from home, deprived of their loved ones' irreplaceable affection, deprived of a ritual burial, cut off from their community, deprived of their wives' embrace as well as that of their earth. Their war of conquest, their imperialism (the criticism of the wars at the end of the fifth century is transparent here), masked behind a language of heroism and patriotism, led them to a moral and political defeat; whereas the Trojans fought to defend a community which highly valued what Cassandra calls "happiness come from within." Troy thus becomes the paradoxical paradigm of a conjugal city—in the largest sense (but it is not without reason that the *Homeric* model of Hector and Andromache is in this version)—where, far from fighting against each other, the *oikos* and *agora* live in harmony; where one can mourn and bury the dead instead of multiplying them in order to offer them, as their only tribute, the *logos* of a funeral oration, a pretext for glorifying a city strained by the anxiety of its own identification. But the Greeks have already burned Troy—a long time ago.

After having overturned History, it remained for Euripides to overturn the meaning of the greatest tragic legend, that of Thebes, city of the Labdacides, fief of autochthony. This is accomplished with *The Phoenicians*. Oedipus is dethroned for Jocasta's benefit and the Thebians for the benefit of their barbaric cousins. *The Phoenicians* is both *Seven against Thebes* and *Antigone* curiously condensed into one single play; but the work has this other peculiarity of playing out these two phases of the legend before the eyes of an aged Oedipus, who has never been to Colone to find his redemption, and an elderly Jocasta, a woman with a shaved head who did not commit suicide after the revelation of incest and will therefore know the destiny of Euripides' women-mothers, designated to carry all the mournings of History. Eteocles is also unrecognizable: the heroic leader, holder of real power (Eteocles means, etymologically, true glory), savior of the city at the expense of his own life, has become a military and political caricature. Oedipus lives in seclusion at the back of the palace. And with him, the mythical origin of this History. It matters little whether he did or did not curse his sons. There is no need to recall this to recognize the civil war at Thebes, the *stasis* that terrorizes the Greek city and which tragedy presents as the natural consequence which always ends up dividing the similar. The disaster is complete, without explanation and without appeal. Common good and love of one's city, which have so often justified war, are sacrificed to the rage of destruction.

It is then that Jocasta appears. She has called together her two sons for a final meeting. She listens to them both, in a very beautiful *agōn*—it is not very often that three people are involved—so as to make heard, in her turn, the voices of reason and political reason. She pleads for the voice of justice, of alternation, which models itself after the natural order; that which makes the night succeed the day, the seasons one after the other. Her voice is obviously not heard. It cannot be, it can no longer be. No more than that of the other willingly sacrificed characters in Euripides' theater—modeled after Iphigenia, Euripides multipled them—who, ironically, are the only ones to find the heroic vocabulary and selflessness that all the leaders around them who are demanding their death have long since replaced with the vocabulary of ambition and cowardice. Like theirs, Jocasta's voice is a relic, a utopia condemned by History. From beyond the grave, like Jocasta who has survived in order to accomplish the most powerful scenic gesture in Euripides' tragedy: having learned that her sons killed each other, Jocasta kills herself, falling across their two bodies. She reconstitutes the enemy brothers' embrace, the city's unity, but she cannot repair the irreparable except by the very gesture of the irreparable. But that is not all. The most Greek tragic myth—Greek because Thebes is the figure of autochthony, city born in the form of an army of warriors, rising up in full warlike order from the dragon's teeth sown long ago by the founding hero, Cadmus—and tragic because, as Aristotle says, the legend of Oedipus is the most fitting for tragedy—is called, in Euripides' version, *The Phoenicians*, not the name of the protagonists but of its feminine and barbaric chorus. Setting itself up on stage in the oriental splendor of its songs and costumes, this chorus renders tragedy exotic. But even more important, it becomes heterochthonic, if I may say. Because the Phoenicians are here visiting their cousins. The theatrical stroke of genius is reminiscent of an older and forgotten version: the founder Cadmus came from Tyr; the Greeks are barbarians.

Secondly, these Phoenicians are not from a country where women are silent; they have their piece to say. They bring their voice; it is the reverse of the scene in *Seven against Thebes* where the hero of the *skēnē* silenced the women in the orchestra. The panic is on stage and it is the chorus that speaks. Now, with them, everything becomes clear; the two faces of the myth come together and reveal: it is the exemplary tragic *anagnōrisis*, their previously secret filiation. The story of Oedipus, the curse of the Labdacides, which up until now seemed to be located at Thebes by accident, are the *manifestation* of the Thebian essence: autochthony becomes *autoktony*, without the two "*h*"s; spontaneous generation which makes men be born in arms; the reciprocal murders of Eteocles and Polynices. For, if the mythical alibis of Apollo and his oracles are relegated to the stores, nothing remains except the story of carnage whose tutelary god appears here in full light: it is Ares, the god of war, whose agent is Oedipus's Sphinx, devourer of men. God, who opposes man against man, transforms them into enemy brothers and makes *polis* and *polēmos*—war—consonant. It is the god, the Phoenicians say, whose retinue is without music, whose enemy is harmony.

The Phoenicians relentlessly oppose another figure to this god consigned by History: Dionysus, he too born in Thebes, in a Thebes before History; a fertile Thebes, rich in running water and green furrows, discovered by Cadmus upon arriving from Tyr before the monstrous dissemination. This entire first Cadmean scene thematizes natural birth: the earth's furrows watered by its own springs, Dionysus born from his mother. Imbued with this memory, the Phoenicians thus oppose the two enemy retinues in the central, eponymous stasimon: Ares' monstrous retinue, cortege of noise and fury, and Dionysus's retinue, cortege of celebration, choruses full of blossoming youth with lustrous hair, the flute's whisper, the whirling of the delirious thyrsus and nebrides, cortege of conciliation, music, and harmony.

But they oppose them to the unreal: why does this latter retinue no longer exist? why has Thebes lost its musical sense? why can the Dionysian way no longer be understood? All that is incarnated in the chorus of Phoenicians—compassion, truth of a history evaluated by its acts (*erga*) and not by its *logos*, the lyricism (one would have to say the aulism) of its song—all this no longer has any place on the tragic and political scene, forevermore condemned to its agonistic tension.

* * *

The conclusion remains, the final scene: that of the *Bacchants*. Scene of Dionysus's return and the triumph of his retinue. But this time, the cortege is murderous: Dionysus turns into Ares. Now *he sows* carnage— the *orchestra* swoops down on the stage and leaves nothing but a heap of rubble. Thebes is ruined. Its leader, Penthea, is dismembered. And the women were the agents of this destruction, the most violent ever shown on the tragic stage. The city sinks with the tragedy.

Here, too, everything is clear. It is the final *anagnōrisis*, the one that lets us, always too late—this is the tragic law—bring story and origin together. A final scene, therefore: once again the city and its leader— here, Pentheus—at war against Dionysus who has come to Thebes to be recognized as a god in the city of his birth. We now know that Dionysus is Thebes' chance. The old soothsayer, Tiresias, knows it, fails to show up for Apollo and decides to leave for the mountains to join the chorus of the Bacchants. But we also know that Pentheus under- stands nothing. Upright, monolithic, fiercely misogynous, intent on his own and the city's salvation, he mocks, insults (especially since this god has an effeminate air about him), and threatens to declare war, to bring the women who have deserted back into their homes by force. He challenges the messager who has come to tell of the Bacchants's happi- ness, chaste beings of a universal maternity which extends right down to the offspring of animals. He tries to imprison Dionysus. But Dionysus *Lusios*, that is, liberator, immediately unties his bonds.

Negotiations are broken off. It is war. Terminal. Exterminating. The war of sons against their mothers; against his mother, Agava, their leader. The war of the city against its repudiated origin. The war of Apollo and his individualized heroes against Dionysus and his syncretic choruses: the war of the *skēnē* —where, as Nietzsche said, the proud dream of an autochthonous city is found, where the *polis* will project its models—and the *orchestra*, where, as Hölderlin said, is sung the "community's hymn."

The victory is stunning. But leaves nothing. Neither sacrificed nor sacrificer, neither victim nor executioner. The *orchestra* founders with the stage. Penthea is dismembered, but the mothers, again become sav- age after not finding a place in the city, instate a reign of terror guided by Dionysus's machinations. There remains only infinite, undifferenti- ated pity.

Tragedy has lost, tragedy has gained. It lost at what it tirelessly at- tempted: to save the city by confronting it with its other. Everything happens as if the Greeks, both captivated and terrified—*deinon*—by their audacity, their invention, their political invention, by their self- institution, had invented tragedy as *katharsis* for their own *hubris*. By replaying the founding scene like Aeschylus, by risking a reconciliation with what History implicated as loss like Sophocles, by setting up figures of a feminine *ethos*—the oxymoron of an Athenian woman—like Euripides. Everything was replayed, but everything was playacting.

Mimesis, which alone, through its lability, would have allowed the city to disengage from its constitution, was able to produce feminine figures. But these figures remained utopian.

Tragedy—genre of a new, mixed, polyphonic genre where there was an attempt at reconciliation between Apollo and Dionysus, lyre and flute, dialogues and chorus—ends with confrontation.

Tragedy lost: this loss is *tragic*. It is Athens's destiny. Tragedy won.

Note

1. *Bouleuetō* is the technical term for the deliberative voice by which the citizen makes the city live.

PORTRAIT OF THE AUTHOR AS A YOUNG WOMAN: BALZAC-CAMILLE MAUPIN, GEORGE SAND, HÉLÈNE CIXOUS

Françoise van Rossum-Guyon

Through the reference to Joyce (*Portrait of the Author as a Young Man*), this title refers to Hélène Cixous's *La Jeune née* and *La Venue à l'écriture*. I am also thinking about George Sand and the portrait she paints of herself in *Histoire de ma vie*. But it is another portrait of a woman writer that interests me here: that of Camille Maupin, alias Félicité des Touches, celebrated woman of the nineteenth century and described at length by Balzac in his novel *Béatrix*[1] where he recounts her "biography": her childhood, education, and all the "circumstances," or, as Hélène Cixous would say, all the "fortunes and misfortunes" of her becoming a writer.[2] It will be a matter then of a fictitious woman, even though inspired by George Sand,[3] and a woman-author created and written by a male author.

This author's portrait as a woman is the product of a literary imagination engaged with the Institution but also struggling with it. A very precise and precisely dated Institution (1839). On the other hand, this portrait is the product of writing. Not only does the text raise questions concerning relationships between women, writing, and society, but it proposes interpretative models that were new at the time and which can still be of benefit today.

For it is, of course, about a problem of reading. If we have been thinking for some time that every reading is dated, we now also believe that every reading is sexed. This is the case for Balzac who, through his character, proposes his reading of woman as author. And it is the case for us who are sensitive to the questions raised in his text precisely because we are asking him our own questions. That is to say

111

that our reading of Balzac's novel will be guided both by what brings it close to us and by the space that distances it. Thus the presence, in the contemporary intertext, of George Sand and, at the horizon of our reading, the twentieth-century woman-author here represented by Hélène Cixous.

Woman of Genius or Monstrosity?

Just as Clara Gazul is the female pseudonym for a man of wit and George Sand the masculine pseudonym for a woman of genius, Camille Maupin was the mask behind which hid for a long time a charming, well-born girl from Britanny named Félicité des Touches. . . . Camille Maupin, one of the few celebrated women of the nineteenth century, was for a long time believed to be a real author because of the virility of her debut. Today, everybody is familiar with the two volumes of plays . . . published in 1822 and which constituted a sort of literary revolution just when the great question of the Romantics and Classicists pulsated in the newspapers. . . . Camille Maupin has since produced several plays and a novel which did not in the least belie the success of her first publication. To explain the series of events which led to the masculine incarnation of a young girl, how Félicité des Touches made herself into man and author and why, more fortunate than madame de Staël, she remains free and therefore more excusable in her fame—will this not satisfy much curiosity and justify one of these monstrosities that rises up in humanity like monuments whose glory is favored by its rarity? For in twenty centuries one can scarely count twenty great women. (p. 688)

Who is speaking here? And to whom? Such is the question that must be asked. Is it the author of *La Comédie humaine*? Certainly, in part. As in all cases where Balzac uses justificatory metadiscourse, the narrator is not without connection to the author of the novel's preface and correspondence. But it is first and foremost the narrator of this particular account who uses auctorial speech to capture the readers' attention, appealing to their curiosity and emphasizing the character's interest.

The passage's tone and the force of the terms used are indissociable from this discursive strategy: only the interest of such an exceptional case can justify an infraction of the novelistic code as defined by "modern poetics" which is intolerant of overly lengthy descriptions and digressions.[4] But this *captatio benevolentiae* is not only a lure: the author will play upon the horizon of expectation that his words have created in his readers (those who think that such women are monstrosities) in order to unsettle their convictions that much better.

The first objective is to rectify the image of Camille presented in the first part of the novel and that we have formed out of the distorted vision of the inhabitants of Guérande and the Guénic family (Calyste du Guénic is in love with Félicité). A monstrous image indeed, forged entirely from fantasies, themselves created by stories, lies, and gossip. In this first part, Félicité is in fact absent from the scene. She appears only as the character being discussed. A fictitious character, consequently, but to the first degree, entirely fabricated by others' discourses and their repercussions. Félicité des Touches is focalized by characters and therefore the object of a partial vision, in both senses of the word; she is also the product of a social discourse, that of Guérande, a small city in Britanny.

Balzac proceeds with a veritable staging of others' speech by reconstructing what has been said in the Guénic's salon. It is in the course of a conversation that the name Félicité des Touches is introduced:

> "Did you receive many people today? the knight said to Mlle de Pen-Hoël.
> - Yes, one of my brother-in-law's cousins. . . . He told me the most unusual things about your neighbor, Mlle des Touches, but so unusual that I don't want to believe them. Calyst wouldn't be so assiduous in his attentions toward her. He certainly has enough good sense to discern such monstrosities.
> - Monstrosities? . . . said the baron, rousing at this word . . . What does she do that is so extraordinary?
> - She smokes, said Mlle de Pen-Hoël.
> - Her land? . . . the baron asked.
> - Her land, the old maid continued, she eats it . . ."
> . . . slattern, hussy, a loose woman . . . involved in the theater, frequenting actors and actresses, eating up her fortune with hack writers, painters, musicians, in short, the devil's society. . . . And, to write her books, she assumes a false name. (p. 674–676)

We see the monstrosity of the character taking shape: she smokes, she is an actress, she writes books, she uses a false name. The effect of such a tirade on a mother's heart is understandable as is her anxiety about her son's passion for such a woman. Developing in her turn an isotopy of the mask and feint, initiated by the parish priest, she imagines her as "a ham actress, a strolling player, a woman of the theater, a writer accustomed to dissimulating her feelings" (p. 678–679). In spite of what Calyste can tell his mother ("she has even more heart than talent. . . . Don't repeat the slander circulating around, Camille is an artist, she is a genius, and leads one of those exceptional lives that cannot be judged according to ordinary lives" [p. 685]), the rumor grows, transforming Félicité into a quasi-diabolical monster.

It is the very process of the rumor—the manner in which it is born and spreads—that the author brings to the fore through the words of different characters:

All of Guérande (the parish priest claims) is in a turmoil over the knight's passion for this amphibious creature who is neither man nor woman, who smokes like a hussar, writes like a journalist. . . . They talk about it in Nantes . . . this morning, this cousin of the Kergarouet's came to see Mlle de Pen-Hoël and sent her reeling with tales about Mlle des Touches that lasted seven hours. (p. 676)

It is this mechanism that the narrator, who finally speaks, will strive to dismantle:

It now becomes necessary to explain the rumors hanging over the individual that Calyste was seeing. These tales, embellished by Breton gossip, poisoned by public ignorance, had even reached the parish priest. The tax collector, the justice of the peace, the customs officer of Saint Nazaire and other well-read people of the district had not reassured the priest in recounting the bizarre life of the woman artist hidden behind the name Camille Maupin. She was not yet eating little children and did not kill slaves like Cleopatra. . . . but for the priest . . . this monstrous creature, who had something of the siren and the atheist about her, formed an immoral combination of woman and philosopher and flouted all the social laws invented to contain or exploit the weaknesses of the fair sex. (p. 687)

To an erroneous discourse, "venomous," without sound foundation, the narrator will therefore oppose a true discourse, revealing "hidden" truths, providing information based upon tangible proofs. Gradually amending the false images that have been created of the woman as well as of the artist. By reemploying the term "monstrosity," the narrator echoes Guérande's discourses but displaces the connotations attached to them. The woman of genius is an exception and, by this token, outside the norm and worthy of being contemplated: "a monument" before which one must "stop a little longer than modern Poetics cares for." By speaking ironically about Camille Maupin's transgression of "all social and moral laws invented to contain or exploit the weaknesses of the fair sex," the narrator prepares his readers to see the character and events differently.

Balzac plays with multiple focalization and vocal polyphony. He brings together fragments of a heterogeneous, diversified, and stratified social discourse and, by the same gesture, addresses himself to different readers. In this dialogical, and even polylogical perspective, the narrator is only one voice among others; caught up in the social discourse, it too carries stereotypes with it. It is, however, a privileged voice, since it controls the actors' interpretation and the characters' destiny and assumes more than any other the communicative function. The narrator thus addresses himself to a much more refined audience than the illiterate of Guérande but who are not without preconceived ideas concerning the woman of genius. If she is not a "monstrosity" as understood by the inhabitants of Guérande to whom a Parisian public is implicitly opposed, as an author and, what is more, a "free" woman, Camille Maupin remains an anomaly, a curiosity. What must be explained is the transformation of a woman into a man: "the series of events which led to the masculine incarnation of a young girl, how Félicité des Touches made herself into man and author?" (p. 688).

The narrator, therefore, assumes the dominant discourse on the woman author: "Camille Maupin, one of the few celebrated women of the nineteenth century, was for a long time believed to be a real author because of the virility of her début." This is what happened to George Sand when her first novel, *Indiana*, appeared in 1832. Considered a masterpiece by the critics, in part because of the virile vigor of its social criticism,[5] George Sand herself knew how to take advantage of this "virilization" and, to a large extent, played the part. Her genius and success immediately placed her beyond the difference between the sexes, as this exclamation of Jules Janin attests: "Who is he or who is she? Man or woman, angel or demon, paradox or truth? Whatever the case may be, she is one of the greatest writers of our time."[6]

"Who is he? Who is she?" The question is typical and Janin heralds, and in a way justifies ahead of time, Balzac's intent in *Béatrix*: "What an enigma, this man, what a phenomenon, this woman! What an interesting object of our affections and fears, this being of a thousand different passions, this woman, or rather this man and this woman! And what critic in this world will ever dare to confront them head on and explain them?"

It is hard to imagine today the astonishment and even the repulsion that the phenomenon of a "woman writer" could inspire at the time. It is an imaginary character, a "type" invested with nineteenth-century fantasies and ideologies. Now, what was problematic, created concern and reprobation when it was not outright horrified rejection, was precisely the sexual difference, the transgression of the barrier between the sexes, the clouding of identities. An 1847 article about women poets in *La Revue des deux Mondes* is emblematic in this respect. What is at stake is woman's role in a patriarchal society and the impossibility of dissociating this role from the use she can make of her body. Writing appears as an activity essentially opposed to her biological function and to such a degree that it becomes impossible to make any room in discourse itself for such an aberration.

What is one to call a creature whose breast, destined for nursing children and containing the joys of motherhood, remains sterile and only beats for feelings of pride, whose mouth, made to give passage to sweet tones, opens to pronounce bold and noisy words, whose eyes, created to smile, to be gentle and ignorant, are thoughtful, severe, and when illuminated by certain flashes, reveal frightening depths, in short, whose every faculty and organ is caught up a destination contrary to what has been assigned to them, how is such a creature to be called? In truth, I do not believe that there exists in any spoken language, and even in those that are written, an appropriate name.[7]

The first transgression which consists in participating in a masculine activity leads very quickly to all inversions and perversions. In becoming a man, the woman author is transformed into a hybrid creature, that is, into a hermaphrodite. This fascinated horror of the hybrid only intensifies during the course of the century as can be seen in the reactions of a certain Barbey d'Aurevilly with regard to Daniel Stern (Marie d'Agoult's pseudonym) in *Les Bas bleus*; or those of an Edmond de Goncourt who goes so far as to write in his *Journal* in 1893: "If there had been an autopsy on women of an original talent like Mme Sand or Mme Viardot, one would have found that their genital parts ressembled those of a man, the clitoris being somewhat related to our penises."

A Polyvalent Portrait

Many of Camille Maupin's attributes correspond to this clinical picture. Not only does she have another name than her own, renouncing, in a sense, the noble lineage of des Touches on the paternal side, not only does she take, in literature, the name of a man, but this name was incapable of not conjuring up in the minds of alert readers well-known transvestic and bisexual characters. Camille refers to the hermaphrodite whose double life is described by Latouche in *Fragoletta* (1829) and Maupin in *Mademoiselle de Maupin* by Théophile Gautier, who himself was inspired by an eighteenth-century actress considered having "other tastes."

Not only does Félicité choose her lovers herself, becoming a sort of "female Don Juan" (p. 699), but her virility is apparent right down to her body:

The chest is broad. The waist is trim . . . The hips swell but little. . . . the curve at the small of her back was more reminiscent of Bacchus than of the callipygian Venus. There you can see [the narrator comments] the nuance that separates almost all famous women from their own sex, for it is there that they bear a vague ressemblance to a man. (p. 695)

The narrator concludes this physical portrait of Camille by emphasizing the unsettling effect she never fails to produce:

> She frightens with her silence and with this look of such profound intensity . . . she has the animal in her . . . of such a leonine nature that a slightly cruel man would regret the composition of such a great mind in a body of this sort and would want it completely feminine. . . . All tremble to meet up with the strange corruptions of a diabolical soul. (p. 696)

The physical portrait of Camille Maupin is therefore reminiscent of the monster denounced by the critics in *La Revue des deux Mondes*, and, along the same lines but even more virulent, the misogynists of the Third Republic. And yet one need only read the text in its entirety to notice just how complex and qualified the portrait is.

The narrator-describer inspects and corrects by attenuation every feature that emphasizes virility:

> The waist is trim *and sufficiently ornate*, the hips swell little *but are gracious*, the curve at the small of the back *is magnificent*. (p. 694)

All the features of the head and face are embellished with predicates which, following Balzac's physiognomic system, variably suggest virility in what it implies of strength and creativity, as well as openness, gentleness, kindness, generosity—attributes qualifying, by a positive valorization, femininity:

> The broad and luminous forehead of geniuses. . . . The arch of vigorously etched eyebrows spread over eyes whose flame sometimes sparkles like that of an unmoving star. . . . The somber eyelids are lined with red fibrils that lend them both grace and force, two qualities difficult to find together in a woman. . . . The strong red margin of the lip full of goodness, full of love. (p. 694–695)

The writer therefore corrects what are perhaps overly rigid elements of the body's semiotic decoding system[8] and proposes more qualified interpretations. Moreover, one must notice that he points out the inevitable partiality of the observer and, by doing so, relativizes the impact of the questions that "everyone" is supposed to ask when confronted with the enigma: "Does this girl not judge instead of feel? does this intellectual force not leave her with a weak heart? does she not crush a sentiment that does not respond to the infinity which she embraces and contemplates? Who can surmount the two precipices of her eyes? One is afraid to find in her something virgin or untamed" (p. 693).

Far from simply reproducing social discourse and its stereotypes, Balzac again plays with it and does so in order to better mock it.

But the author is not satisfied with this task. What he constructs, through the effects of writing, is a new figure engendered by terminological polysemy and play of rhetorical figures: metonymy, metaphor, comparison. This portrait must be read as it is written: as a work of art produced by art.

Putting on airs, in a sense, Balzac profits from quoting fragments word for word from a text that Théophile Gautier had devoted to the *Belles Femmes de Paris*. Among them is the great and beautiful actress, Mademoiselle George, whose name, of course, recalls the other George, which brings us back to the model actress, this time the incarnation of an artist capable of expressing all feelings. Moreover, Balzac borrows his descriptive material from all domains of art, particularly sculpture: the shine of ivory, "granite of an Egyptian statue softened by time," "bronze framed in gold," unchanging marble. He associates Camille with the mythical figures of Diane the hunter and Isis, the great goddess of Nature and mysteries. The description's internal dynamic far surpasses the accuracy of any referent. It is also not satisfied with reproducing previous codes. This literary portrait is emminently composite. The writing simultaneously emphasizes contradictions, animates tensions, and integrates them in a new and superior harmony, transforms them into a hyperbolical representation, a veritable "monument" proposed for the readers' admiration.

An Exceptional Existence

The biography of Félicité des Touches has the explicit aim of understanding the "anomalies" of her existence. The narrator fulfills the wish Calyste expressed to his mother: that she be judged as an artist.

The manner in which the narrator-biographer justifies Félicité's rejection of marriage and maternity is, from this point of view, characteristic: "Her superior intellect refused to accept the abdication by which a married woman begins life, she keenly felt the price of independence" (p. 692). We can hear the echo of conversations Balzac had with George Sand on "the vital questions of marriage and liberty" (from a letter, March 2, 1838, to Madame Hanska). The number and quality of Camille's works attest to a prodigious fertility, the ability to "conceive" and "carry out" which, according to Balzac's theory of artistic creation, implies bringing a "cerebral maternity" into play.

Félicité des Touches is an orphan. Born in 1891, she loses her parents and her brother, then her religious aunt to whom she had been entrusted at the age of two in dramatic circumstances linked to the Terror. This misfortune allows her to escape paternal authority as well as the "circle drawn by the futile education given to women by the maternal teachings on grooming, hypocritical decency, and huntress charms characteristic of their sex" (p. 692). But one can just as well note that she is also marked during childhood by political violence. Thus we later see her "accustomed to managing things on her own," becoming familiar with "actions which seem exclusively assigned to men" (p. 692). She brings herself up "alone as a boy," that is, she has unrestricted use of her uncle's library. "At twenty-one, a girl with this will was the equal of a man of thirty. She had a very broad mind, and her critical habits allowed her to judge men, arts, affairs, and politics fairly" (p. 691). All these qualities do not prevent her from remaining a woman, experiencing emotions, wanting to please and doing so—"she had nothing of the woman author" the narrator is careful to tell us (p. 699)—, full of pity for the unfortunate and excessively generous. She is as well a striking beauty. Félicité therefore escapes the laws of nature: "Eighteen years had passed over her with respect," the narrator concludes, "At forty she could say she was only twenty-five" (p. 693).

We can see, therefore, to what degree Camille Maupin is idealized as a woman and an author. Far from appearing as a diabolical being, Félicité turns out to be sublime. If she refuses biological maternity, it is to better exercise a spiritual maternity over Calyste. She rejects the young man's love as much out of wisdom as out of heroic virtue, she treats him as her child and becomes the "mother of his intelligence." Whereas at the dénouement, in a definitive gesture of total renunciation (even abandoning her books), she enters the convent, leaving her entire fortune to her protégé.

Sublimination and Birth into Literature

This process of sublimination has not failed to be interpreted as a concession to the dominant ideology.[9] However, this form of sublimination (entering the convent after an unhappy love affair) is not woman's fate in Balzac's writing, as Albert Savarus also concludes. If the system of values which is in place in *La Comédie humaine* is taken into consideration, a system that is certainly mobile and susceptible to inversions but which nonetheless remains hierarchically organized, one can see that this move toward spirituality corresponds to the author's thought (see *Pensées de Louis Lambert*). Moreover, at this time George Sand was rewriting *Lélia* and destined her heroine to the convent. It is definitely a matter of sublimination, in the psychoanalytical sense of the term: indeed, Balzac very carefully recounts the process which leads the subject to compensate for lack with another derived activity, to transform psychological sufferings into a work of art or heroic action by the elaboration of an energy recognized as sexual. This energy strays from its path because it is deprived, in a way, of its "normal" object. In this genesis of an author, which is what the biography of Camille Maupin is, the narrator thus brings out the role of affects and psychological traumas in the coming to writing. The narrator observes that once abandoned for an Italian, "Félicité died and Camille was born" (p. 698). The metamorphoses of Félicité des Touches are thus described as a process that implies death and rebirth: "misfortune is the midwife of genius" (p. 698). It is finally in her inability to recount her sorrows a second time—this time caused by Calyste, madly in love with Béatrix— that she finds the solution: "she stifled earthly love with divine love" (p. 808). One can see that this description which speaks of the complex paths and avatars of a libidinal economy makes Balzac one of Freud's predecessors. It is, however, these "operations of sublimation" that Hélène Cixous challenges today: "Writing is always first a way of not managing to grieve death," she declares in *La Venue à l'écriture*. "First she dies. Then she loves . . . she does not give herself in the text of derived satisfactions. She does not transform her desires into works of art, her sorrows and solitude into costly objects."[10] But Camille/ Félicité is a being of fiction and, what is more, a novelistic character of the nineteenth century. For her, "as for some infinitely rare men of genius, love is not what nature made it (but) what Christianity made it: an ideal realm" (p. 751).

"The Illustrious Hermaphrodite" or Portrait of the Author as a Woman

In all respects therefore, Camille Maupin appears as a hyperbolical figure of genius, the archetypical great writer—several times in *La Comédie humaine* and in a striking manner in *Illusions Perdues*, as seen through the eyes of the young apprenticed poet, Lucien Rubempré. "Beautiful and sublime girl," "charming girl," "illustrious hermaphrodite,"[11] the qualifications do not contradict each other, they are complementary to the point of merging. If beauty and a gentle smile are perhaps the woman's characteristics, generosity and fertility are just as much those of a man. These qualities engender the hermaphrodite who, as a mythical figure, brings about the union of opposites. Thus Camille Maupin reunites in one sublime figure aristocratic greatness and modesty, values of the past (Guérande) and confidence in those of the future (Paris, modern art, the civilization of the nineteenth century); all relate her to these "infinitely rare men of genius," among whom is, of course, her creator.

That is to say that this portrait of a woman-author is just as much a portrait of the author as a woman. A disguised, displaced, transposed, sublimated portrait, but a portrait all the same: George Sand's, written as a watermark, but also that of the creator of *La Comédie humaine*. The author as he would have liked to have been: well-born, glorified, handsome; but also as he is: innovative, brilliant, prodigiously productive. How else can one explain the privileges enjoyed by this woman as an author—or this author as a woman—as manifested in the character of Camille Maupin? Fictitious character, thoroughly constructed, implausible, and utopian in so many respects but who, more than any other in the work, incarnates the author as artistic writer and creator? Perhaps because it is a question, precisely, of a woman, that is to say, the other, the different, and of the writer as an artist whose own experience is that of being essentially different, literally of another species than his fellow creatures, fundamentally misunderstood if not taken, he too, for a monster in the eyes of others, as in the "portrait of the artist as a young man": *Louis Lambert*.

Also—but there is undoubtedly a connection—because Balzac is fascinated by superior women and, in particular, by women of genius as are, in his consideration, George Sand and Mme de Staël. He admires them because they represent the "modern" writer, who, like him, incarnates the spirit of synthesis by effecting the union of opposites in the aesthetic realm. But it is also because, like him, they possess the faculties of both sexes. For Balzac's fantasy is certainly that of a sublime hermaphrodite, a being capable of "uniting in their powerful heads the woman's breasts with God's strength" (*Le Curé de Tours*, p. 244).

Balzac assumes, then, if not usurps the powers of femininity in their specificity: creative maternity. Well-known and typical masculine gesture that once again, it will be said, appropriates the feminine so as to better repudiate women. I would prefer to say that if, for Balzac, it is perhaps still "preferable to be a man to make a good androgyne,"[12] times are beginning to change. It seems to me that we can be grateful to the author of *Béatrix* for having eluded the traps of the dominant discourse on women and, more generally, for having questioned the traditional equivalence between paternity and creation. In giving the character Camille Maupin such importance, to the point of making her the greatest writer of *La Comédie humaine*, he shows that such an exception is not only possible, but admirable. Great artists are prophets. Let us take, then, this portrait of a sublime woman as it is given to us. As fiction, certainly, but also, for this very reason, as anticipation.

Notes

1. All references refer to the Pléiade edition, P. G. Castex editor (Paris: Gallimard, 1976), Vol. II. Introduction and notes by Madeleine Ambrière. See as well Maurice Regard's introduction to the Garnier edition, 1970.
2. See "De la scène de l'inconscient à la scène de l'Histoire: chemin d'une écriture," in *Hélène Cixous, Chemins d'une écriture*, F. van Rossum-Guyon and M. Diaz-Diocaretz editors (Amsterdam: Rodopi; Paris: Presses Universitaires de Vincennes, 1990).
3. See the introduction to *La Muse du Département* by Bernard Guyon (Paris: Garnier, 1970), p. 112–117.
4. Françoise van Rossum-Guyon, "Des nécessités d'une digression: sur une figure du métadiscours chez Balzac," *Revue des Sciences humaines*, no. 175, 1979.
5. "Les enjeux d'*Indiana*, métadiscourse et réception critique," in *George Sand. Recherches nouvelles* I, F. van Rossum-Guyon editor, Amsterdam, C.R.I.N., nos. 6–7, 1983.
6. J. Boilly and A. de Montferrand, *Biographie des femmes auteurs contemporaines*, Armand Aubrée, 1836.
7. Quoted by Christine Planté, *La Petite Soeur de Balzac. Essai sur la femme auteur* (Paris: Éditions du Seuil, 1989), p. 23–24.
8. See Bernard Vannier, *L'Inscription du corps* (Paris: Klincksieck, 1972), and Roland le Huenen, "L'écriture du portrait dans *La Cousine Bette*," in *Balzac et les Parents pauvres*, F. van Rossum-Guyon and M. van Brederode, editors (Paris: SEDES, 1976).
9. Nicole Mozet, *Balzac au pluriel*, PUF, 1991, and Lucienne Frappier Mazur, "Balzac and the Sex of Genius," *Renascence. Essays on Values in Literature*, no. 1, autumn, 1974.
10. *La Venue à l'écriture* (Paris: UGE, 1977), p. 45–47.
11. Balzac, *op. cit.*, Vol. IV, p. 865, 871, 877.
12. Nicole Mozet, *op. cit.*, p. 170. For feminist criticism on androgyny, see, among others, Domna C. Stanton, "Women's Studies," *Tel Quel*, nos. 71/73, autumn 1977.

RACHILDE.
REVERSAL OF TWO.
INFERNAL TWO. ANSWERS.

Charles Grivel

The Two Sexes

The serialization and mechanical reproduction of the philosophically and technically elaborated person during the course of the nineteenth century not only abstracts its "aura" (this is a point, incidentally, that would require discussion), but spirits away its distinction. Because the genealogical rationalization evoked presupposes two corollary interpretive measures affecting *sex* and *language*, fundamental for us since, at the end of the century onward, they are the basis of all writing efforts.

Indeed, positive genealogy is constructed—and not surprisingly—upon a functionalization of the sexual. In opposition to what prevailed under the Ancien Régime, where sex was devoted to either reproduction (multiplication of childlike images of God) or debauchery (rebellious squandering of pleasure). Positive genealogy *connects the sexual to the series* and turns it into the ultimate evolutionary motor: the historical progression of humanity, of the human race itself, is the product of a sexual activity thought of (naively) as a competition of excellence (the most beautiful female goes to the strongest male).[1] Sex (actions and representations) is genealogically reduced to a cog in the wheel of the species in its finality and positivity. It simultaneously instates and assures its value and preeminence. It chooses the ultimate, converts to the best. Schopenhauer: the beautiful, which alone is capable of eliciting desire, leads to the good which is the essence of the species (it would be necessary to read what Victor Cousin has written on this subject).

Genealogical sex induces a subject totally implanted in the series, subservient to it, to its rhythm, to its demands. From Michelet to Darwin, the only pleasure (both possible and permissible for this subject, be it male or female) is *that of inscription of and in the species*: I

123

climax only in accomplishing it; if I accomplish it, I accomplish myself, and I am only accomplished as mother or father, obviously.

The Two Languages

Genealogy turns the subject back onto its body and assimilates its language into its emotive expression: it is not without reason that Darwin wrote a theory of the emotions. Or that Duchêne (of Boulogne) and Mantegazza proposed their theory of expression. These authors (along with many others) appear obsessed with the idea of a subject entirely "seized" by its body and the idea of an entirely "speakable" body: they posit an exact science of the body's language (or languages): one or several pathognomies. The (true) personality would be knowable by its "tracks." Entirely resolved in its very substance, since it would be possible to detect these tracks, directly and inexorably, on the skin, through muscular contractions, various lines and folds working the envelope. A body would be entirely manifested by its expression (still genealogical and still demonstrative of genealogical positivity). Mediation would be complete. Semiologization achieved. Such a subject is of course without a soul: it corresponds to its support, it "is" this support which expresses it, *the same of the same and also the same of the other.*[2]

Of course, this theory is nothing other than fine fiction. Controversial fiction. Fiction to which is opposed *two*, law of desire and law of counter-desire: literature ensures this. Here is the point I wanted to make: it is an encounter, a duel, between the heavy, scientific (theoretical) edifice of the genealogical system and the unbound, derived, unbelieving subject—without territory and without finality. The end of the century position, therefore, is this: two representations are fighting over the person, or rather, the person lives as two, right side and wrong side, until there suddenly appears—under the theoretical, ideological, positive, schoolish self—another: more profound (or so it seems), more powerful, irrepressible, and "veritable." It is a notion, therefore, of a subject inhabited by turbulence for whom it will no longer suffice "to be." A situation that, a century later, I believe, we recognize perfectly as our own. Foucault: "There is no absolute subject"; Barthes: "I write myself as a presently badly placed subject"; Sibony: "The subject leaves no other trace than that of its absence, and the space made for it is most precisely a literally unbearable, empty space."[3] Muted struggle, more or less perceptible, more or less valorized through interposed literature in particular; between the *given* subject and the *arisen* subject, between ideological representation and its remainder, supplement and negation: a "body of socialization"—such is the function of its genealogical version — stumbles over a *second* body, intimate, inapplicable, inadmissible. Scandalous, it goes without saying. *A lusting body.* An elusive body. Inalienable and unqualifiable. Of which sex? Of the other sex, exactly!

Rachilde, Not One, Not Two

Rachilde, a second-rate author, writes in these circumstances. Her novels accommodate — it is said — "all the odds and ends of fashionable and traditional beliefs";[4] they are quite obviously lacking a little in anecdote: one can easily see that, scarcely disguised, it is always the same story revolving around the same couple — named and adorned a little differently each time. Rachilde, a woman writer of dubious reputation. Provocative, she makes her debut in literature with a scandal — *Monsieur Vénus* — and then errs in drawing from the same vein throughout her long life: *La Marquise de Sade, L'Heure sexuelle, Les Hors-Nature, La Sanglante Ironie, L'Imitation de la mort, Au Seuil de l'Enfer, Le Grand Saigneur, Dans le Puits ou la vie inférieure,* and many more. Blithely allying sex with blood. Testimony of the priest Béthléem, established censor: Rachilde's literature is "perverse, lascivious, blasphemous, infernal, and reprehensible"! What could be more enticing?

Of dubious reputation — if we read what colleagues had to say about her — for another reason: *Rachilde is a woman who is a male writer*: she says so herself (in her stories), she maintains it (in her life), even though she is duly married to Auguste Vallette, founder-director of the *Mercure*. In reading her, Gourmont, a close friend and éminence grise of her husband's periodical, believes that, in spite of what he considers obvious weaknesses, he is examining "pages . . . [which] show that a woman can have phases of virility, can write at such a time without concern for the usual affectations or customary poses, make art out of nothing except an idea and words, create."[5] Similar strains can be heard in her biography: "Rachilde does not disguise herself; she wants her *genius* to be naturally masculine" (Claude Dauphiné, p. 46). Incidentally, in 1928 she will sign, in perfect keeping, a thundering "Why I Am Not a Feminist?"

Rachilde or contradiction. But . . . moderate contradiction. However provocative and "inverted" (?) the foundations of her writing may be, the stories themselves are prudish, even modest, scarcely gallant, not licentious, never pornographic. *Rachilde or contradiction within contradiction.*

All the critics, the first being Maurice Barrès who, in 1888, prefaced *Monsieur Vénus* when it appeared, cry out virtuously at the paradox: a young girl, a young woman, a *woman* would never think of, even less write, the horrors that one can discern in her books (p. xi). Question—a man's question: how can a woman conceive of something that she has never experienced? Answer—which leads to the abyss—from Lorrain's account, this equally astonished specialist of debauchery who, after exclaiming over the languor of her eyes, their radiance, their limpidness, as well as over the incredible lushness of her eyelashes, exclaims: "eyes that know nothing, leading one to believe that Rachilde does not live with those eyes but that she has others in the back of her head which look for and discover the violent spices with which she seasons her works" (p. xiii). Still Barrès: "Whoever composes such books is perhaps no more in control of herself than a double monster; it is too fine a case of teratology" (p. xxii). Periscopic or unconscious detection: there is certainly no confidence in Rachilde!

Rachilde, "double monster": this is precisely what intrigues me. The biographers report that the woman of letters limped slightly. So slightly, however, that it was not noticeable and could be taken for another charm of her bearing. *Something is seen which is not seen; something spoken which is not said*: such contortions, I believe, target the meaning I mentioned. Let us *now* see how it can be done in her books.

In the system which regulates the relationship between the subject and its body, its body and its sex, its sex and its being, Rachilde instates disorder three times by the three distinct strategies alluded to above: the first strategy is the elementary *negative path*; the second (still little exploited by today's contemporaries), *inversion*; and third, the most enigmatic, the *symbolic graft*. Let us proceed in order.

1. Bad Two

In the genealogical system in place here, the sexual must be something like the driving belt in the impetus of meaning (causalities); insofar as the son (the daughter) accomplishes the system, the procreative instrument (which is profane, however) is positive. However, the Rachildian text lavishly demonstrates that it is nothing of the sort. According to Rachilde, sex is *negative* and perverts the constraints inside the "familial" system: far from engendering, it intervenes against the series. *Barren*, it shatters the conditions of its practice.

Of course, this is not the first time one holds such a discourse: it is even, literally, the most constant one held. As proof, I refer to the statement Marc Angenot made concerning the contemporaries of the *Mercure*'s lady: there is plenty of evidence that sex was seen as a "total and degrading" passion, disturbing, alienating, pathological, indicating the irresistible return to animality (p. 123, 125, 153, 154). But it is the first time, I believe, that we are told that the body exists for sex and that this negative and unproductive sexuality is accomplished (without being accomplished, moreover) *without the slightest pleasure*: the Rachildian body is a neutral body equipped with a fearful and destructive sex.

No longer the body of genealogy, fiction's body exists "for sex," without referential truth; it is occupied, permeated through and through by a desire or aimless energy, which is sex. It is from an unknown, irrepressible, and deadly nature that it speaks as sex. Its sex is neither role nor function, it is an elusive sign, an unassignable, an inexpressible. No discourse can grasp it but neither is any discourse capable of doing without it. In short, this sex constitutes a supplement of silence given back to the body. It is much less an organ than the *signifier*, which we must qualify as absolute, *of the body as such*.

Of the subject in its body and the body in its sex, seeking the other, unrecognizable, unexpected, untouchable, profound. *Sex is that of the other*. The other of the principle of this body which is given back to me. Inside, but outside. Equivalent but different. Sex: individual difference from subject to subject. As though the break had to take this path. Here I cite Lacan: "Everything that is written stems from the fact that it will always be impossible to write the sexual relationship as such."[6] The relationship is included in the founding instrument of "relationship," that is the problem.

Rachilde: sex does not think, does not speak, does not represent: it *acts*, it *agitates*. It is not seen: neither space nor form, truly unassignable. It is an action which leaves no trace. Turmoil. An operator of energy with a hidden source and whose undecided terms ("perversity," "desire") situate it straight away outside of any meaning and as hyperbole (sex is always the most action of a given possible subject). This originating point constitutes the principle of instability in people, that which secretly or manifestly governs their behaviour: devastating revelation is the mode of being of this sexuality: I am the prey as well as the profiteer of my desire. This desire has no name, respects no species, submits to no function. This is precisely what makes it equally horrifying and fascinating: *it signifies nothing, leads to nothing, implicates nothing, if not the physical, "orgasmic" suspension of the person who consents to it*; the person who consents to sex is "dead." From an action without end or motivation. Pure signifier without pleasure — negative and positive. From a blank act, in sum, that excludes the community since the community is founded upon the renunciation of sex (or at least upon its normed moderation). There would be a declaration in sex with which one would have to comply entirely, thus already entailing self-deprivation.

Undoubtedly in complete literary utopia.

Let us take an example. *L'Homme roux* (in the series (?) entitled "The Forgotten"), 1889. The theme is simple: a man (the husband's employee) wants a woman (the employer's wife); a woman wants nothing to do with this man. Or she decides for all kinds of good reasons not to yield to him. Does she want him, does she really not want him? Indecisive. In any case, this is a story of resistance. Like Monsieur Seguin's goat, she surrenders, or rather succumbs, on the point of death, whereas he is halfway up the gangway of the ship that is to take him off to America. Alas, the servant (faithful to the image that the virtuous woman was able to give of herself) intervenes with the child that the "red-headed man" had had from his own, legitimate wife (the sister of Ellen, the heroine). The problem is that the child of this unwanted man, conceived in the womb of her sister who is given back to him (after the seduction, however), *resembles her as much as it does him*. It is, then, before an accomplished fact that she does not yield. Moreover, at the very beginning of the adventure, the red-headed man took advantage of her while she was bandaging his burnt arm, marking her, on her bared bosom (revealed by a kerchief gone askew), with a kiss she will never forget. The kiss of a red-hot iron. A vampire's kiss.

Let us think: *a man wants a woman*. This man is a "red-head," which is to have already signed his passion-warrant (as is known, red-heads are partial to sex). He is, incidentally, described as "handsome" but nameless (an orphan, of course): "James." "James" lives and loves, just as Ellen observes and demurs. The strategies are in place; he has none: he is ardent ("passion is the rapture of life," p. 206), a gambler, drinker, great lover of women, but, above all, "handsome." This mandatory constellation of epithets is completed by a look that brings everything together. This look is fixed. Unspeakable. It too is infernal (p. 218). Emanating from eyes beneath indomitable eyebrows — like leeches, according to the text: who is drinking whom? What blood, from which source?

In this novel, normal men (those who get married or should marry: the foundry's owner, the family doctor), respectable men, those who kiss on the temple and those who do not kiss at all, are not likeable (the husband may well read Byron, and the doctor [who aspires to become Ellen's husband once she is widowed] gives up drinking), and both fall down the hatch of the narrative. As for the "forgotten" man, "a-natural," he is fascinating precisely because of *all the abjection he displays*. This abjection has a name: it is sex.

It is also from this enemy that its designated victim attempts to protect herself: the strategy of she who finds herself plunged "live into hell" (p. 77) is refusal; her problem: *how to stop being a desirable object?* The disposable arsenal is simple: keep out of sight; introduce a third into the game; bind the recalcitrant man by the bonds of marriage (Ellen has him wed her sister whom he seduced); ensure that this new wife becomes a beauty; take care in turn to render oneself progressively more ugly; rouse the seductor's paternal sentiments; fall ill and cough up blood; wed an unloved man in order to give substance to the obstacle, etc. All these projects fail, and the pretender returns to take up the challenge anew, confirmed in his will. *However, it turns out that in the narrative, his will no longer has any object.* It has become "empty." This book has emptied it. The book can end.

2. Reversal of Two. Infernal Two.

Rachilde: from a writing of perversion to a writing of inversion. Sex, which is the sign of the other—its fascinating negativity—, is *not* the one one thinks: the other is not other, neither man nor woman. The other is not represented by his or her sign—sex. Makes neither one nor two with it, dare I say, but separates itself from it, flaunts and denies it. Position and deposition. Display and restraint. The likeable characters in Rachilde's fiction are . . . inverted: men are beautiful like women, women are handsome like men; "beautiful" and "handsome" mean "similar to." War of attributes, articles, genders: monsieur Vénus is "beautiful" and Raoule de Vénérande is "handsome"!

Sex does not manifest the sense of being of the other but, on the contrary, denies this being. *Sex is not the one we think.* It assigns no ego to any subject: it is displaced sex—eloquent in its displacement; a man is a woman, a woman a man, or rather: a man *represents* a woman and vice versa (by means of makeup, clothing, perfume, haircut, lifestyle, habits, attitudes, and love roles).

There is none desirable apart from this *duality* (between being and seeming), apart from this *equivocality* (between sex and role); there is no pleasure (taken and given) apart from this reversal. *It is the feeling of no place and yet of two roles.* Not in the series but through genealogy. Against the law, which does not permit woman to ape man (or man woman), but with the law, which determines what is "a-natural." For the "a-natural" constitutes the space of pleasure: roles remain and the sexes permute only in their representation. For the body of fiction exists as a body-for-the-other *"in the representation of the other" that it is not, however: man makes himself loved by woman by representing to her the woman he is not.* The body is two bodies: one that is in use plus another of the opposite sex that is worn in effigy. The body is lived with its other body. Two. The body is two, addition, subtraction and scission, version and inversion. Positive and contrary. Male in its female, female in its male.

Now, a few examples, first of all the one furnished by *Monsieur Vénus*, "sulphurous" novel, scandalous, and successful, which dates from 1888. Received at the time, quotes Angenot (p. 152), as "an opaque and fascinating cryptogramme" and found "unreadable" a century later by the same scholar, it is a perfect illustration of the inversion I defined: *inverting and representing the inversion is its only object.*

SHE.—"No middle ground! Either nun or monster! God's heart or the heart of sensuality! It would perhaps be better to shut it away in a convent since we lock up hysterics in the Salpêtrière! She doesn't know vice, she invents it!"

SHE.—"She dropped her coat onto a chair and came forward, svelt, her chignon twisted up high, dressed in black fur with coiled coat-tails and adorned with rich trimmings. This time, there was no glittering of jewelry to brighten this almost masculine outfit. Only a cameo signet ring set with lion's claws on her left hand.

When she reached for Jacques' hand, he was scratched. In spite of himself, he was overcome by a sense of terror. This creature was the devil."

HE.—His body is her body. Details: "Lying motionless on the floor behind the curtain, she could see him without having to move. The candle's gentle glow fell softly on his pale flesh which was covered with fine down, like a peach. He was facing the back of the room and playing the principal role of one of Voltaire's scenes where he describes in detail a courtisan named Bouche-Vermeille.

Worthy of the callipygian Venus, this slope of the back where the line of the dorsal spine disappeared into a sensual plane and rose up again, firm, full, in two adorable contours, looked like a Parosian sphere shimmering with amber lights. The thighs, a little less strong than a woman's, were, however, of a solid roundness that obscured their sex. The high calves seemed to buttress the entire torso, and this impertinence of a body seemingly unaware of itself was all the more enticing. The arched heel rested upon an imperceptible spot, it was so round.

Two pink indents could be seen in the elbows of his extended arms. Between the line of the underarm and much further down from this line could be seen a few tangled golden ringlets. Jacques Silvert told the truth. He was covered in it. He would have been mistaken were he to swear that that was the only attestation of his virility."

HE.—(Jacques Silvert, florist by profession, arranger and painter of frivolities)—"Because he is handsome, will a man of the people not also have to be abject?" Answer: yes! It is better that way.

HE. (simple)—"She did not seek to explain the strength emanating from this simplicity, she let herself be swept up in it, just as a drowned person is swept up by the waves after a final struggle, abandoned forevermore to the current."

SHE.—(to a "real" man who proposes conjugal union—incidentally, he will have an affair with the "artist's" sister—a prostitute by profession—and will not be insensitive to the florist's strange charm whom he beats, for fun, in a duel)—she argues: "I have always found myself alone although I was two."

SHE to HIM.—"Suddenly, she threw herself upon him, had him at her feet before he had time to struggle; then, grabbing his neck revealed by the open collar of his white flannel jacket, dug her nails into his flesh.

—I am *jealous*! she roared wildly. Have you finally understood? . . .

—Jacques did not move, he had placed his two clenched fists, that he did not want to use, over his tearful eyes.

Sensing that she was hurting him, Raoule's grip slackened.

—You must see, she said ironically, that I do not have florists' hands like you and that, of the two of us, I am always more the man.

Without replying, Jacques looked at her out of the corner of his eyes, the edges of his lips twisted in a bitter grimace.

His feminine beauty stood out even more in the inertia imposed upon him, and a mysteriously attractive power emanated from his perhaps willful weakness.

—You're cruel! . . . he said very softly. . . .

Raoule kissed his fine golden hair that was like strands of gauze, wanting to breathe her monstrous desire through his skull. Her imperious lips bent his head forward, and she bit him fully on the back of the neck.

Jacques writhed with a cry of lovestruck pain. . . .

—Jacques, Raoule answered, I have made *a god* out of our love. Our love will be eternal . . . My caresses will never tire! . . .

—Is it true then that you find me handsome? that you find me worthy of you, the most beautiful woman? . . .

—You are so handsome, darling creature, that you are more beautiful than I! Look over there in that slanted mirror, your neck is white and pink like a baby's! . . . Look at your marvelous mouth, the wound of a sun-ripened fruit! Look at the clarity distilled by your eyes as deep and as pure as the day . . . Look!

She had lifted him up a little, opening his shirt with her feverish fingers.

—Do you not know, Jacques, do you not know that fresh and healthy flesh is the unique power of this world! . . ."

SHE.—A "new Sapho" seeking to eliminate within herself the femininity she exposes (hidden, however, since she wears pants). (Yet, this "femininity" hatefully brings her back to herself, "regularly" . . .)

HE.—"I want to be vile."

HE. — A sleeping concubine — his mouth is "radiant" — (even) seduces a "real" man (a regiment officer!).

She bloodies him with her nails to the point of rendering him unfit for the service he is expected to perform.

SHE to HIM. — You make me a man, my caresses are — in vain — of either sex. "Raoule threw herself upon the bed of satin, rediscovering the white and supple limbs of this amorous Proteus who had no longer preserved anything of his virginal modesty.

For an hour, nothing could be heard in this temple of modern paganism apart from long, shuddering sighs and the rythmic sound of kisses; then, all of a sudden, the agonizing cry of a demon who had just been vanquished rung out.

— Raoule, cried Jacques, face twisted, teeth biting into his lips, his arms flung out as though he had just been crucified in a spasm of pleasure, Raoule, are you not then a man? Can you not be a man?"

ELLE. — Once dead, she has "a German artisan" make a portrait-substitute of him, reminiscent of Des Esseintes, and which she takes pleasure in contemplating, hidden away in her room.

3. The Graft

Possibility (1) sex is not assigned positively to any body; possibility (2) sex passes from one to the other like an object of amorous fascination; possibility (3) woman can be grafted onto man, sex can be doubled, and played, by itself!

Fiction on fiction on fiction!

Tireless writing of the same!

A tatooing which would be truly absolute — a successful excess: *das Fremde im Eigenen.*

One in the other so as to produce division yet intimate reunion.

This ingestion implies castration. Castration and decapitation. Rachilde writes it. The graft is a cannibal's dish. Let us open *La Tour d'amour*:[7] woman's sex, potted, in place of tulips and in the form of her head, is revealed to man at the window of the lighthouse (in Brittany) in which he lives and is in the process of restoring (sic): take from one side, put on the other. This done, climax, then death.

The book's theme: Jean Maheux, a simple man of not even thirty, is appointed assistant lighthouse keeper somewhere along Brittanny's most forsaken coasts; the lighthouse is isolated and impossible to reach when the sea is up. Already there is an eccentric old man to whom he is to act as assistant and who has become half or completely mad in his solitude. Initially excited by this unhoped for promotion, the hero is soon prey to anguish: something is brewing in the sinister place. But what? One day, a shipwreck. Suspicious excitement on the part of the old man. The tide leaves within sight upon the flat rock a woman, undoubtedly naked. The bizarre man forbids giving any assistance. The following day, the body has disappeared. The climate of suspicion and terror reaches a pitch. The assistant keeper brushes against death in what appears to be only an accident. The lighthouse requires repair. Suspended outside the edifice for his work, Jean Maheux spies through an unused window a woman's head, planted in a crystal pot, its blue eyes wide open, watching him. Terror, blackout, search: the secret is known. The assistant, abandoned by the one he thought was his fiancée, murderer of a too enterprising and pitiful prostitute, ends up mad. The old man, his companion in agony, obliges him to throw the much-desired head into the sea.

The book's thesis: *the other lacks; man's sex lacks woman.* In the body-lighthouse-phallus that man is unaware of possessing, there is no sex, no knowledge. The strategy consists in his integration of the misunderstood and disposessed sign by sealing it within him, in the very substance of his "edifice," in the name of his "renovation." Fiction serves this purpose: the sign of castration, which is woman, preserved in alcohol inside a jar filled with flowers, will be consumed by transparency. There is integration in absence: woman, man's unknown sex, only sexualizes him inasmuch as she makes him lose either reason or life. A potted head, an erection whose name is castration—here indeed is an unqualifiable symbol but which must still be formulated beforehand.

Two Eyes

Rachilde writes these three constraints: perversion, inversion, graft. Rachilde's desire-writing establishes itself on the circulation-tension implied by these constraints: all her books vary and verify this. From one denial to another: the bad die but what they incarnated is perpetuated (they die for "nothing," their death is meaningless in any case). Rachilde's three fictive constraints constitute pleasure in representation. This triple (and wandering) pleasure is no longer subjected to Damocles' moral sword of an appropriate epilogue: the heroes die, certainly, but they die unpunished.

The three performances presented are performances of fiction. Rachilde does not imagine real accomplishment (she has harsh words for Sade ["You have to be senile to try that," *Madame de Lydonne*]), but all the evidence shows that she herself strived to take on the appearance of the role she staged. In any case, it matters little. The pleasure of the three orders which are in question is only acquired at the performance, as a performance.

Fiction as a theaterization of possibilities from a delirium produced, perhaps, by secular, genealogical elaboration. Galloping de-symbolization and re-symbolization. Disassembling and reassembling. Shuttle between what is wanted and what is possible as opposed to that which constitutes the obligatory. Shuttle sufficiently *alive* so that a *disaccelerated* subject is never inscribed in any body. Rachilde: "I have not a single deep feeling" (Dauphiné, p. 388). Fiction maintains superficiality. Write to disinscribe, detach man from man, him from him, her from her, as feeling is produced: as soon as a hero is going to be capable of loving, let him die! From a sexuality "on empty" for a desexualizing, "dense" representation.

We can decide that it is out of nostalgia for the *One* (as Albert Béguin believes in his essay on *L'Androgyne*),[8] we can decide that it is out of a taste for the *multiple infinity*. Or, concurrently, the *two*.

Notes

1. I believe, therefore, that Marc Angenot simplifies things when he writes that the end of the century sexual "dysfunction" that he examines through interposed literature is not the result of observation but of allegory or synechdoche "serving as a global image of a society gone amok" (*Le Cru et le Faisandé. Sexe, discours social et littérature à la Belle-Epoque*, Brussels: Editions Labor, 1986, p. 118): sex and its various forms are the expression of a system which determines (and also interprets) their possibilities.
2. See Charles Grivel, "Der siderale Körper. Zum Prinzip der Kommunikation," in J. Hörisch and M. Wetzel (eds.), *Armaturen der Sinne* (Munich, Fink, 1990), p. 1, 3–4, and 8.
3. Michel Foucault, "Qu'est-ce qu'un auteur?" *Bulletin de la Société française de philosophie* (July–September 1969), p. 102; Roland Barthes, *Le Plaisir du texte*, Paris, Editions du Seuil, 1973, p. 99; Daniel Sibony, "A propos des mathématiques modernes," *Tel Quel* 51, 1972, p. 89.
4. Claude Dauphiné, *Rachilde* (Paris: Mercure de France), 1991, p. 350.
5. Rémy de Gourmont, *Le Livre des masques*, 1923, p. 192.
6. *Encore. 1972–1973. Le Séminaire*, book 20 (Paris: Editions du Seuil, 1975), p. 34.
7. 1899. Edition used: *Le Tout sur le tout*, 1980. In conformity with that of 1916.
8. In *Minotaure*, 11, p. 66.

THE MATERNAL IDOL IN A SYSTEM OF BOURGEOIS POETICS

Anne-Emmanuelle Berger

O Poetry, o my dying mother.
BANVILLE, "Ballade de ses regrets pour l'an 1830."

The "Sons' Republic"

"It will probably be more difficult for women to liberate themselves from the son than from the father who, in my mind, does not exist as such: difficult to renounce being Jocasta, to escape passion according to Oedipus," says Antoinette Fouque in an interview published in the periodical *Le Débat*.[1] It is the filiarchate, and not the patriarchate—which, according to her, does not exist (or perhaps *no longer* exists) "as such,"— that would constitute women's greatest adversary—women "as such"— in their attempt to access a symbolic autonomy.

On this note, let us now turn to the community of French poets, contributors to popular almanacs as well as established authors who, from the 1840s to the end of the 1870s, subscribed to a cult of the maternal idol which, in its intensity, remains unrivaled in the history of poetry.

The Parnassian leader Banville dedicates his entire work to his mother: from *Les Cariatides* to *Exilés*, his discourse is nothing but an immense ode to the one who, living or dead, "sees him." "To the One Who Sees Me," title of the last poem in the augmented edition of the *Cariatides*, published in 1879: "Oh dis-le que parmi les éthers remplis d'ailes/ C'est toi qui me prendras entre tes bras fidèles,/ . . . Et qu'enfin délivrés de toute angoisse amère/Nous vivrons, ô mon Ange, ô mon espoir, ma mère!" November 19, 1878.[2]

Lamartine also composes a monument for his mother and, in 1858, establishes an edition of her personal diary which will appear in 1871 under the title *Le Manuscrit de ma mère*.[3] In *Contemplations*, Hugo inscribes his family's legend and sings of his domestic tragedies; from *Les Misérables* to *La Légende des siècles* he writes, in prose or in verse, the nineteenth-century épopée featuring the mother and child as heroes. In Rimbaud's works, we are familiar not only with the conflictual relationship he had with his mother but also with the importance of the maternal figure and signifier. Playing the game of literary history, let us also mention the minor poet and Rimbaud's "Belgian big brother," Paul Demeny, addressee of numerous letters from the great poet-child in the years 1870–1871 and, in particular, of the so-called "Letter from the Seer." In 1870, Demeny publishes a collection of verse, *Les Glaneuses*, which constitutes a veritable manual of composition for popular Parnassian apprentice poets of the time. The entire volume is placed under the aegis of the mother, starting with the dedication: "A ma mère/Si mon coeur bat, aime et soupire/Si les beaux rêves lui sont chers,/Ton âme seule a pu l'instruire/*C'est toi qui fis mes premiers vers*."⁴

The eponymous poem of the collection, "Les glaneuses," clearly refers to the one so often represented with the characteristics of a "destitute gleaner," maternal, wandering bird, come from the sky and the people to glean food for her children on man's cultivated earth: Marceline Desbordes-Valmore. This "mother of sorrows," "muse of mothers in mourning" as her grateful readers called her in common pity over the lost child, died in misery in 1859. In the decades following her death, however, she enjoyed great popularity among the poets who celebrated in her a universal mother: the sons shed tears over she who wept so much when alive. The misogynist Baudelaire is one of the first to water her tomb with studied tears; in an article devoted to her in 1861, written as a sort of posthumous crown, he claims his filiation:

> . . . only in passionate Marceline's poetry will you find the warmth of a maternal nest whose delicious memory has been kept alive by a few of the woman's sons, more grateful than the others.

Let us finally mention Mallarmé, "hungered by the azure virgin's air," and who settles into beauty as into a virginal and maternal bosom.

In 1978, Hans Robert Jauss published a study devoted to a phenomenon inherent in what interests me here.⁵ At the end of a systematic enquiry into lyric production in 1857 (the year *Les Fleurs du mal* appeared), he presents the following conclusions: an examination of this period's lyric discourse reveals a "sweetness of the home" motif, expression borrowed from Baudelaire's "Crépuscule du soir" to designate the insistent representation of a certain domestic happiness. Jauss is able to demonstrate poetic discourse's ability to transmit what he calls "social norms" (p. 278) by sanctioning certain modes of historically determined daily interaction.

But if he points out the aptitude of neo-Romantic poetry for speaking about historic reality, the "information" that this reality conveys still creates problems, as the interpreter himself recognizes. Indeed, Jauss observes that lyricism "[represents] the home, a space of happiness in the bourgeois world, as a realm of feminine sweetness where the man, the father, is invested only with a subordinate role . . . (p. 287). The sweetness of the home functions, then, as an antonomasia for the maternal universe. Now, according to Jauss, all historical facts confirm "the omnipotence . . . of the husband and head of the bourgeois family" of this era. Jauss therefore interprets this "parricide by omission" in lyric discourse as a maneuver of "ideological dissimulation of the real." In the real, the father rules; in the poetic model of the home he would, in Jauss' very words, be "excluded," "repressed," or "censored" (p. 287–290). He generally believes that the nostalgic celebration of "the sweetness of home" suits bourgeois ideology: the happy image of home, which presupposes the institution of the family and bourgeois conjugality while presenting itself as universal norm would serve, for example, to mask role transformations and the splintering of the family occasioned by the industrial revolution and the proletarianization of the masses.

Jauss is undoubtedly correct in underscoring the coincidence of the "sweetness of home" paradigm with the cultural primacy of a historically determined family model. It remains to be asked why poetry chooses to "transmit" this norm rather than another. And since the idealization of the home establishes the maternal figure's preeminence in particular, and lyric discourse accordingly seems to distinguish itself from other literary discourses (the novel or bourgeois theater), poetry certainly summons us to think about the particular connection (or cord) that attaches the poet to the mother.

This poetic configuration is, first of all, in harmony with a certain Historical imagination, and in this respect Jauss's analysis probably remains too partial, in both senses of the word. The father obviously dominates a certain "real" and rules as master over the private sphere as it is sanctioned or defined by the Napoleonic civil code. But, on a European scale, the nineteenth century also sees the development or resurgence of a cult of the mother which touches all spheres — religious, artistic, political — and which, in France, is expressed in particular by the formidable growth of the Marian cult, described and analyzed in Stéphane Michaud's fine book, *Muse et Madone (Visages de la femme de la Révolution française aux apparitions de Lourdes)*. In France, the

Saint-Simonians decree 1833 the "year of the Mother"; in one of their brochures we read: "Woman! Here is the Redeemer, the Queen and Mother of the people."[6] Toward the end of the 1830s, their main ideologue, "Père Enfantin" (so appropriately named), departs on an expedition to Egypt in search of the great Mother. 1854: the dogma of Immaculate Conception, Christian faith's definitive article which up until then had remained controversial. Mary emerges desexualized but glorified. In 1858: apparition of the Virgin in Lourdes. From then on, she and Christ make a couple, displacing the Father, Son, and the Holy Ghost ménage à trois. Appearing in 1960, Renan's *Life of Jesus* attests to this inflection of the Christian imagination. Christ, protorevolutionary figure, simultaneously feminine and childlike genius of History, takes after his human mother much more than his divine father. In emphasizing maternal ascendence, Catholicism, be it reactionary or social, and utopian socialism paradoxically agree to diminish paternal power, already twice shaken by revolutionary regicide and the fall of Napoleon who carries his dreams of modern chivalric glory with him into the grave. The Horace-son and Horace-father alliance is no longer acceptable, and even if, from one Napoleon to another, the new bourgeois order looks for letters patent of paternity, the aristocratic patriarchate's downfall must have favored the mother's assumption in the son's name.

In this respect, the course and discourse of those in whom Rimbaud, in 1870, does not recognize putative fathers but rather fraternal "masters"—our masters of 1830—clearly show the complex stakes of the new filial order. *Confession d'un enfant du siècle* inaugurates the century of the child. We know that Musset imbues his childhood with a value symptomatic of the collectively contracted historical illness described in his first three chapters. He who is "only a suffering child" writes in the name of all the century's children. The autobiographical (or autoneurographical) genre immediately attains the dimensions of political allegory. And what is this child suffering from? He is suffering from the collapse of the Napoleonic dream which deprives the sons of the shining Imperial warriors of their passage to virility. The heroicophallic father, with whom the son identified, is dead or mutilated. There remain only weeping wives and sons, new Hippolytes severed from future glory, a people of stillborn children that History condemns to never reach the age of man.

Other interesting filial configurations which also traverse poetic and political territory: Lamartine and Hugo. Only son (he has, incidentally, five sisters) of a monarchist mother of aristocratic origin, Lamartine becomes a Republican in an avowedly filial relationship with his mother. The contradiction is a superficial one and is explained by the commentaries with which Lamartine burdens his mother's manuscript, mixing his voice with hers in a semiposthumous literary duo. In this strange work, Lamartine reaffirms his allegiance to his mother at the same time as he explains their political differences: "In religion and in politics, a son has his mother's sentiments but not her dogmas" (*op. cit.*, p. 227). It is through sentimental loyalty to his monarchist, Catholic mother, then, that he is her liberal and deist son. We can add that the mother-son alliance is sealed by a mutual resentment of Napoleon.

Hugo's well-known journey is not entirely different from Lamartine's. It has often been said that his evolution from maternal legitimism to republicanism marked his reconciliation with his father, an Imperial soldier. But he may identify less with his warrior father, an aristocratic regime's emmissary, than with the Revolution's son and standard-bearer. We know well Hugo's hatred of Napoleon III because he usurped the Republic's throne, protective mother of the people, instead of placing himself in her service. Indeed, Hugo himself will be a father figure in exile for the Second Empire poets and republicans. But it is a rather maternal father, as grandfathers often are, and as is especially the hero of *Les Misérables*, Jean Valjean, whose first redeeming gesture consists in taking over the care of Cosette from Fantine, a fallen and abandoned unwed mother. The charitable convict simultaneously identifies with his adopted orphan-child and with the mother-pariah whose place he takes. As for Gavroche, maternal orphan, Cosette's masculine and Jean Valjean's childlike double, he adopts two little brothers, two tiny little children shaking with cold in a glacial winter and shelters them in the stomach of a colossal wooden mammal, the elephant of the Bastille. We are familiar with the frequence of the orphan theme — the "homeless" — in the populist literature of the time. Archetypical figure of the miserable working-class condition, the orphan is the ultimate motherless child whose salvation and maturation depend upon the miraculous intervention of a maternal messiah of "humanity" who fills its material and emotional needs.

However, if the mother-child complex with socialist tendencies functions in literature as an allegory of humanity's progress, if bountiful liberty leading the people (represented by Gavroche) has, like the insurgent commune celebrated by Rimbaud in "L'Orgie parisienne . . . ," "the head and two breasts thrust toward the Future," the adoration of the mother can certainly favor an expression of regressive tendencies, those that Jauss, for example, discerns in the poetic discourse of Baudelaire's era and which he considers reactionary. Referring to Banville, Baudelaire writes "All lyrical poets fatally carry out a return to the lost Eden." Discourse of loss, fatal regression in the direction of unattainable origins, lyricism would be the royal voice [*sic*][7] of melancholy and which it indeed is in the nineteenth century. Now, one could easily show that the nostalgic recollection of a maternal interior, of a harmonious intimacy both cornerstone and antisocial ["*ante et antisocial*"], is the bourgeois, or let us say urban transposition of the Edenic dream: dream threatened with obsolescence by the progress of an industrial civilization that Romantic and Neo-Romantic poets experience as directly affecting their chosen domain, their green, childlike paradise.

Whether the poet appeals to Mary or Marianne, his return to the maternal bosom, be it progressive or regressive, attests in any case to a refusal to live in the Historical present and functions well, in this sense, as an allegory of enunciation's lyrical position.

For Herself and By Herself?

"When woman's infinite bondage is broken, *when she lives for herself and by herself*, . . . she too will be a poet!" Rimbaud proclaims in his May 15, 1871 letter written at the height of the Commune's battle against Versailles.

Now, the mother does not live "for herself and by herself." She is mother by and for the child. She is only a poet for him, in the secret intimacy of their exchange, or by him, that is, metaphorically, by the son's intervention who claims to be writing not so much in her name — she scarcely has one — but in her place. From this viewpoint, Lamartine's edition of his mother's personal diary offers some interesting insights, half *in vitro*, into the engendering of incestuous fiction. A work entitled *Le manuscrit de ma mère* establishes the son as speaking and seeing subject. Publishing his mother's personal diary is in itself a complex gesture because it proclaims an authorized or unauthorized penetration into her intimacy and then couples this infraction with the public's interference in the maternal secret. Lamartine claims that it is 'a private work whose "lines will only be read by the light of this mother's home and by eyes that have cried." Yet this is contradicted by the editorial and literary machine set up around the journal, or is given a more figurative than literal value. Meaning that Lamartine addresses his mother's manuscript to a public familiar with the image of the mother as constitutive of the home. Finally, without ever stating it clearly, Lamartine only presents (self-) selected fragments of the manuscript. This selection process is no doubt just as significant as the tenor of the text offered to the public. This work of omission is usually passed over in silence, but Lamartine does occasionally refer to the editing and thereby reaffirms his exclusive right to the maternal text as against his rivals, the readers. Speaking of his mother's "true intoxication" upon learning of her son's literary glory, Lamartine justifies the exclusion of the intoxicated pages in these terms: "They are too intimate to be cited, it is a secret between God and her heart." The "secret," displayed as such, will thus remain shared between God, the mother's heart, and the machinator, Lamartine, who necessarily occupies the self-designated places of the maternal heart and God. The secret, by whose virtue Lamartine assumes the right to exhibit, or, on the contrary, to retain certain passages, is still the same: the mother's sublime passion for her son. In their happily immodest candor, Lamartine's words confirm the great narcissistic profit he derives from this.

What kind of figure of woman emerges from such a manuscript? Precisely a very Marianne figure. Preceding the journal's excerpts of melancholic evocations, there is a series of scenes where we see the mother "[cast] her eyes *shining with a celestial light* over everything around her." "When they fall upon me," notes Lamartine, turning to a narrative present which eternalizes the scene, "they stop and soften. It is a mother contemplating her son's happiness" (pp. 9–10). The son is rapturous before this mother who contemplates him. Pages imbued with Christian suavity follow. In these pages, perhaps because Lamartine omitted them, there hardly ever appear references to trivial events and concerns of everyday life or, even more important, comments about the woman's relationship with her husband or with the opposite sex in general. The only love mentioned is a mother's love for her children. The husband-father remains an abstract figure, liminal, who provides and represents the conjual context within which is played the scene of matrifilial union. It is therefore with an ideal mother, sexless, desireless, that the son, alone except for his infantile partners, consumates an imaginary union which takes the form of a reciprocal identification since no breach, sexual or otherwise, seems to generate any difference between them. The mother is the one the son-poet wants to be, not to have. On November 7, 1828, shortly before her death, Madame de Lamartine notes in her diary: "Alphonse sent me some verses he just composed that truly moved me; he says precisely what I think: *he is my voice* . . .; but God who listens to me does not need my words; I thank Him for having given them to my son" (p. 273).

Anybody who is familiar with poetic production under the Second Empire knows that the poets of the time adored angels and entrusted them with their dream of maternal paradise. Angels often appear with the characteristics of an angelic mother, watching over the sleep of a very fetal child. One could, incidentally, put the transports of dream, sleep's child, in Romantic and Neo-Romantic poetry in relationship with the desired reconstitution of the maternal universe. Rimbaud, dreamy Tom Thumb, expressly invites us: in the last stanza of "Étrennes des orphelins," a "cradle's angel" brings, by way of a Christmas present, a joyous dream into the soothing sleep of little grieving children: cradled by the dream, they see before their very eyes medallions appear in the place of the lost mother "Bearing three words engraved in gold: 'To our mother!'" The dream, grief's magic alchemy, transmutes the maternal body into verbal gold. The "three words engraved in gold," first words of the gift of writing, enable the children to produce and preserve their mother's sparkling and unchangeable trace. By the second stanza, the narrator of this moving scene has already defined the dream's function: "*The maternal dream* is the warm carpet. The cottony nest where children . . . sleep their gentle sleep *full of white visions!*" The "maternal dream" is, as suggests the ambiguous semantic relationship between the noun and adjective, a *mother's dream* and a *dream-mother*. "*What good arms*, what beautiful hour will give me back this region whence come my sleep and slightest movements?" nostagically exclaims the poet of *Illuminations* at the end of his dreamlike crossing of "Villes II."

But, inversely, the angel can replace the dead child, the Crucified's modern avatar and little brother of the century's castrated child whom the poet resuscitates and gives back in this form to the tearful mother. Maternal and childlike angels agree in any case to overcome grief and melancholy by reconstituting the sexless couple of mother and child which replaces the predominantly phallic couple, very sexed and sexual, the couple, in courtly poetry, formed by the singer-knight and his Lord and Lady.

We can, in this context, see the significance of Rimbaud's appeal to woman, future poet, who will live for herself and by herself. What is more, Rimbaud subverts the maternal cult's terms from inside by reintroducing what its vocation was to eliminate: the role of sexuality, acknowledgment of the mother's body as an erotic body and, consequently, the play of differences. "Credo in Unam," poetry Rimbaud sends to Banville in soliciting his admission into the poets' fraternity, effectively celebrates the cult of the "divine mother." But it is not a question of Mary: contrary to what the Latin title maliciously leads him to believe, it is to Venus that the "little Eros" addresses his prayer: "I believe in you! I believe in you! Divine mother, maritime Aphrodite!" swears the apostate believer in the second stanza. Addressing himself to an ambiguous deity (Venus or Christ?), the believer mimes the movement of the idealizing exaltation of "Woman" and claims to celebrate the value of virginity and spirituality so as to execute, at the end of his transfiguration, an unexpected reversal: "Et l'Idole où tu mis tant de virginité, / Où tu divinisas notre argile, la Femme. / Afin que l'homme pût éclairer sa pauvre âme,/ . . . *La Femme ne sait plus même être Courtisane.*"[8]

The consecration of the Idol, therefore, ironically coincides with the fall of "Woman" far below the paradoxically valorized state of "Courtisan." Rimbaud thus denounces the amorous body's debasement and burial which is executed under the cover of the Idol's establishment. For the young poet, adoration of the Mother does not imply abasement or fore-closure of the feminine sex but, on the contrary, her assumption *in Unam*, a Woman possessing the truth in a soul *and* a body. At the other end of the work, setting herself up in the Illumination "Being Beauteous," appears a "mother of beauty." The Illumination's autograph is on the same sheet as "Antique," desiring portrait of a body "in which sleeps the double sex." In its turn, "Being Beauteous" orchestrates the confusion or the fu-sion of a "tall Being of beauty" with the "mother of beauty":

> Standing before snow, a tall Being of Beauty. . . . black and scarlet wounds shine forth in superb flesh. . . . Shivers rise and rumble, and the frenzied flavor of these effects are charged with the mortal sibi-lance and hoarse music that the world, far behind us, throws on *our mother of beauty—she steps back, she stands up. Oh! our bones are clothed in a new amorous body.*

This text scarcely describes the harmonious union, prenatal or post-mortem, of mother and child. A new version, in a barbaric language, of the simultaneous birth and giving birth of an extraordinary Venus under the voluptuous ascendancy of a maternity at work, the Illumina-tion notes the precarious and violent emergence of a uterine body which attracts and engenders others.

Of course, the Being of beauty (in which, because of the alliterating liaison, one can also hear "u*ne n*eige u*n* être" like "un 'Naître de beauté,'" ["a Birth of beauty"]) who merges with the mother of beauty in a relationship of reciprocal engendering, is neither man nor woman, just as the mother's child, an angel for her just as she is an angel for him, wishes to be neither a boy nor a girl. In the evocation of this erected body, then, we can recognize a strongly eroticized "transsexual" varia-tion of the fantasy of regressing back to an undifferentiated, preoedipal stage through which the poets affirm their social dissidence at the same time as their melancholic attachment to poetry.

As for the Girls

Is it the same, would it be the same for the woman poet? In this filial concert where the son sings with his mother's voice, we have scarcely heard the girl.

Desbordes-Valmore, like her contemporary Lamartine and their lyric inheritors, celebrates the maternal house, birthplace of her poetry. (Only a dead mother is good, perhaps—for making poems grow on her tomb.) She too "drank heartily while playing in the courtyard" of her mother's "harmonious strains of love," echoed in her poems. She too is a mother's child, and, moreover, unlike her brother poets, a mother of children, girls and boys. In the posthumous edition of her works, the poems where mothers and children converse have been gathered together in a section entitled "The Book of Children and Mothers." But, even though Desbordes-Valmore herself uses the undifferentiated term "child" to designate her "child life," spent with her mother or relived through her daughter, this daughter-mother and mother-daughter relationship, staged in its duality by the poet, differs perhaps from the mother-son union, even as it is represented in her own work. Sons appear less often than daughters in her maternal discourse; however, the poet fulfills the roles of comforter and cradler (Notre Dame of dreams) assigned to her by their desire. Let us leave, then, the mother at the little boys' bedside— one of her poems is entitled "A Little Boy's Bedtime"—and sketch, by way of a conclusion, a few steps on the girl's side in order to open a chapter of history that has scarcely begun to be written. Ondine's joyful leaps inspired the poem entitled "My daughter":

> Ondine! enfant joyeux qui bondis sur la terre,
> Mobile come l'eau qui t'a donné son nom,
> Es-tu d'un séraphin le miroir solitaire?[9]

In these first verses, we see the play of feminine and neuter, the angel theme variation, the meeting of water and sky, the merging of the enunciative instance with "water" since both have the power to name "Ondine." Following her daughter's evolution and resulting from it is the evocation of her own childhood dances. Daughter gives back to mother her own childhood by "prolonging" it, and, because of this involuted childbirth, the mother becomes her daughter's daughter: "Viens! Mon âme sur toi pleure et *se désaltère*. / Ma fille, ils m'ont fait mal! . . . Mets tes mains sur mes yeux, / . . . O ma blanche colombe! entr'ouvre-moi ton aile: / *Mon coeur a fait le tien; il s'y renfermera*."[10] The mother drinks the waters of her daughter's womb and seeks refuge in her bosom, wing, or heart. In this context, "My daughter, they have hurt me" almost sounds like "*Mother*, they have hurt me," and the generic designation of a masculine enemy confers to the mother-daughter alliance a dimension of women's solidarity fully aware of the sexual aspects.

The end of the poem confirms the genealogical reversibility that characterizes their exchange: "Sur tes traits veloutés j'aime à boire tes pleurs;

/ C'est l'ondée en avril qui roule sur les fleurs,"[11] says the tearful mother to her weeping daughter. "The flowers" upon which roll the April showers can designate Ondine, her mother's flower-daughter, just as well as the mother herself, or, again, the poetic flowers of the mother's garden of writing that Ondine's shower makes blossom and grow. Due to the metaphors borrowed from germination's natural cycle, that which could have been a realistic scene—a mother drying her daughter's tears—thus becomes an allegory of their mutual fecundation.[12] This scene of mingled tears, not terribly melancholic, however, concludes with the consumation of a textual union bearing homosexual connotations: "Embrassons-nous! . . . Sais-tu qu'il reste bien des charmes / A ce monde pour moi plein de ton avenir? / Et le monde est en nous: demeure avec toi-même . . ."[13] The speaker and interlocutor of this lyrical discourse are gathered together in the embrace of "us" in such a manner that the injunction to "stay with yourself" does not imply their separation. The one designated by "yourself" prolongs the one who calls her according to generalized expressions of inclusion which precede the injuction: the world is pregnant with the daughter ("full of your future") and it is also *within us*: in (her) you and me.

But is there really a difference between this scenario of mother-daughter fusion, of a daughter made mother, and the Lamartine mother and son duo in which one says in silence: "You are my voice" while the other sings: "I am your voice." To me, the final words of the poem suggest a provisional answer: "L'oiseau pour ses concerts goûte un sauvage lieu: / L'innocence a partout un confident qui l'aime. / Oh! ne livre ta voix qu'à cet écho: c'est Dieu!"[14] The mother-poet first defines the situation propitious to the emergence of the poetic word by way of impersonal maxims. The bird, Valmorian allegory of the poet—but with her it is a sparrow or a dove rather than an albatros—, needs a wild place, and the poet's or the child's innocence must only be entrusted to a loving ear, this nondeforming echo, sonorous mirror, that Desbordes-Valmore, close in this respect to Hugo, calls "God." This is just what the mother-poet did in addressing Ondine: "Enfant! je ne veux pas méchantiser ton coeur, / . . . Garde-le plain d'écho de ma voix maternelle: / Dieu qui t'écoute ainsi m'écoutera."[15]

But in enjoining her daughter to stay with herself in the intimacy of "one" ["soi"], which includes the world and her mother, so that she may "entrust her voice" in complete freedom and security, she treats her in turn as a poet, offering to serve as her echo in an indentificatory reciprocity such that she annuls or is unaware of the difference of their positions, thus preventing their structural redistribution in opposing couples on the vertical axis of generations. When Madame de Lamartine writes:

"He is my voice," she stays silent. And when the poet says to his mother: "I am your voice," he also counts on her silence. Now, if Desbordes-Valmore lets her daughter in on poetry's secret, it is to encourage the birth of her own voice. When one sings, so does the other; when one listens, so does the other. In any case, it is the dream the daughter inspires in her mother, both daughter of her mother *and* her daughter. It remains to be seen how the daughter will respond to the invitation.

Notes

1. "Femmes en mouvements: hier, aujourd'hui, demain," *Le Débat*, no. 59, March-April 1990, p. 138. "The Sons' Republic" is the title of another article by Antoinette Fouque published in *Passages*, no. 38, 1991.
2. Date of his mother's death. ["Oh say that among the wing-filled ether / It is you who will take me in your faithful arms / . . . And that delivered at last from all bitter anguish / We will live, o my Angel, o my hope, my mother!"]
3. *Le Manuscrit de ma mère* [Mme P. de Lamartine], with comments, prologue et epilogue, by A. de Lamartine [preface signed: L. de Ronchaud] (Paris: Hachette/Furne/Jouvet/Pagnerre, 1871).
4. "To my mother / If my heart beats, loves, and sighs / If beautiful dreams are dear to it / Your soul alone could have been the teacher / *It was you who wrote my first verses.*"
5. *Pour une esthétique de la réception*, "La douceur du foyer: la poésie lyrique en 1857 comme exemple de transmission de normes sociales en littérature," trans. C. Maillard (Paris: Gallimard, 1978), p. 263–299.
6. Quoted by Stéphane Michaud (Paris: Editions du Seuil, 1985), p. 145.
7. [In French, the usual expression is "*voie* royale," "royal path" as compared to "*voix* royale," "royal voice."
8. ["And the Idol where you placed so much virginity / Where you rendered our clay, Woman, divine / So that Man could enlighten his poor soul / . . . *Woman no longer even knows how to be a Courtisan.*"]
9. ["Ondine! joyful child who leaps upon the earth / As mobile as the water that gave you your name, / Are you a seraph's solitary mirror?"]
10. ["Come! My soul cries over your soul and is *quenched.* / My daughter, they have hurt me! . . . Put your hands on my eyes, / . . . Oh my white dove! open your wing for me: / *My heart made yours; there it will enclose itself.*"]
11. ["From upon your soft features I love to drink your tears; / They are April showers rolling on flowers."]
12. Here my reading owes much to Michael Danahy's excellent article, "MDV and the Engendered Canon" (*cf. Yale French Studies*, no. 75, 1988, p. 129–147).
13. ["Let us embrace! . . . Do you know that there remain many charms / In this world that is for me full of your future? / And the world is within us: stay with yourself . . ."]
14. ["The bird prefers a wild place for its concerts: / Innocence has every-

where a confidant who loves it. / Oh! give your voice over only to this echo: it is God!"]

15. ["Child! I do not want to harden your heart, / ... Keep it full of the echo of my maternal voice: / God, who listens to you will thus listen to me."]

SHATTERED GENRES

Claudette Sartiliot

In *Le Corps-à-corps avec la mère*, Luce Irigaray recommends the dissolution of genres so as to subvert, indeed, reject the oppositions theory/fiction, truth/art. Her work, as well as her career as psychoanalyst and woman, illustrates this opposition to genre laws. In her texts one finds a mixture of elements belonging to feminist liberation discourse (contraception, abortion, environment) as well as poetic, fictional, and especially mythical elements. For her, refusing the opposition between truth and fiction which, as she says, has no meaning for women, is much more than just a dissolution of genres: it is a dissolution of categories, of hierarchy.[1]

As Jacques Derrida has shown in his essay "La loi du genre," as soon as the notion of genre appears, it brings in its wake notions of class, classification, separation, borders, and exclusion: "As soon as a genre is announced, one must respect a norm, not cross a limitrophic line, not risk impurity, anomaly, monstrosity."[2] Like Irigaray and Hélène Cixous, Derrida points out the impossibility of not mixing genres: he illustrates this desire to move beyond the borders that genre laws impose upon the always multiple and protean nature of the "one." Crossing a border is always risky. You can always be told that you cannot go over or that things do not go over (happen) ["(se) passer"] like that. This is the case of what is still called *French Theory* in .the United States, or, for Cixous or Irigaray, what they like to call *French Feminist Theory*. This is all going badly: something sticks in your throat. And this bit that cannot be swallowed, that cannot be either received or repressed, is what undoes the borders of genre laws. Here I allude to Derrida's texts *Glas* and *La Carte postale*, among many others, that do not seem to belong to any "recognized" genre, which extend beyond the domain of philosophy and have the audacity to "toll the knell" of the classic and of classification.[3]

As for Cixous's works, one can see a movement from writings that can be qualified as "critical" or "theoretical" to texts often called "feminine writing" but whose genre is difficult to determine: should they be called "novels," "fiction," "narratives," "autobiographies"?

In an interview with Alice Jardine and Anne Mencke on the question of the rapprochement of different disciplines in France, Cixous and Irigaray deny the existence of such a movement, yet that is what they both practice and advocate. Both, however, mention Derrida's name as an example of the border breakdown in philosophy, a philosopher, says Cixous, whose texts resonate in the language of poets.[4] That is why today I can place between them the "philosopher" who expresses his desire "to write with a woman's hand" so as to demonstrate that the desire to transgress the law, or rather the impossibility of not transgressing it, is, as Cixous tells us, feminine.

These transgressions of genre laws are, incidentally, much more than simply calling into question literary genres, or masculine and feminine genders, with respect to their purity or contamination. They question an entire way of thinking, question Western thinking itself. This much talked-about feminine writing is based on an entirely different way of thinking and apprehending the world. However, this way of thinking is not new, but, on the contrary, very old. Speaking about feminine writing, Luce Irigaray remarks: "This style does not favor the look but takes all figures back to their tactile birth . . . Touching, touching oneself . . . desire for nearness rather than 'ownness.'"[5] Discounting vision, or at least relegating it to the background—this privileged sense of logocentric philosophy—, Irigaray and Cixous return to the senses that philosophy and psychoanalysis have had a tendency to control, repress, indeed, to ignore, especially hearing, smell, and touch.

Unlike vision which separates, divides, and establishes borders between self and other, outside and inside, the senses of hearing, smell, and, of course, touch, reduce or annul this distance. This feminine knowledge that prefers closeness to "ownness," that merges "prehend" with "comprehend" is necessarily a perpetual transgression of the law of ownership and of property based upon the gaze and upon self-consciousness. Derrida describes this archaic thought in an essay entitled: "Télépathie:"

> Yes, touching, sometimes I think that before "seeing" or "hearing," thought touches, puts its paws on, and that seeing or hearing comes back to touching at a distance—very old thought, but the archaic is necessary in order to access the archaic. Touching, then, the two ends at the same time, touching on the side where science and so-called technical objectivity take hold of it now instead of resisting it like before . . . , touching also on the side of our apprehensions because we let ourselves be approached without losing or understanding anything and because we are afraid. (*Psyché*, p. 247)

Turning away from modern and sociological knowledge based on numbers, things, and categories, Irigaray's and Cixous's texts take us toward this archaic knowledge. Thus they both return to the myth of Demeter and Persephone which they relate and reinterpret. Interest in this pre-Hellenic myth is explained by the fact that it stages the primitive proximity between mother and daughter as well as between woman and earth, a proximity which precedes the fall into the masculine world of vision. This myth gives them the opportunity to recall reciprocal mother-daughter love, affection often ignored or passed over in silence by psychoanalytical and philosophical phallocentric theories, and to re-establish the tie between human beings and the exterior world—a tie symbolically broken since Descartes.

Contrary to the myth of Oedipus, chosen by Freud to explain the father-son relationship and leading the way to separation, opposition, and death, the myth of Demeter and Persephone present feminine love, the proximity between mother and daughter, between woman and the fruits of the earth. Moreover, this myth circumvents the theoretical scene of the sociological struggle for gender equality and leads to an unconscious scene in which woman can finally see what one would like her to forget.

Irigaray returns to the myth of Demeter and Persephone to show woman a means of escaping imprisonment in masculine language and to teach her to get closer to the natural world of which she has always been a part. For Cixous, every woman has always been a Demeter or a Persephone for, as she writes, women are not so much human beings ["êtres humains"] as they are beings with hands ["êtres à mains"] who have always had to touch to understand and who have since then al-ways transgressed the masculine law which prohibits certain objects (especially flowers and fruit) and which interrupts the natural relation-ship between woman and nature.

In *Le Temps de la différence*, Irigaray thus describes what she calls "the beginning of our (hi)story":

> There was once à time when mother and daughter represented a natural and social model. This couple was the guardian of nature's fertility in general and of the relationship with the divine. At this time, food consisted of the fruits of the earth. The mother-daughter couple therefore assured the safeguarding of human food and the place of the oracu-lar word. This couple protected the memory of the past: daughter respected mother, her genealogy. It also took care of the present: food was produced by the earth in peace and tranquility. Provision for the future existed thanks to the relationship of women to the divine, to the oracular word.[6]

This harmonious relationship between daughter and mother, woman and earth, divine and natural, the past, present, and future is illustrated by the relationship between Demeter and Korè, the daughter sacrificed by the establishment of the patriarchate. This is perhaps just a myth, but myths are needed to respond to other myths—be they masculine or feminine. In Irigaray's interpretation, the rape of Korè becomes emblematic, as it were, of the difference between masculine and feminine thinking. Korè corresponds most simply to the beauty of natural elements, yet she is stolen and raped by the imposition of a transcendental meaning imposed by man on the natural. Korè allows herself to be seduced by what, for her, is only a flower. At the moment of cutting the flower, she is cut off from the natural and maternal world and deflowered. For the daughter who is unaware of the symbols that masculine knowledge associates with the narcissus and pomegranate, the punishment will be burial, loss of independence, and separation from the mother and the earth. In *Amante marine*, Irigaray describes the scene:

> Korè has let herself be seduced, is lost because of ignorance. Her attraction for the flower and the fruit, still "natural," became confused in the power of resemblance—the end of the young girl torn from her mother, brought unto death by the contemplation of Narcissus, and her taste for the seed. But without knowing the properties of these analogies. Ravished by surprise, in secret, by her lack of knowledge, of appearance's technique.[7]

For Irigaray, Korè's rape represents not only the girl's loss of independence but also the separation of mother and daughter and the breakage of the woman-nature bond by the imposition of a masculine law on the natural relationship between woman, flower, and fruit. The establishment of the patriarchate is therefore effected by a sacrifice: that of "Korè's virginity and Demeter and her daughter's love. It has imposed silence upon the daughter. It has dissociated her body from speech, her pleasure from language" (p. 212).

Cixous's interpretation is, although similar, noticeably different. What interests Cixous in this particular myth is precisely the impossibility of separating mother and daughter, earth and seed. Contrary to Irigaray, for whom Korè's abduction by Dis, with Zeus' complicity, represents the daughter's rape and her necessary separation from the mother so as to establish the patriarchate, for Cixous, Korè's seduction by Dis doesn't really break the telepathic bond that ties the daughter to her mother. The breakage both takes place and does not take place: "The scene which could have taken place is that of a young girl's rape in the flower of her youth."[8] In fact, the separation takes place on the surface, in the world of vision and light, but there is no deep separation since Demeter and Persephone can communicate at a distance by ear, voice, and body.

Which is why, for example, Demeter, who was not present when her daughter was raped, heard what she could not hear (the muffled cry) and senses the disappearance in her entrails. Cixous sees this separation as a screen veiling the first separation of birth:

> Did the disappearance of the daughter occur at the moment she picked a white flower or a flower or at another moment? Or else is the moment she bent over not just a moment of hiding? A disappearance having taken place before, this one, at which none of us were present, only being the second version of the first? Or the realization on earth of a disappearance already executed in another place? (p. 79)

This late and superficial separation is nothing since a first physical and tangible separation—birth—has already been experienced. Moreover, in order to be born, to exist, the daughter must physically detach herself from the mother. To be born, in Greek *gigomai*, is to separate from the earth and from the mother, but to know (*gignosco*), is to recognize the link with the mother and the earth and to delight (*gaio*) in its gifts. In the myth, Demeter is the earth and Korè the seed, the fruit. Her disappearance from the world of light is then nothing but a return to the earth's entrails. This "separation" can therefore be interpreted as a return to a prenatal union, and the opening of the earth, which seems to signify death, can also signify a new birth as in the myths of vegetation.

Opposing Freud's theory according to which the daughter must detach herself from the mother, even hate her, and turn toward the father as love object in order to become a woman, Cixous presents a primordial vision of the mother's attachment to the daughter and of women amongst themselves:

> And, like so many other lightfooted young women who have never betrayed their mother, she scorns the power of Love, definitely preferring the love of love, and lives among her friends, without class or race distinctions, delighting in a same science of gaiety, possessing the wisdom beyond that which women transmit amongst themselves in lush spots sheltered from the symbolical sun by crowns of leaves, where all of nature is a veil which does not provoke, does not serve as hymen, dispenses freshness, keeps the voyeur at bay, while, in the forest's rooms, in the depths of lakes, in the fields' tender, green bosom, they satisfy the need for happiness without limits of reality or intensity. (p. 42–43)

In this feminine environment, protected from the blinding light of the sun and the father's gaze, there is neither language nor memory and therefore no separation, no limit. Contrary to man's love, Love with a capital, that is, love based on the law of the hymen which, although it establishes bonds between man and woman, also separates them, the love of women ("love of love") is free and limitless. It is in perfect harmony with the benevolent, protective, in a word, maternal attitude of nature.

Our entire history tells us, and Irigaray and Cixous remind us, that woman must touch, *prehend* in order to *comprehend*. This touching is presented as a natural response to the gifts of the mother and the earth. In *Limonade tout était si infini*, Cixous recalls the myth of Eve: "And why did all of history begin with a fruit? And the most important thing in the world: daring to eat a fruit?"[9] Our response to the mother and the earth's call falls immediately under the law's prohibition whose aim is to separate, and especially to separate women from flowers and fruit. The law of the father, whether he is called Zeus, Dis, or God the Father, transforms the call into a ban. He literally places his "no" ["non"] and his name ["nom"] between woman and fruit. In doing so, he transforms the gift into property. The gift is not a gift, because he only leaves it in order to come back to it as his property. "It was therefore a fruit. But the proof consisted in not taking it as a fruit . . . History says: pay no attention to fruit . . . It suffices to think that there was a no before the yes. The law's desire is to separate" (p. 112). This prohibition that denies woman's pleasure is marked by the passage from the natural to the symbolic. Thus, *a* fruit becomes *the* fruit. With the definite article, the fruit disappears as a natural reality in order to signify that with which it has no relationship.

Cixous and Irigaray seem to accept the traditional association between woman and flower. In fact, they go back to the beginning of this association and use it to reinforce the impossibility of *not* transgressing genre laws. Thus, for Derrida, Cixous, and Irigaray, flower and woman are tied to the opposition of the law of "ownness" and ownership. In *Glas*, a text which illustrates the inevitable mixing of genres, Derrida writes: "the practical deconstruction of the transcendental effect is at work in the structure of the flower as of every *part*, insofar as it *appears* and grows *as such*" (p. 146). If it is enclosed in the symbolic, the flower disappears as living multiplicity. That is why Derrida quotes Genet: "flowers symbolize nothing." In the beginning, they are part of a chain of signifiers without end or origin. Moreover, flowers are always implicated in a process of dissemination and metamorphoses which subvert the oppositions between masculine and feminine, innocence and crime, etc.

Like woman, the flower or plants in general have always been subjected to man's dominating and classifying gaze, beginning with the botanist whose work it is to recognize and name. Under the subjugating and desubjecting gaze of a botanist like Rousseau, for example, the flower is inevitably cut so as to be dried in the pages of a book. The same characteristics have been applied to flowers and to women: immobility, silence, passivity, and even, in a contradictory fashion, innocence and seduction. For a long time botanists refused to recognize flowers as sexed. As in the case of women, one has always seen their purpose not in themselves but in others. For an aesthete like Ruskin, the flower is beautiful so as to be admired by man; for Darwin, the bright colors of its corolla are to attract insects and thus preserve the species.

Like Derrida, Irigaray refers to plants in the context of a critique of phallocentrism and of occulocentrism (*Speculum*). A passage in *Ce Sexe qui n'en est pas un* describing woman also seems to mark the destiny of flowers at the hands of men:

> Separating light from the night comes down to renouncing the levity of our mixture. To hardening these heterogenes who so continuously make us one/everyone. To dividing into watertight compartments, to dissociating us into parts, to cutting us in two and more while we are always one or the other at the same time. (p. 216)

As we have seen in the myth of Demeter and Korè, man separates the world of light from the world of darkness and relegates flower and woman to the subterranean world when, as the myth emphasizes, they belong simultaneously to both realms, crossing and recrossing this border, for them nonexistent, between the two.

In a seventeenth-century treatise, Thomas Hall tells of the punishment of Flora. Flora is banished from the city for having introduced "confusion and disorder into the Church and State."[10] Banishing the flower, reducing woman to silence, driving the poets from the city is always a temptation, but an impossibility: the impossibility of not transgressing genre laws. Each in their own way, Derrida, Irigaray, and Cixous show us what is at work in this repression.

With Cixous, the woman-flower identification is complete and personal. In *Illa*, she writes: "We have always known that women are flowers. We have all lived one or two flowers" (p. 157). With regard to herself, she repeats that she was born in the Jardin d'Essais in Algiers where she learned to let things blossom freely. For Cixous, the vegetal also becomes a physical representation of writing: more precisely, pollinization often serves as a metaphor for literary production. It is in these terms that she describes the inspiration she receives—at a distance—from Clarice Lispector:

> She [Clarice Lispector] breathes on my being a pollen-laden wind. I am covered in it. She has her dust over her entire body, on her eyelids,

on her eyelashes, on her lips I feel her dry gold delicacy under my
teeth, she licks and I swallow her incredibly fine dust, she reads everything through her tasteless, straw-colored wind, she sees everything through the provocative movement of her clouds of thought in
a high storm, I am the tracks of the great Clarice with golden foot-
steps, she writes in the light of great lunary night resonant with the
treasures of the stars. (p. 185)

Like Clarice Lispector, Cixous, whose name is almost an anagram of
care ["souci"], is the color yellow which is also the color of pollen.
Moreover, in Lispector, she isolates the phoneme "lis," the name of a
flower and of reading.[11] It is therefore through reading Lispector that
Cixous is pollinated so that her work may grow. In a talk presented in
California, Cixous mentions the inscriptions that Kafka and Lispector
had left at the time of their deaths, reflections that reveal their preoc-
cupation with the well-being of flowers. She notes that "at the time of
their death, these two heroes of writing recognized the bond that tied
them to vegetation, to the earth, to the subterranean world of roots.
Their works exhort us to remember them."[12]

For feminists, especially American feminists struggling for equality
of power between the sexes, these visions could appear too "poetic,"
too mythical, too "idealistic." In fact, these feminists whose first aim is
to "attack masculine institutions" and to "fight against masculine culture by direct action" have accused Cixous and Irigaray of "revalorizing
feminine stereotypes which for all time have been convenient for men."[13]
Both have been reproached for idealizing the mother and maternity.
There again, they have not been read correctly, understood correctly, or
read entirely. The mother-daughter relationship in the myth of Demeter
is in fact a perfect harmony that Irigaray hopes we can come back to.
She also knows the mother-daughter relationship is difficult and the
subject of many psychoanalytical treatments, especially on the part of
the daughter, because, as she shows in *Et l'une ne bouge pas sans
l'autre*, the mother is the phallic mother, almost entirely emprisoned in
the father's discourse. Moreover, for her, being a mother does not simply come down to bringing children into the world; we procreate in
creating something else besides children: love, desire, language, society,
politics, religion, etc. But this creation, this procreation has been prohibited for centuries and we must reappropriate this maternal dimension that belongs to us as women.[14]

It is true that for Cixous and Irigaray, woman should not compete
with man's power but instead recognize the power she has always
possessed but whose repression by masculine discourse is symptomatic.
This calling of woman back to her true strength should precede social

transformations. That is why Irigaray and Cixous both reject the "feminist" category, all the more so because for them, the "feminine" is not woman's prerogative. It is a way of apprehending the world that should be liberated and valorized for the good of men and women. Because liberating the feminine, in this sense, is in fact liberating the unconscious as well as the ties between writing and the unconscious. As Cixous remarks, "poetry is simply taking strength from the unconscious and . . . the unconscious, this other limitless country, is where the repressed live: women, or as Hoffman would say, fairies."[15] It is a program which banishes borders and trangresses genre laws, a program that can lead to the hope that one day the word "feminism" will no longer be necessary and that we will no longer be able to talk about the battle of genders/genres or sexes, but of their peaceful cohabitation.

Notes

1. Luce Irigaray, *Le Corps-à-corps avec la mère* (Montreal: Editions de la pleine lune, 1981), p. 45–58.
2. Jacques Derrida, "La Loi du genre," *Psyché. Inventions de l'autre* (Paris: Galilée, 1987), p. 253.
3. Jacques Derrida, *Glas* (Paris: Galilée, 1974), et *La Carte postale: de Socrate à Freud et au delà* (Paris: Galilée, 1980).
4. "Shifting Scenes: Interviews on Women, Writing and Politics in Post-nineteen sixty-eight France," Alice Jardine and Anne M. Mencke, (eds.) (New York: Columbia University Press, 1991).
5. Luce Irigaray, *Ce sexe qui n'en est pas un* (Paris: Editions de Minuit, 1977), p. 76.
6. Luce Irigaray, *Le Temps et la différence* (Paris: Poche, 1989), p. 30.
7. Luce Irigaray, *Amante marine de Friedrich Nietzsche* (Paris: Éditions de Minuit, 1980), p. 121.
8. Hélène Cixous, *Illa* (Paris: des femmes, 1980), p. 143.
9. Hélène Cixous, *Limonade tout était si infini* (Paris: des femmes, 1982), p. 103.
10. Quoted by Lesley Gordon, in *Green Magic, Plants and Herbs in Lore and Legend* (New York: Vintage, 1977), p. 23–24.
11. ["Lis" signifies "lily" and is also the second person singular form of the verb "lire," "to read."]
12. René Wellek Lectures, University of California, Irvine, spring 1989.
13. Diana Griffin Crowder, "Amazons and Mothers? and Theories of Women's Writing," *Contemporary Literature*, vol. 24, no. 2, p. 143; Domna Stanton, "Language and Revolution: The Franco-American Connection," *The Future of a Difference*, Hester Eisenstein and Alice Jardine (eds.) (New Brunswick: Rutgers University Press, 1985), p. 86.
14. Luce Irigaray, *Le Corps à corps avec la mère, op. cit.*, p. 27–28.
15. Hélène Cixous, *La jeune née* (Paris: Union générale d'éditions, 1975), p. 182.

Aspects of the Evolution of Feminine Titles in French: From Miresse and Ministresse to the Generic Masculine

Marie E. Surridge

Feminists' attitudes toward the feminization of words serving as titles for women's employment, positions, and social roles have undergone a radical change over the course of the last few decades. Until comparatively recently (between 1920 and 1960, according to Trudeau),[1] women regularly chose to assume the titles given to the men holding the positions for which women were by then competing: *directeur, médecin, professeur, docteur, maître*. At that time, the assumption of such titles represented a victory for women. Since 1980, at least, a less elitist feminism has aimed to change not the status of a small number of gifted and privileged women but the status of women in general. According to this new attitude, women as a group should be valorized in the eyes of the world and have their role made explicit in language.

It is easy to see that the degree of sexism varies from one language to another. The recent movement in favor of feminine titles in French shows that a given language can evolve as far as linguistic sexism is concerned. The history of *they, their* as generic singular pronouns in English would be another indication. But the historical aspects of sexism as well as its variations in successive synchronic states of language have not received the attention they deserve. If we want to attain better understanding of linguistic sexism and the factors that govern it, we need to look from this point of view at the history of languages whose past is well-documented. To this end, the present study examines the semantic ecology of the French suffix *-esse/(-eresse)*, which was long used to feminize nouns but which feminists and women in general today tend to set aside in favor of other methods of feminization.[2] This suffix, very commonly used without emotional color in French up to the sixteenth century, undergoes a curious change: in the eyes of modern feminists and others, it assumes a strong pejorative connotation and undergoes a dramatic reduction in frequency. No satisfactory explanation for this drop in popularity has so far been proffered.

In order to set out and compare the semantic ecology of the suffix in the sum total of the derivatives which can be formed by it, I propose to examine two corpora of nouns ending in -esse/-eresse, one representing modern French and the other Old French. The verb *form* is used here in a synchronic sense. The previous existence of a suffixed form produced by a speaker is not pertinent to the process of derivation: it is not necessary to have heard the derivative in order to use it. Furthermore, the nouns which form the contemporary corpus are not necessarily of recent date. They nevertheless serve as a pool of examples showing the semantic characteristics of the available fund which provides a model for the formation and interpretation of "neologisms" using this suffix.

The Suffix -esse/-eresse in Modern French
(Corpus A)

Corpus A, which represents the models available in contemporary French, was established from the following sources: Juilland's *Dictionnnaire inverse de la langue française* (The Hague: Mouton, 1965); *Grevisse, Le Bon Usage* (1986, para. 486) and Marina Yaguello's *Le Sexe des mots* (1989).[3] Names of animals are included, in part because they undoubtedly serve to establish the semantic connotations of certain of the suffixed words, and in part because they are ambiguous, applying either to a woman or to a female animal.

In order to evaluate the connotations that this suffix may convey in our time, I have divided the corpus into five sub-categories: (I) Words of more or less neutral meaning, formed from [BASE NOUN] with the modified trait [+ male]. (II) Words with a meaning implying that the person denoted is respected for herself. (III) Those with pejorative or devalorizing meaning. (IV) "The wife of [BASE NOUN]." (V) "The female of the animal denoted by [BASE NOUN]." However, it is not always easy to judge whether a noun is pejorative or devalorizing. A question mark in the table indicates doubt. Certain nouns having more than one meaning can appear in several categories.

Corpus A

NOUN	I	II	III	IV	V
I. bailleresse	x				
chéfesse	x			x	
chasseresse	x				
clownesse	x				
codemanderesse	x				
contremaîtresse	x				
défenderesse	x				
demanderesse	x				
doctoresse	x				
hôtesse	x				
mulâtresse	x				
peintresse	x				
poétesse	x				
II. abbesse		x	x		
chanoinesse		x			
déesse		x			
diaconesse		x			
druidesse		x	?		
enchanteresse		x	?		
prêtresse		x	?		
prophétesse		x	?		
III. abbesse			x		
ânesse			x		x
borgnesse			x		
bougresse			x		
devineresse	x		x		
diablesse			x		
drôlesse			x		
faunesse			x		x
ivrognesse			x		
mairesse		x	x	x	
maîtresse		x	x	x	
négresse			x		
ogresse			x		
pauvresse			x		

Corpus A — (Continued)

NOUN		I	II	III	IV	V
	sauvagesse			x		
	singesse			x		x
	scélératesse			x		
	tigresse			x		x
	traîtresse			x		
	vengeresse			x		
IV.	archiduchesse	x			x	
	comtesse	x			x	
	consulesse	x			x	
	dogaresse	x			x	
	duchesse	x			x	
	mairesse	x		x	x	
	maîtresse	x		x	x	
	ministresse	x			x	
	notairesse	x			x	
	pairesse	x			x	
	princesse	x			x	
	vicomtesse	x			x	
V.	ânesse			x		x
	bufflesse			x		x
	faunesse			x		x
	lionesse					x
	singesse			x		x
	tigresse			x		x

A few remarks are called for:

1. The meaning "the wife of [BASE NOUN]" is indissolubly tied to respectability except in two ambiguous cases: *mairesse, maîtresse.*

2. Of the eight nouns indicating that the designated person is respected for herself and not by virtue of her status as a wife, only one (*abbesse*) possesses an established pejorative meaning. Four others (*druidesse, enchanteresse, prêtresse, prophétesse*) are associated with paganism which is not necessarily to be interpreted as a negative connotation and which definitely attributes a certain power to the person designated.

3. Of the twenty nouns in group III, some do not carry an exclusively pejorative sense. *Faunesse, singesse, tigresse* also designate

the female animal. However, there is scarcely any ambiguity as far as use is concerned: if the noun designates a woman, the value is pejorative. On the other hand, whereas if the term *négresse* were used in speech today, the offensive value would be inescapable, this is not necessarily so in literary usage where it may retain the neutral sense it was capable of carrying in the past. Finally, *abbesse*, *mairesse*, *maîtresse* have a double meaning. The majority of the nouns in category III, however, are scarcely ever used in a non-pejorative sense.

If the distribution of the sub-group of nouns in Corpus A considered non-ambiguous is analyzed, it can be seen that they are divided as follows: (a) nouns with exclusively neutral meaning (12), (b) nouns exclusively implying respect (3), (c) nouns of exclusively pejorative or devalorizing meaning (12). Furthermore, category V includes nouns designating animals thought to be stupid (*ânesse*), large and ferocious (*bufflesse*, *tigresse*), or lascivious (*faunesse*), and which are all regularly used to designate women. In fact, the ambiguity of which they are capable is not a variation between pejorative and neutral. Given that they are always pejorative when applied to humans and that when they designate animals the animals are assumed to have undesirable characteristics, these nouns could just as well figure in III.

It is obvious that present-day women have excellent reasons for rejecting nouns feminized by means of this suffix: about 50 percent of the corpus of contemporary models is made up of pejorative nouns. Let us now compare this state of affairs with what is to be found in the corpus based on Old French.

The Suffix -esse/-eresse in Old French
(Corpus B)

In Old French the suffix *-esse/-eresse* serves to create feminine forms from masculine nouns and adjectives. The group of words which may serve as bases for the suffixed forms consists of:

1. nouns, or adjectives serving as nouns, designating a human [+ male] which end in a consonant followed by a feminine *e*. The feminine *e* is deleted and *-esse* is added (*apostresse*, *barnesse*);

2. nouns or adjectives ending in *-eor*, *-eur* where the existing suffix is replaced by *-eresse (acheteur, acheteresse, avoer, avoeresse)*;

3. some cases that do not correspond to this description, but which are recognizable as suffixed forms (*harperesse*, *medecineresse*).

In her partial history of the suffixe *-esse* in the Middle Ages, Leena Löfstedt[4] explains some phonomorphological variations, recounts the development of the suffix -eur/-euse, and shows that -euse ultimately displaces -eresse. Löfstedt, however, mentions only in passing the semantic fields represented by words with the feminine suffix, and the importance of such words in the history of the representation of women in French. These matters are dealt with in the remainder of this article.

In order to address these questions, I established a corpus of nouns attested in Old French, formed with the suffix -esse/-eresse, and representing a woman or a girl. This corpus was obtained from the *Dictionnaire inverse de l'ancien français* (Gorog, 1982).[5] Gorog's sources are the *Lexique de l'ancien français* (Godefroy, 1901) and the first ten volumes of the *Altfranzösisches Wörterbuch* (Tobler-Lommatzsch, 1925–). It includes words attested from the eleventh to the sixteenth centuries, although the latter is only thinly represented. Löfstedt identifies 169 nouns ending in -esse using only Tobler-Lommatzsch as her source, whereas I was able to establish a corpus of 502 nouns, divided as follows: -esse: 91; -eresse: 367; -erresse: 44.

The corpus established for the present study is remarkable for the preponderance of the variation ending in -eresse/-erresse which plays an important role in the Middle Ages before almost completely disappearing, leaving only a few examples in contemporary French.

The definitions cited below for the Old French forms are mainly derived from Godefroy; some also draw on Tobler-Lommatzsch or on *Le Petit Robert*.

Analysis of the Data

For our present purpose, there are two questions of interest: what are the occupations, roles, positions in society that this derivative method allows to express in old French? And what are the implications for the history of the French language in general?

We look first at the titles in which the suffix designates "the wife of [NOUN BASE]," even if the nouns in question are capable of bearing another meaning:

Corpus B

TITLE	MEANING
conestablesse	constable's wife
favresse	woman who forges, blacksmith's wife
mairesse	mayor's wife, superior in a religious house
ministresse	woman who accomplishes or carries out something, servant, minister's wife
miresse	woman who conducts medical examinations, doctor's wife

Corpus B—(Continued)

TITLE	MEANING
ostesse	innkeeper's wife
patriarchesse	Patriarch of Jerusalem's wife
prest(r)esse	priestess (in antiquity), priest's wife
senatresse	senator's wife
vidamesse	vidame's wife
voeresse	wife of a *voe* (*'lawyer, defender'*), one who carries out the office of *voé*

We also find some terms expressing rank. The meaning can be either "wife of [NOUN BASE]" or "woman holding the rank of [NOUN BASE]": *comtesse, empresse, princesse, vavasseresse, vicomtesse.*

It will be seen that the number of terms in this category is remarkably modest in comparison with the categories to which we now turn: terms usually expressing unambiguously a status or role directly attributed to a woman without reference to her husband (or to her father). The following are not included in these lists: nouns designating women of questionable lifestyle, flirtatious women, or nouns expressing a judgment on a woman's sexual life. They are few and without particular interest in this context. On the other hand, nouns expressing a criminal or reprehensible role are included, since this category indicates the existence of functions for women which, even if blameworthy, are potentially active and independent. Similarly, it is interesting to note the number of available terms in old French for "witch" because of the strong association between witches and power. Certain of the roles represented are neither surprising nor distinctive: they have been included so as to ensure that the range of occupations and positions attributed to women and expressed by means of words formed in this way is fully depicted.

The titles serving to express the independent roles of women are divided into seven semantic categories: criminal or reprehensible roles, terms for "witch," warlike roles, commercial roles, agricultural, industrial, or manual occupations, nouns indicating a legal status, other societal occupations and roles.

Table 1—Criminal or Reprehensible Roles

arderesse	female arsonist
beveresse	drinker
blasfemeresse	blasphemer

Table 1—Criminal or Reprehenisble Roles continued on p. 164

Table 1—(Continued)

degasteresse	debauchee
dissiperesse	debauchee
empoisonneresse	poisoner
enfraigneresse	law-breaker
engigneresse	liar
forfaiteresse	transgressor, rapist
imposteresse	impostor
larronnesse	thief
menaceresse	one who utters threats
mordrisseresse	murderer, assassin
poitevineresse	counterfeiter of money called *poitevine*
rapineresse	plunderer
ravisseresse	ravisher, abductor
violaresse	rapist

Table 2—Terms Designating Witches

cauresse
charmagneresse
charmeteresse
charoieresse
sorceresse

Table 3—Warlike Roles

championeresse	woman who serves as a champion (in the primitive medieval sense: one who fought in an enclosed field to defend a cause [*Petit Robert*])
conquesteresse	conqueror
guerroieresse	warrior
vindicateresse	avenger

Table 4—Commercial Roles

acheteresse	buyer
changeresse	money changer
ciresse	one who sells wax
détailleresse	retailer
faneresse	one who sells hay
floreresse	florist

Table 4— (Continued)

forneresse	baker
harengresse	herringmonger
heridesse	woman responsible for cleaning in houses where a death from plague has occurred
moneresse	miller
olieresse	one who sells oil
pagesse	female page
paieresse	payer
peseresse	weigher
pesteresse	baker
pétrisseresse	kneader
poteresse	one who sells pottery
sauneresse	one who sells salt
usufructueresse	usufructuary
venderesse	saleswoman, merchant

Table 5—Agricultural, Industrial, and Manual Occupations

acesmeresse	woman in charge of adorning others
baconneresse	woman who carves up carcasses
carderesse	carder
cortilleresse	gardener
coutiveresse	cultivator
dispenseresse	one who dispenses
estouresse	woman who combs out knots in wool
escorcheresse	skinner
estenderesse	stretcher
estofferesse	seamstress
fileresse	spinner
forbisseresse	furbisher
froteresse	masseuse
gaaigneresse	cultivator
garnisseresse	decorator
glaneresse	gleaner
harperesse	harpist
herbilleresse	grass cutter
laneresse	woman who prepares wool

Table 5—Agricultural, Industrial, and Manual Occupations continued on p. 166

Table 5— (Continued)

maçonnesse	mason
mailleresse	woman who works with a hammer
messaneresse	harvester
orgneresse/oinderesse	anointer
orbateresse	goldsmith
orfevresse	silversmith
orderesse	weaver
peigneresse	comber (of wool, etc.)
pelucheresse	peeler
pescheresse	fisherwoman
planteresse	planter
poigneresse	hewer
porpoigneresse	woman who makes doublets
priseresse	estimator
racleresse	scraper
recuiteresse	metal firer
retonderesse	shearer
roleresse	roller, *cf. rouleur/euse*, "worker who rolls ore, casks" (*Petit Robert*)
rooigneresse	goldcutter
sarcleresse	hoer
semeresse	sower
soieresse	harvester
tenderesse	woman who hangs out freshly-dyed sheets
tieuleresse	tiler
tonderesse	shearer (wool, animals)
torderesse	twister (cords, chains)
torteleresse	pie maker
touseresse	woman who twists (curls?) hair
traieresse	stretcher (iron thread, brass wire)
traîneresse	trainer, *cf. traîneur/euse*, "person who pulls, cart-puller" (*Petit Robert*)
tresseresse	weaver, braider
vacheresse	cowgirl

Table 6—Nouns Indicating Legal Status

apauteresse	feminine of *apauteor*, "one who mortgages a feudal property"
apeleresse	appellant

Table 6— (Continued)

arbitresse	arbitrator
aquesteresse	inheritor
avoeresse	feminine of *avoeor*, meaning "defender, solicitor, ombudsman"
executeresse	executor
fiefferesse	woman who grants fiefs
garantisseresse	guarantor
hoiresse	legatee
legateresse	testator
plaideresse	litigant
possesseresse/	
possideresse	possessor
procureresse	authorized representative, proxy, person with power of attorney, caretaker, a nun who temporarily deals with the interests of the convent
responderesse	one who vouches for another
restitueresse	one who makes restitution
testamenteresse	executrix
tesmoigneresse	witness

Table 7—Other Occupations or Roles in Society

abeesse	abbess, director of a house of prostitution
apostresse	announcer (*cf. apostre*)
apothicaresse	nun who works for the poor
clergeresse/clergesse	educated woman, nun
edefieresse	woman who edifies, educator
intrepreteresse/	
interpreteresse	interpreter
fondatresse	founder
hermitresse	hermit
inquisiteresse	researcher
inventeresse	inventor
jugeresse	judge
liseresse	reader
mairesse	superior in a monastic house
medecineresse	woman practicing medicine
megeresse	woman practicing medicine

Table 7—Other Occupations or Roles in Society continued on p. 168

Table 7—(Continued)

messageresse	messenger
mesureresse	assigner
miresse	woman who performs medical examinations
moieneresse	mediator, procurer
moinesse	nun
moveresse	instigator
pardoneresse	pardoner
peintresse	painter
penseresse	thinker
philosophesse	philosopher
prieresse	woman who prays, comes to pray, invites others to services and funerals
proclameresse	proclaimer
reconteresse	teller
recommanderesse	one who recommends, chooses wet nurses, servants
relieresse	binder
sauveresse	one who saves
semonceresse	woman who delivers invitations
sourmonteresse	dominator
troveresse	finder, inventor

The important points which emerge from this corpus can be summarized as follows. According to this lexis, women occupy positions at all levels: in the area of witchcraft which is, of course, a significant source of power (*cauresse, charmagneresse, sorceresse*), but also in occupations requiring a certain physical strength (*baconeresse, coutiveresse, mailleresse, recuiteresse*) or the ability to direct a commercial enterprise (*changeresse, détailleresse, olieresse*). During the period covered by our corpus, women worked in professions that would be closed to them for many centuries to come: for a long period, the roles of teacher, lawyer, philosopher, and doctor, to name only a few notable examples, would not be open to them. From the end of the Old French period to the beginning of the current movement towards nonsexist language, the linguistic system, increasingly subject to close normative control, for the most part sanctions only masculine generics for a high proportion of the roles represented by feminines in our corpus.

A particularly striking aspect of Corpus B is the difficulty of finding a synonym in modern French for many of the nouns ending in -*esse*. For the most part, one can only express their content by using a relative sentence or a periphrasis relating the feminine to the masculine equivalent: "feminine of x" or "wife of x." Examples are *acheteresse*, expressed as *"féminin d'acheteur"*; *changeresse* expressed as *"femme qui fait l'office de changeur."* It is clearly apparent that, although the suffix *-euse* has indeed replaced *-esse/-eresse* in the morphological system, this is not the case over the lexis as a whole.

Overall, the most notable feature of Corpus B is its rich, varied, and positive semantic content. Corpus A, in comparison, is marked by the limited and pejorative semantic potential of the words which constitute it.

Conclusion

Women's rejection of the modern suffix *-esse* is justified, as we have seen, by the pejorative semantic connotations now attached to this method of derivation. In contrast, the bank of *-esse/-eresse* suffixes in old French provides models connoting for women a series of important and respected positions in society.

No morphological obstacle prevented the suffix *-euse* from assuming the function of *-esse/-eresse*, and yet this is not what has occurred. The suffix *-euse* allows the creation of many feminine [+ human] nouns, but it simply has not, for example, produced suffixed forms to replace *avoeresse, championeresse, inquisiteresse, inventeresse, jugeresse, medecineresse, megeresse, miresse, penseresse, philosophesse,* or *sauveresse.*

The area of medieval and postmedieval French vocabulary examined in this study proves the existence of social and linguistic systems that are surprising in that they attest to a more broad-minded spirit, on the part of a society we are accustomed to regard as somewhat primitive, than exists today.

In discussions for and against the use of a neutral, nonsexist French language, the examples we have seen have a special, perhaps critical role to play. Those who oppose the creation of femininized titles justify their belief by pointing to the violence they say this innovation will inflict upon the spirit of the French language. In fact, the data presented here indicates that if the spirit of the language is opposed to the production of explicitly feminine titles, this opposition is of comparatively recent date. The characteristics of terms ending in *-esse/-eresse* between the eleventh and sixteenth centuries clearly show that factors preventing free feminization of titles must be sought elsewhere.

Is the fate of our suffix *-esse/-eresse* an isolated case? I do not think so. Vaugelas believed that the symbolic value of linguistic gender was representative of sociological gender as is shown by his statement concerning fluctuations in the gender of certain nouns:

"Aage" ... most women (and, in questions of language, their number is not small) commonly make this word feminine ... and, not surprisingly, they give the same gender to several other words with this ending, like "ouvrage," "orage," "gages," "étage," and to still others which are usually in the masculine without counting those with a different ending that they also make feminine *from a particular affection they have for their gender.*[6]

It will be observed that the era in which so many feminine titles are eliminated coincides approximately with the age in which a grammarian of the standing of Vaugelas so strongly identified feminine gender with women. It also coincides with the time at which the routine use of personal pronouns and determinants was established in French, bringing with it a major increase in instances of the feminine being absorbed in the so-called generic masculine. It is especially difficult to conceive of such masculines as neutral when they are seen in the light of a statement such as Vaugelas's, which was certainly not unique. Nor is the moral outrage of traditionalists convincing when they declare that the creation of feminine titles disrupts the lexical morphology of French, with potentially disastrous results, since we now know that a radical change in the opposite direction has taken place in French in historical times.

This study has given us a glimpse of changes brought about by the earlier morphological "revolution" although much remains to be discovered about it. In the light of the facts we have seen, it is difficult to see the downgrading of the suffix -*esse/-eresse* otherwise than as the product of a rise in linguistic sexism which inculcated a new and negative attitude towards the feminine. The movement to establish feminine titles, looked at from the historical point of view, seems to be merely a reversion to a former, less sexist state of the French language.

Notes

This article is a revised version of "Religieuses, Travailleuses, Poétesses et Notairesses; aspects de l'évolution des titres féminins en français" published in *Du féminin*.

1. Danielle Trudeau, "Changement social et changement linguistique: la question du Féminin," *The French Review*, vol. 62, no. 1, 1988, p. 77–87.
2. The suffix -*ice*, which is also rejected, undoubtedly merits similar study.
3. Marina Yaguello, *Le Sexe des Mots* (Paris: Belfond, 1989).
4. Leena Löfstedt, *La Désinence féminine -esse* in Maher, J. Peter, Allan R.

Bombard and E. F. Conrad Koerner, 1982, Papers from the conference on historical linguistics (Amsterdam: John Benjamin B. V.), p. 217–233.
5. Gorog, Ralph Paul de, 1982, *Dictionnaire inverse de l'ancien français* (Binghampton, New York: Centre for Medieval and Renaissance Studies).
6. Quoted by Jean-Yves Belliard, *La notion du genre grammatical chez Vaugelas et ses continuateurs*, Master's thesis, Queen's University, 1978, p. 65. My emphasis.

WOMEN'S PLACE IN THE LITERARY INSTITUTION, OR THE LESSONS OF RELATIVE INTEGRATION

Nicole Mozet

For Colette Julien-Bertolus.

If I have chosen to deal with the literary institution, it is because I do not think that writing is a solitary activity—at least, solely—and that one does not become a writer simply by writing. But I use the term "institution" in a very broad sense, encompassing, for example, literary genres and the texts themselves. It is a matter, then, of a study which uses certain tools from the sociology of literature but which allows itself to take a number of excursions beyond the usual borders of this type of analysis.

As for the second part of my title, it obviously indicates that I chose to broach the study of the literary institution by taking sexual difference into account. Let us straightaway make clear that I prefer to speak about sexual identity rather than sexual difference so as to avoid theoretical problems tied to the concept of difference. But if I have decided to emphasize the importance of the parameter of sexual identity, it is not only because of a militant viewpoint seeking to reveal certain mechanisms of exclusion or marginalization which victimize women. This is too well known to be dwelt upon further. What interests me more is that the place, or rather places, reserved for women inside the institution inform us about the institution and, consequently, about writing itself. My ambition is to contribute to visibly modifying the most common conception of literature which is still essentially based on an overly simplistic opposition between good and bad authors, quality texts and so-called consumer literature. In the past, these categories were de-

172

nounced as issuing from an elitist conception of literary practice. It is most informative to note that these arguments convinced no one, not even those who used them! And rightfully so, because it is impossible to read without preference and judgment. This is true not only of the literary institution but especially of ourselves as reading professionals. What I am proposing, then, is simply a refinement of certain criteria and a diversification of categories so as to better apprehend the complexity of the literary phenomenon.

Why women? If my first intention is not militant, why choose this minority group which is at the same time so heterogeneous? Precisely because it is a heterogeneous minority: studies are easier when there are few, and diversity guarantees a certain representativeness of the samples. Of course, these two arguments will not be able to support a credible analysis if I do not manage to show that there exists a common denominator among the members of this group which is directly tied to value judgments of the quality of women's texts and their more or less "regionalist" character. The very purpose of my study is to suggest that there is something exemplary — and, as a consequence, equally applicable to male authors — in the situation of women striving to become writers.

Two preliminary remarks. The first is that literature is, by vocation, the privileged place of tension between two contradictory forces: on the one hand, there is the tendency which consists in transporting the relations of power which underlie the social body in its entirety into the symbolical and aesthetic domain, and, on the other hand, the reverse tendency which consists in making the questioning of these power relations the very subject of literature, especially in its most innovative areas. As far as sexual difference is concerned, a factor which cannot be ignored is the combination of the writer's sex and the textual sex, if I may say, of word-beings forged by him or her.[1] The second remark, which is complementary, is that literature is the ultimate theater of disguise where authors and readers step with varying degrees of pleasure into the characters' shoes. That is why it seems paradoxical to me to speak about literature without taking into consideration the parameter of sexual identity.

1. Corpus: A Catalogue of Authors, Works, and Editors of French Literary Production Between 1945 and 1950

We will be looking at an ongoing research project which has been conducted over the past few years at the University of Paris VII under the direction of Marcelle Marini and myself. Based on the postulate of exhaustiveness, its task is to consider all titles which appear in the *Bibliographie de la France* under the heading *Littérature*.[2] Of course, exhaustiveness, even relative, always implies attendant drastic limitations: we have therefore eliminated reeditions and translations so as to retain only works written in French, published for the first time, and only in France. This classification already entails considerable work. But it gives us a vertical slice of a moment of literary production that plunges to its depths, to this zone, unexplored by literary criticism, where writing wavers between amateurism and professionalism. This is why we have a series of authors of only one book, often published at the author's own expense or by a tiny publishing house, and even a book of which there remains only its title! It is the baseline of literature, the lower limit under the tip of the iceberg. Then comes the even more intimidating underworld where lie the corpses of all the texts rejected by publishing house reading committees. The second original aspect of this research—and, I would say, its essential merit—is that we decided to take into consideration the authors' sex. These two decisions have more in common than one would think, because it is in distancing ourselves from the average threshold of recognition that we begin to discover more and more women. But this is also where we ran into our greatest problems: how is some unknown person who left no trace to be identified? how are we to even decide upon the sex of an author who can always be suspected of having used a pseudonym? We saw fairly quickly that no man had taken a feminine pseudonym[3] and we could therefore, with an almost nonexistent margin of error, classify as women all those who had feminine first names. There remained, however, totally unknown women who had taken a masculine pseudonym as well as the question of ambivalent names such as Dominique and Claude. In a total of approximately 6,600 authors, there were about one hundred undecided cases. I chose to account for a quarter of these as feminine and the rest as masculine. The numbers we propose can therefore be considered as sufficiently reliable.

2. Analysis of Some Statistical Facts

The entire catalogue, that is, the six years from 1945 to 1950 inclusive, represents about 11,000 titles (I have rounded off the numbers so as to ensure a small, inevitable margin of error). The number of authors is obviously inferior: 1,300 women as compared to 5,300 men. Apart from Colette and a few women writers at the beginning of the century like Rachilde or Jeanne Galzy, the most well-known (today) are Beauvoir, Duras, Sarraute, and Elsa Triolet. We can also mention

Françoise d'Eaubonne, Dominique Arban, Gisèle Prassinos, Béatrix Beck, Dominique Aury, Andrée Chédid, Germaine Beaumont, or Violette Leduc. What appears significant to me is the disparity between the number of relatively important women writers and the tiny number of those who achieved true symbolic recognition. Here it is useful to look at a manual of literary history. I chose the *XXe siècle* (Nathan) in Henri Mitterand's collection because it is one that appears to be most open to a diversified concept of literature and can therefore be considered as a rather accurate reflection of the literary institution's evolution. His "chronologies" are even more revealing. In 1940, among the four titles cited, only one is that of a woman's work, Colette. In 1943, twenty-two titles, including one Beauvoir and one Triolet. For 1944, nine titles, one Colette and one Beauvoir. As for the period which corresponds to the catalogue, subtitled "Sound Post-War Values," there is not a single woman. Things move a little after 1951 with Françoise Mallet-Joris and Marguerite Yourcenar, but with no Pauline Réage.

This situation lends itself easily to different interpretations. For my part, I wonder if, in the French literary tradition, there is not a quasi-structural inability to accept more than one woman per century: Germaine de Staël, George Sand, Colette. What is at work around 1950 is Colette's succession. In a section on the novel entitled "A Return to Real-Life," the *XXe siècle* cites a book by a woman twenty-two times out of a total of sixty-five for the period 1959–1988, an unprecedented ratio of one to three.

The years 1945–1950 are interesting because they fall between a still very sheltered literary practice and the upheavals characteristic of the second half of the twentieth century. The war had a two-pronged effect: it brought the debate on literature down to the question of commitment which, befitting the times, evoked the Platonic theme of the poet as either being in or outside the city; however, the simultaneous discoveries of extermination camps and the atomic apocalypse compounded the effects of World War I and thus rendered the prewar world obsolete. Women writers, whose legitimacy in speaking about the war was not a given, first suffered from this situation. But again, it is from this historical fissure that a movement of liberation, which had previously touched only a minority, extended to all of society.

From the point of view of literary criticism, our period is situated just before the great upheavals that preceded and followed 1968, but the sense, often mixed with fear, that a profound change was occurring can be perceived in the titles of many essays on literature: in Gaëton Picon's *Panorama de la nouvelle littérature française* (1948) as well as in Pierre de Boisdeffre's *Métamorphose de la littérature* (1950) or in

La Révolte des écrivains d'aujourd'hui (1949) by Albérès. Also, 1950 is the year of Nathalie Sarraute's *L'Ère du soupçon* which, in a way, is the founding text of our modern conception of literature, deconstruction and postmodernism included. Starting with first-rate writers like Beauvoir, Duras, Marie Noël, or Yourcenar, it would be fascinating to look more closely at the role women played in these profound transformations; this would be in the same vein as Susan Suleiman's research on the relationship between women and the avant-garde[4] for example, or the issue of the journal *Avant-Garde* coordinated by Françoise van Rossum-Guyon.[5] Out of the six years covered by our general list, one scarcely finds 1.4 books per woman writer, whereas with men the ratio is almost two to one.

Apart from the year 1950, for which we gathered a sufficient amount of data, I am not in a position to carry out more refined analyses on my corpus because authorial identification is not yet complete, especially as far as men are concerned. I will begin, then, by giving global figures for 1950 which have a minimal margin of error. First, we confirmed that a quarter of the writers, even a little more, are women. The numbers are as follows: titles: 1,346; authors: 1,132; women: 230; men: 893; couples (man-woman): 4; unidentified authors with no first name: 5.

In 1950, therefore, the number of women writers was far from negligible. However, the ratios change considerably when it comes to familiar names: even among romance novels, it is difficult to find more than ten representatives of reasonably established woman writers in the cultural tradition. Here I will mention, in alphabetical order, the names which appeared most significant to me because they mix generations and types of notoriety as well as the extremely variable eras when women were recognized: Béatrix Beck, André Corthis, Delly, Duras, Jeanne Galzy, Daniel Gray, Magali, Claude-Edmonde Magny, Hélène Parmelin, Gisèle Prassinos. Of course, on the male side, well-known names of novelists, poets, and playwrights abound, such as Adamov, Anouilh, Bataille, Blanchot, Camus, René Char, Claudel, Gide, Edmond Jabès, Klossowski, Mauriac, Michaux, Prévert, Salacrou, Simenon, Roger Vaillant, Boris Vian—to name but a few.

In order to better understand this phenomenon, or distortion, between number and reputation, or, if you prefer, in terms that are not mine but that I do not challenge, between quantity and quality, we must look closer.

Our initial classification enables us to divide the 230 feminine names in 1950 into two large categories: authors that we have clearly identified and those we believe to be women judging by their first names—a category which, as we will see, is not the least interesting of the two.

The women whose sexual identity, at least, is indisputable number 140. Among them, those who achieved a certain degree of recognition were all published by major Parisian publishers: Gallimard (seven): Béatrix Beck, Edith Boissonnas, Marguerite Duras, Jeanne Galzy, Edmée de La Rochfoucault, Lydia Chweitzer, Georgette Henry. Le Seuil (three): Claude-Edmonde Magny, Dominique Rolin, Raymonde Vincent. Fayard (one): André Corthis.

Plon is less selective: next to Thyde Monnier, who was a writer of large print runs, as was Delly, we find unknown authors like the journalist Suzanne Chantal, or Colette Henri-Ardel (pseudonym: Henri-Ardel). Julliard, who practiced an editorial policy of promoting young authors, published as established a writer as Jeanne Galzy as well as someone like Elizabeth Barbier in 1950. The two well-represented publishing houses in this list are Tallandier and Ferenczi (twenty-eight titles), specialists in romance and children's literature. This distribution corresponds exactly to the distribution of literary genres: out of the 146 titles on the list, we have thirty-two that are officially catalogued—including six Delly—as a romance novel. A woman like Josy Ambroise-Thomas, who published fourteen books between 1932 and 1957, all of them romance or children's literature, is very representative of a specific form of writing primarily reserved for women. There are in fact only six authors of romance novels for the 898 names identified as masculine or taken as such by default. Only two identifications are definite, whereas the other four names—Marcel Artigues, Th. Bernardie, Arthur Bernède, and Jean Demais—could be women's pseudonyms. This difference allows us to better appreciate Duras' genius in having understood, particularly in *L'Amant*, that the romance genre, somewhat like erotic or pornographic literature, corresponds to reading needs that are not really met by official literature.[6]

Apart from the romance novel, the most homogeneous and also the most interesting category is poetry: a fifth are women, whereas the proportion is more than a quarter for men (234 out of 893). And if we take into consideration, as we do for the men, clearly identified women as well as those only assumed to be women, we move to a global figure of 53 out of 230, that is, less than a quarter. It is clear, then, that in 1950 women were writing less poetry than men.

Directly linked to poetry, a difficult genre to publish, we come up against editions with no other publisher than the author him or herself. The proportion of this self-publishing, which lies on the border between private and public, is, incidentally, for all genres taken together, the same for men as it is for women: 2.5 percent for the former (twenty-three out of 898), 2.6 percent for the latter (6 out of 230). We see again, therefore, that in the mid or lower zones of the literary institution, women are on par with men. It is only in the upper spheres that they appear less suited—at least in 1950—to playing a leading role.

Thus, if we examine the place of publication based on the opposition between the provinces and Paris, a city which, as we know, has always played an essential role in French cultural life, we can see that all the duly authenticated women from our first list were published in Paris with the exception of eight titles for 140 authors, that is, 6 percent, whereas the proportion is close to a quarter (twenty-one titles for ninety authors) on the second list which includes very few known publishing houses. The list of men offers a global, intermediary percentage of 20 percent for texts published outside Paris (a little less than 200 titles for 900 authors), but with the essential difference again having to do with the number of works: established writers like Michaux, Paulhan, or Ponge published, in the same year and *at the same time*, in Paris and in the provinces; this radically changes the significance of the place of publication.

It is time to consider the main trends: they clearly show that even if the number of women whose occupation is writing is greater than generally thought, the literary institution in France in 1950 is far from being truly mixed. The handicap of femininity lies in a number of sometimes imperceptible overdeterminations, reminiscent of a spider's web: almost invisible but frightfully efficient. Not only is it more difficult for a woman than a man to put the plan of publishing into action, but once this step is made, many other obstacles remain to be overcome for which women writers are always a little less well-armed, a little less well-prepared than their male counterparts—except for when the long series of trials has endowed them with incomparable strength and freedom of bearing.

How are we to interpret this quantitative element which initially seems to have nothing to do with literary quality? If the consideration of individual cases is unimportant, statistical truth is different: on the institutional scale, quantity is almost always a determining element, whatever the sector of production, be it a romance or mystery series, or a more ambitious work. The combination of quality and quantity is the keystone of literature's very foundation, and especially of what is called a writer's works. Lacking in our research is the essential parameter of print run figures, usually impossible to obtain. A literary work must be managed and this management produces effects that spill back over onto the writing, for better or for worse, depending on the case. But it is impossible to manage everything in writing, so much so that the writer needs assistance, preferably at the management stage. There, perhaps, is the Achilles' heel of women writers because the power of writing depends in part on the emotional environment and on one's social circle, be it modest, even marginal.

Judging by our catalogue, one can imagine the many situations in which women's writing initiatives were simultaneously encouraged and impeded. Wives and mistresses of famous or recognized writers, often hidden behind a pseudonym, can no longer be counted. How many became famous solely on their own merit? Gérard d'Houville was the daughter of Hérédia and Henri de Régnier's wife: who, even among French literature specialists, still remembers her name? Come a certain age, a writer also need disciples. This is something that even celebrated writers have lacked, especially in France. George Sand benefited from an extraordinary entourage of friends, lovers, and children during her lifetime, yet, until recently, posthumous links have been strangely weak. She has still not seen the consecration of her writing in a "complete works" edition—indispensable element of survival—whereas every half-century has produced one or two sets of Balzac's "collected works." A literary work must be managed and promoted, but it must also be orchestrated, most often in the context of a scholarly institution like the university. The fact that today there are more women in all levels of publishing firms and newspapers as well as in universities constitutes an essential factor of integration in literary production and allows less acrobatic women to more easily clear each hurdle in the successful literary career's long, treacherous journey, including the very problematic passage into posterity.

Conclusion: Integration and Complexity

In spite of the temporal and spatial limitations of this study, I believe that it nonetheless indicates some general trends. The first is that even when tolerated or legalized, integration continues to be frightening, and this fear engenders underhanded yet efficient new methods of exclusion, classification, and marginalization.

In order to move beyond this pessimistic observation, I would like to suggest that it is not only the feminine which frightens in integration, but integration itself in what it necessarily implies about learning complexity—now recognized as the basis of all areas of scientific study. In this respect, the literary institution is exemplary because it is very much informed by the aristocratic temptation to assimilate the complex into the difficult. This reductionist sleight-of-hand is nothing other than a quick solution. Moreover, it constitutes a mode of exclusion characteristic of our times which is upheld by an exaltation of the nonwarlike exploit, just as commercial, scientific, or athletic successes are privileged. The literary exploit—masterpiece or bestseller—is all the more fascinating because it is magic, entirely fabricated from words. This phenomenon is perhaps most noticeable in French literature because of its history of always having been dominated by a very strong separation between highbrow and popular culture.[7] I prefer to contribute to the construction of a new image of the literary institution, more supple and more complete, that takes into consideration social determinants as well as the specificity of the literary enunciation. To the extent to which literary reading[8] presupposes verbal learning at the same time as a very strong relationship to imagination, it seems to remain the best school where "all sorts of people," as Apollinaire says, may have access to a certain dose of complexity, necessarily varying from one individual to the next. In other words, I think that it is better to read bad books than no books at all, like the characters in Marguerite Duras's *La Pluie d'été* who are so passionate about reading and rereading *La Vie de Georges Pompidou* that they salvaged from a dust bin. . . . Just as psychoanalysis has elaborated the concept of a "sufficiently good" mother, perhaps it would be appropriate to set into movement the notion of a *"sufficiently good"* literature that would favor freedom of choice without falling into total indiscrimination or pure repetition.

Notes

1. Denise Brahimi, *Appareillages. Dix études comparatistes sur la littérature des hommes et des femmes dans le monde arabe et aux Antilles* (Paris: Deux Temps Tierce, 1991).
2. This is in section 10 of the *Bibliographie de la France*; the exact title is "Linguistique. Littérature," as distinct from scientific, legal, and historical publications, but also from philosophy, fine arts, and religious sciences.
3. Except in the area of erotic literature: Armande du Loup, who published twenty books of about 250 pages each in six years, is the pseudonym of someone designated as a man in the preface of one of these works.
4. Susan Rubin Suleiman, *Subversive Intent: Gender, Politics, and the Avant-Garde* (Cambridge, Mass.: Harvard University Press).
5. *Avant-Garde*, no. 4 ("Femmes, Frauen, Women"), Françoise van Rossum-Guyon (ed.), (Amsterdam: Rodopi, 1990).
6. See Marcelle Marini, "La mort d'une érotique," *Cahiers Renaud-Barrault*, no. 106, September 1983; Mireille Calle-Gruber, *L'Amour fou femme fatale. Marguerite Duras: une réécriture des archétypes littéraires* in R. M. Allemand (ed.), *Nouveau Roman en question(s)* (Paris: Minard, 1992).
7. Renée Balibar, *Les Français fictifs, le rapport des styles littéraires au français national* (Paris: Hachette), 1974, and *L'Institution du français. Essai sur le colinguisme des Carolingiens à la République* (Paris: PUF, 1985).
8. "Lire pour lire. La Lecture littéraire," revue *Textuel*, no. 23, 1990.

LIST OF CONTRIBUTORS

Hélène Cixous. Since the publication of *Dedans* (winner of the Prix Medicis in 1969), she has written some thirty works of poetic fiction, critical essays, and eight plays, including *L'Histoire terrible de Norodom Sihanouk* and *L'Indiade* (performed at the Théâtre du Soleil). Cixous's works have been translated into over ten languages. Since 1968, she has been professor of literature at the Université de Paris VIII which she helped establish. There she is also director of the doctoral program and the Centre of Research in Feminine Studies. She also teaches at the Collège International de Philosophie.

Mireille Calle is professor of French literature at Queen's University (Canada) and a writer. She has written numerous articles and books on literary theory (*L'effet-fiction. De l'illusion romanesque*, Nizet, 1989), on the "nouveau-roman," and on feminine writing ("l'ecriture féminine") (*Photos de Racines*, co-authored with Hélène Cixous, des femmes, 1994). She is also the author of several works on Michel Butor and Claude Simon. Mireille Calle has just published her third novel, *La division de l'intérieur* (L'Hexagone, Montreal, 1996) and is completing a book entitled *Les Partitions de Claude Ollier: une écriture de l'altérité*.

Philippe Lacoue-Labarthe is currently professor of philosophy and aesthetics at the University of Strasbourg. He has worked at the National Theatre of Strasbourg with Michel Deutsch on coproductions of Sophocles's/Hölderlin's *Antigone* (1978–1979), Euripides's *Les Phéniciennes*, as well as at the Centre Dramatique des Alpes and at the Théâtre National de la Colline in a production of Michel Deutsch's *Sit venia verbo*. He is the author of numerous works which include: *L'Absolu littéraire* (with J.-L. Nancy), 1978; *Portrait de l'artiste en général*, 1979; *Le Sujet de la Philosophie (Typographies I)*, 1979; *L'imitation des modernes (Typographies II)*, 1986; *La Poésie comme expérience*, 1986; *La fiction du politique*, 1987; and *Musica ficta (Figures de Wagner)*, 1991.

Maroussia Hajdukowski-Ahmed is an associate professor at McMaster University where she teaches literature in the French Department and feminist theories in the Women's Studies Program. She is also a Principal Investigator in the McMaster Centre for the Promotion of Women's Health—on a grant from Health Canada and the Social Science and Humanities Research Council of Canada—where she conducts health promotion projects with immigrant women. She has published essays and articles on women writers of Quebec and on Bakhtin and feminist theories (epistemology, ethics, and cultural theory). She is presently working on the relevance of Bakhtin to a transdisciplinary approach on the issue of women and health (critical theory, discourse analysis, participatory/action research, theories of development, health, and culture).

Eberhard Gruber received his doctorate in the Philosophy of Education from the University of Marburg/Lahn (Germany) and is currently a translator and researcher at Queen's University (Canada). He is the author of numerous articles on philosophy, sociology, and literary theory as well as of several books, including *Un trait d'union* with Jean-François Lyotard, 1994; *Hyphen: Between Judaism and Christianity* (Humanities Press, forthcoming); plus an essay entitled *La fin du chômage* (German translation Krämer Verlag, Hamburg, 1996).

Verena Andermatt Conley is professor of French at UCLA. She has written on Hélène Cixous (*Hélène Cixous: Writing the Feminine*, Nebraska University Press, 1984 and 1992). She is currently interested in problems of feminism, technology, and ecology. Recent publications include *Rethinking Technologies* (Minnesota, 1993) and *Ecopolitics* (Routledge, 1996).

Gayatri Chakravorty Spivak is Avalon Foundation Professor in the Humanities at Columbia University. She has published *Of Grammatology* (1976), a critical translation of Jacques Derrida's *De la Grammatologie*, and *Imaginary Maps* (1994), a critical translation of Mahasweta Devi's fiction. Her own books include *Myself Must I Remake* (1974), *In Other Worlds* (1987), *The Post-Colonial Critic* (1988), *Outside in the Teaching Machine* (1994), and *A Spivak Reader* (1996).

Lynn Kettler Penrod is President of the Social Sciences and Humanities Research Council of Canada, located in Ottawa. Author of three books on French literature and Canadian chidren's literature in French, Dr. Penrod has also published various articles in scholarly journals on Simon de Beauvoir, George Sand, J. M. G. Le Clézio, feminist theory, and the intersections of law and literature.

Claire Nancy is professor of Classics in Strasbourg. Her publications include "Le mécanisme du sacrifice humain chez Euripide" in *Théâtre et Spectacles dans l'Antiquité*, USHS, 1981; "Euripide et le parti des femmes" in *Quaderni Urbinati di Cultura Classica* 2, 1984; "Medée la Juste" in *Livret du spectacle*, Bob Wilson, Opéra de Lyon, 1984; and "La voix du choeur" in *Annali della Scuola Normale di Pisa*, 1986.

Françoise van Rossum-Guyon is professor emeritus and Director of Research at the University of Amsterdam. She has published *Critique du roman* (Gallimard 1970, 1995) and numerous articles on the "nouveau roman," Balzac, and George Sand. Member of the Centre of Feminine Studies in Paris VIII, she has directed several collective works. Mme van Rossum-Guyon has been president of the Scientific Committee of the George Sand International Centre since 1995. Forthcoming is *Le coeur critique: du nouveau roman à l'écriture féminine* (Rodopi).

Charles Grivel is professor at the University of Mannheim in Germany. He is the author of *Le fantastique* (Mannheim Analytiques 1, 1983), *Production de l'intérêt romanesque. Un état du text, un essaie de constitution de sa théorie* (Mouton, Paris, 1973) as well as numerous articles on writers as diverse as Zola, Aragon, Jarry, George Bataille, and others.

Anne-Emmanuelle Berger is Associate Professor of French Studies at Cornell University (USA). She is the author of *Le Banquet de Rimbaud. Recherches sur l'oralité* (Champ-Vallon, 1992) and of numerous articles on subjects such as modern poetry and poetics, the literature of the Enlightenment, women writers, and contemporary thought.

Claudette Sartiliot is the author of *Citation and Modernity. Derrida, Joyce, and Brecht* (1993). Other publications include *Herbarium Verbarium: The Discourse of Flowers* (1993), "Telepathy and Writing in Jacques Derrida's *Glas*" (*Esprit Créateur*, 1990), and "Reading With Another Ear: Derrida's *Glas* in English?" (*New Orleans Review*, 1989).

Marie E. Surridge is professor in the Department of French Studies at Queen's University (Canada), a department which she chaired from 1983 to 1993. She is a linguist whose research interests include historical lexicology as well as all aspects of linguistic gender and the expression of "real" gender in French.

Nicole Mozet is professor at the Université de Paris VII and the director of the Groupe International de Recherches Balzaciennes. Author of several books on Balzac and a specialist of nineteenth century French literature, she is currently completing a work on the fictional writings of George Sand which is to appear in 1996 (Klincksieck). She has also edited several issues of *Romantisme: le bonheur d'écrire*, 1992–93; and *Pouvoir, puissance: qu'en pensent les femmes?*, 1993–94.

INDEX